THE JURIDICAL UNCONSCIOUS

Shoshana Felman

THE JURIDICAL UNCONSCIOUS

Trials and Traumas in the Twentieth Century

Harvard University Press

Cambridge, Massachusetts, and London, England   2002

Library of Congress Cataloging-in-Publication Data

Felman, Shoshana.
The juridical unconscious : trials and traumas in the
twentieth century / Shoshana Felman.
p.   cm.
Includes bibliographical references and index.
ISBN 0-674-00931-2 (cloth : alk. paper)—ISBN 0-674-00951-7 (paper : alk. paper)
1. Law—Psychological aspects.   2. Trials—History—20th century—
Psychological aspects.   3. Law in literature.   I. Title.

K346.F45 2002
340'1'9—dc12   2002068521

Contents

Acknowledgments

This book could not have been written without the ongoing critical feedback of two people whose proficiency and expertise in two specific areas (here conjoined and thought together) is greater than mine: Michal Shaked for jurisprudence (and legal thinking); Cathy Caruth for trauma theory (and its conceptual implications). I thank both for their rigor, which was for me a guiding inspiration, and for their help in sharpening the concepts here developed. Other precious interlocutors and guiding readers were Barbara Johnson, who, along with Eyal Peretz, assisted me in the concluding process of thinking through the synthetic structure of the introduction, and Rivka Spivak, who helped me and accompanied me in thinking through the synthetic theoretical framework of Chapter 1. Winfried Menninghaus solicited the first version of the text on Benjamin, and made me benefit from his outstanding erudition and from his ear for the nuances of the German language in Benjamin's texts. My path into Benjamin owes much to his friendly encouragement. Idit Zertal read early versions of Chapters 1 and 3 and contributed her literary acumen and a historian's perspective and stamp of approval. Dori Laub offered expert and discerning psychoanalytic feedback on early versions of Chapters 3 and 4. Irad Kimhi followed the evolution of the manuscript chapter by chapter and contributed his generous and unfailing philosophical attention, interest, and insight. Pnina Lahav thoughtfully and liberally gave time and legal feedback, in reading early versions of Chapters 2 and 3. Her open-minded, sympathetic, and responsive comments encouraged me to pursue the project further. I am grateful to Elizabeth Rottenberg for her faith in the book and for the preparation of the index. Finally, I wish to thank Dalia Tsuk for her highly discriminating, expert legal and historical assistance in the supportive and wide-ranging interdisciplinary research of Chapter 2.

*   *   *

An early version of the second half of Chapter 1 appeared under the title "Benjamin's Silence" in *Critical Inquiry* 25 (Winter 1999): 201–234.

An early version of Chapter 2, entitled "Forms of Judicial Blindness, or the Evidence of What Cannot Be Seen: Traumatic Narratives and Legal Repetitions in the O. J. Simpson Case and in Tolstoy's *The Kreutzer Sonata*," appeared in *Critical Inquiry* 23 (Summer 1997): 738–788.

A revised and extended version of this essay, entitled "Forms of Judicial Blindness: Traumatic Narratives and Legal Repetitions," appeared in *History, Memory, and the Law*, ed. Austin Sarat and Thomas R. Kearns (Ann Arbor: University of Michigan Press, 1999), pp. 25–94.

An early version of Chapter 3, entitled "Theaters of Justice: Arendt in Jerusalem, the Eichmann Trial, and the Redefinition of Legal Meaning in the Wake of the Holocaust," appeared in *Theoretical Inquiries in Law* 1 (Tel Aviv University Law School journal), special issue *Judgment in the Shadow of the Holocaust* (July 2000): 465–507.

A revised version of this essay, entitled "Theaters of Justice: Arendt in Jerusalem, the Eichmann Trial, and the Redefinition of Legal Meaning in the Wake of the Holocaust," appeared in *Critical Inquiry* 27 (Winter 2001): 201–238.

An early version of Chapter 4, entitled "A Ghost in the House of Justice: Death and the Language of the Law," appeared in *Yale Journal of Law and the Humanities* 13, special issue *Cultural Studies and the Law* (July 2001): 241–282.

THE JURIDICAL UNCONSCIOUS

Introduction

> The hour of justice, . . . the hour of institutions empowered to judge, of states within which institutions are consolidated, of Universal Law . . . , and of citizens equal before the law . . . is the hour of the Western World. The hour of justice [is] required, however, by charity . . . It is in the name of that responsibility for the other, in the name of that mercy, that kindness to which the face of the other man appeals, that the entire discourse of justice is set in motion.
> —Emmanuel Levinas, "The Other, Utopia and Justice"

> Must not human beings, who are incomparable, be compared? . . . I must judge . . . Here is the birth of the theoretical. But it is always starting out from the face, from the responsibility for the other, that justice appears.
> —Emmanuel Levinas, "Philosophy, Justice and Love"

This book deals with the hidden link between trials and traumas:[1] two topics that in previous generations have existed as two separate phenomena, but that have begun to be to be linked, I will argue, in the second half of the twentieth century.[2] Trial and trauma have become—I claim— *conceptually articulated* ever since the Nuremberg trials attempted to resolve the massive trauma of the Second World War by the conceptual resources and by the practical tools of the law. In the wake of Nuremberg, the law was challenged to address the causes and consequences of historical traumas. In setting up a precedent and a new paradigm of trial, the international community attempted to restore the world's balance by reestablishing the law's monopoly on violence, and by conceiving of justice not simply as punishment but as a marked symbolic exit from the injuries of a traumatic history: as liberation from violence itself.

The twentieth century—an era of historic trials—was in effect a century of traumas and (concurrently) a century of theories of trauma.[3] Since Freud first published at the threshold of the First World War his "Thoughts for the Times on War and Death" (1915); since war and death destructively and catastrophically returned and repeated their traumatic devastation in the holocaust of two world wars; since the traumatic and protracted repercussions of the Vietnam War; since the totalitarian revolutions of the first half of the century and their new forms of organized enslavement, massacre, massive deception, and large-scale brutality and horror; since feminists first grasped toward the end of the millennium that the renewed manifestations of domestic violence and of deceptive intimate brutality and private horror are in fact collective traumas; since the appearance of new forms of political, racial, and sexual persecution and their historical translation into legal claims, trauma quite visibly today invades the law in all its forms. In an era in which trials—televised and broadcast—ceased to be a matter of exclusive interest to jurists and penetrated and increasingly invaded culture, literature, art, politics, and the deliberated public life of society at large, the hidden link between trauma and law has gradually become more visible and more dramatically apparent.

I therefore argue that this absolutely crucial link—which hitherto had remained hidden or legally unreadable—historically came to the fore as a result of three interrelated twentieth-century occurrences, whose interaction I will try precisely to think through: (1) the discovery of psychoanalysis and, with it, the discovery of trauma as a new conceptual center, an essential dimension of human and historical experience and a new type of understanding of historical causality and of historic temporality; (2) the unprecedented number of disastrous events on a mass scale that wreaked havoc on the twentieth century and whose massively traumatic ravages were rendered possible by the development of weapons of mass destruction and technologies of death that allowed for unprecedented human assaults on the human body; (3) the unprecedented and repeated use of the instruments of law to cope with the traumatic legacies and the collective injuries left by these events.

The twentieth century has thus brought to the fore the hidden link between trauma and law. The aftermath of the events of September 11, 2001, in the United States has dramatized the same connection for the twenty-first century. In his September 20 address to the nation, President George W. Bush described and named the shock and the collective trauma of America:

On September 11, enemies of freedom committed an act of war against our country. Americans have known wars, but for the past 136 years they have been wars on foreign soil, except for one Sunday in 1941. Americans have known the casualties of war, but not at the center of a great city on a peaceful morning.

Americans have known surprise attacks, but never before on thousands of civilians.

All of this was brought upon us in a single day, and night fell on a different world . . .

I will never forget the wound to our country and those who inflicted it.[4]

But no sooner had collective trauma ("the wound to our country") been named than its link to law and justice has emerged or reemerged as a reparative and healing mode of a community's recovery of meaning.

Our grief has turned to anger and anger to resolution. Whether we bring our enemies to justice or bring justice to our enemies, justice will be done.[5]

As a pattern inherited from the great catastrophes and the collective traumas of the twentieth century,[6] the promised exercise of *legal* justice—of justice by trial and by law—has become civilization's most appropriate and most essential, most ultimately meaningful response to the violence that wounds it.[7]

At the turn of the century and at the turn of the millennium, contemporary history can thus be said to be crystallized around these two poles: the trial (law and justice), on the one hand, and trauma (collective as well as private trauma, trauma and memory, trauma and forgetfulness, trauma and forgiveness, trauma and repetition of the trauma) on the other hand. There has never been so tight a relationship between justice and trauma as the one that has developed in the past several decades.

* * *

This book revolves around an examination of two specific trials—very different from each other—whose legal memory and whose concrete historical examples I here view as paradigmatic for thinking through the interaction of law and trauma in the twentieth century. These trials—among the many called "the trial of the century" in their day (indeed, perhaps the proliferation of that epithet is itself a symptom of the twentieth century)—are the 1961 Eichmann trial, which took place in Jerusalem, and the 1995 O. J. Simpson trial, which took place in Los Angeles. Two events that frame and stand behind my understanding of those two trials and of their larger twentieth-century contexts are the 1945–1946 Nuremberg trials and the story of Walter Benjamin's suicide in September 1940. By setting a highly public story (and dilemma of justice) alongside a highly private story (and its biographical dilemma of justice), I will think through the new relations between the public and the private that the two trials (as two embodiments of the relation between law and trauma in our time) historically and allegorically entail.[8]

I argue that the trials of Adolf Eichmann and O. J. Simpson, however different they may seem in terms of their legal history, their cultural context, and their particular legal agendas, mark a structurally similar professional predicament and historical challenge. What characterizes these trials (a characteristic that they share, in fact, with other trauma trials but that they quite spectacularly magnify and amplify) is that in them the law—traditionally calling for consciousness and cognition to arbitrate between opposing views, both of which are in principle available to consciousness—finds itself either responding to or unwittingly involved with processes that are unavailable to consciousness or to which consciousness is purposely blind. What has to be heard in court is precisely what cannot be articulated in legal language.

Thus, in the case of the Eichmann trial, the law finds itself called upon to respond to claims that go far beyond the simple conscious and cognitive need to decide about Eichmann's individual guilt or innocence; it must respond, in a larger manner, to the traumatic historical experience of the Holocaust and juridically confront the very trauma of race, of being a Jew in (Hitler's) Europe. In the case of the O. J. Simpson trial, the legal system, which initially was summoned to decide a personal case of murder, found itself entangled with, and called on to judge, something else. On the side of the prosecution, the issue that made its claim in court became the trauma of abused women, and on the side of the defense, the issue that imposed itself was yet another trauma, here again the massive fact of race: the trauma of being black in America.

Thus, both these trials, as well as the Nuremberg trials, found themselves turning into something different from a simple litigation or a simple controversy over legal issues: they have turned into veritable theaters of justice. They were *critical* legal events, both in the ways in which they dramatized or triggered an emblematic crisis in the law, and in the ways in which the legal crisis each of them enacted represented also a transcendent, vaster, and highly traumatic (if not always conscious) *cultural crisis*. These trials staged paroxistic spectacles both of the drama of the law and of the drama of culture. They encapsulated, therefore, each in its own way, a crisis of legitimacy and a crisis of truth that organized themselves around a *critical traumatic content* that, like a magnet, polarized the cultural, the political, the moral, and the epistemological crises of their generations. It is not a coincidence that all these trials were dubbed, at the time of their occurrence, "trials of the century." In different contexts, they were all perceived and should be remembered as the defining trials of their era and of the different cultures of which they externalized the crises.

In examining through these paradigmatic legal events the interaction of the law with the introduction of trauma into the court, I will explore three main perspectives:

1. I will look at the ways in which the law tries to contain the trauma and to translate it into legal-conscious terminology, thus reducing its strange interruption. Uncannily, however, while the law strives to contain the trauma, it often is in fact the trauma that takes over and whose surreptitious logic in the end reclaims the trial. I thus show, for example, that when a jury or a court confronts the trauma in the courtroom, it is often inflicted with a particular judicial blindness that unwittingly reflects and duplicates the constitutional blindness of culture and of consciousness toward the trauma. A pattern emerges in which the trial, while it tries to put an end to trauma, inadvertently performs an acting out of it. Unknowingly, the trial thus repeats the trauma, reenacts its structures. I will thus show how, like society itself and despite its conscious frames and rational foundations, the law has quite conspicuously and remarkably its own structural (professional) unconscious.[9]

2. I will look at the ways in which the law and legal procedures nevertheless seem to be transformed by their interaction with trauma, a transformation that calls for a reformulation and reconceptualization of what it is that the law and trials are about. A dialogue of law and trauma does occur, albeit in nonconventional and nontraditional ways. I analyze this dialogue and try to demonstrate and show concretely how the shock of the encounter with the trauma penetrates the trial and impacts the structures of the law in unpredictably reshaping the proceedings and in giving to the trial (to the drama of the law) a new jurisprudential dimension.

3. I will demonstrate and analyze the ways in which the introduction of the dimension of trauma into the court unsettles the stereotypical division between the public and the private and requires a rethinking, in particular, of the relationship between what is presumed to be private trauma and what is presumed to be collective, public trauma.

Within the larger category of significantly symptomatic "trials of the century" whose legal traumas and legal dramas have defined the end of the millennium, I focus on the Eichmann case and on the O. J. Simpson case, not only because they embody two exemplary and mutually illuminating paradigms of race trials (abuse of blacks: abuse of Jews; traumatic memory of slavery: traumatic memory of genocide) but, more generally, because they concretize a *structural* dichotomy, or two distinct *conceptual poles*, of trauma trials. The first pole is the pole at which the law sets out to deal with *private trauma*. The second pole, diametrically opposed to the first, is the pole at which the law undertakes to deal with a *collective trauma*. Notwithstanding their exemplary embodiment of these two poles, the Eichmann and Simpson trials also demonstrate how in contemporary trauma trials the two poles of private and collective trauma cannot be kept apart but, rather, keep reversing into one another.

The Simpson trial initially set out to deal with private trauma and with a private injury. The trial was supposed to be the trial of an intimate violence that ultimately led to (private) murder. Although a criminal case is always of course "public" or "collective" in the sense that prosecution takes place in the name of the community, initially the only matter of collective interest in this affair was the glamorous celebrity of the accused. But as the trial lingered on, and as the adversarial stories of the prosecution (about the trauma of a battered, murdered wife) and of the defense (about the trauma of an innocent man accused and lynched only by virtue of his race) unfolded and confronted each other, the private injuries under dispute (the harm done to the wife or to the husband) gave rise to such an immense *collective* echo, and provoked such an intense *collective* identification, that the private traumas litigated in the courts received from the passions of the audience—as from a chorus—their own dramatic and conceptual *generalization;* so much so that the trial of the private trauma of domestic violence and of the private murder of a wife by her ex-husband gradually and retrospectively became a leading, archetypal legal drama of the historical (collective) trauma of the persecutions, the abuses, the discrimination, the murders, the administrative murders, and the legal murders suffered by African Americans, along with and in confrontation with the historical (collective) trauma of the persecutions, the abuses, the humiliations, and the murders suffered by women (and by battered wives). The private traumas have become the emblems or the icons of collective (publicly shared, unexpectedly common, unexpectedly omnipresent) traumas: the two cardinal societal traumas of race persecution and gender persecution.

In contrast, the Eichmann trial was typically and from the start a trial of collective crime (and of an archetypal perpetrator of that crime). At stake from the beginning was the collective racial persecution of the Jews and the way in which this history of persecution reached its climax in the

Holocaust. By project and design, the Eichmann trial therefore set out to deal with *collective trauma,* with collective injury and with collective memory. But it was also a conscious and deliberate attempt to transform an incoherent mass of private traumas (the secret, hidden, silenced individual traumas of the survivors) into one collective, national, and public trauma, and thus to give a public stage to a collection of individual abuses and private traumas, to render public and politically transform into public, abuses that were lived as private and hidden away by the individual traumatized subjects, who had become, in their own self-perception, "the bearers of the silence." The trial was a conscious legal effort not just to give the victims a voice and a stage, to break the silence of the trauma, to divulge and to uncover secrets and taboos, but to transform these discoveries into one national, collective story, to assemble consciously, meticulously, diligently, an unprecedented *public and collective legal record* of *mass trauma* that formerly existed only in the repressed form of a series of untold, fragmented private stories and traumatic memories. The Eichmann trial therefore was the trial of the granting of authority (articulateness and transmissibility) to trauma by a legal process of transformation of individual into collective trauma, and by a parallel process of legal translation of the "private" into "public." I contend that, both by the role it gave to victims and by this conscious abolition of the dichotomy between private and public, the Eichmann trial anticipated by several decades legal developments to come.

This book thus makes the Eichmann trial and the Simpson trial face one another. Both trials demonstrate the indivisibility and the reversibility between private and collective trauma. The Simpson trial starts as a private criminal case but moves from private trauma to collective trauma. The Eichmann trial starts as a collective criminal case but moves from collective trauma to a sort of liberation of the private traumas, to which it restores consciousness, dignity, and speech. Analyzed here side by side, these two case studies illustrate two idiosyncratic and yet structurally archetypal paradigms of trauma trials. Together, these two legal events encapsulate at once the central traumas of the twentieth century and the two ends of the legal spectrum of traumatic trials, the two dynamic poles of the relationship between trial and trauma in our era.

* * *

My theoretical framework is an articulation of three contemporary visions that are seldom brought together. The three thinkers whose diverse conceptual frameworks underlie this book are Sigmund Freud,

Walter Benjamin, and Hannah Arendt. They are usually viewed separately, unrelated to each other. This book consists in an attempt to integrate their insights, to assemble the conceptual tools they have provided,[10] and effectively to bring their visions and their concepts to bear on one another. My proposition is to view these theorists essentially as three groundbreaking thinkers of memory. I suggest, indeed, that there are ways in which Freud, Benjamin, and Arendt could all be seen (elucidated, understood profoundly) as *theorists of trauma*. This is thus not just a book on trials (and on the link between trials and traumas in the twentieth century): it is also a book about three groundbreaking readers of the twentieth century, three cultural witnesses who turned trauma as experience into insight and whose innovative concepts have given us new tools with which to think our times.

*   *   *

Another dimension through which I read the cultural significance of these historic trials is the complementary dimension of literature. Literature emerges from the very tension between law and trauma as a compelling existential, correlative yet differential dimension of meaning. An encounter between law and literature—understood in new ways and methodologically conceived in utterly noncustomary terms—will thus beckon in the background of these trials. I analyze the ways in which the testimony of some literary writers in the face of trauma and in the face of the events of law corroborates and complements the testimony of the critics and the thinkers, the theorists of trauma. I will show how, in these two trials as in every culturally symptomatic and traumatic case, legal meaning and literary meaning necessarily inform and displace each other. The complexity of culture, I submit, often lies in the discrepancy between what culture can articulate as legal justice and what it articulates as literary justice.

What indeed is literary justice, as opposed to legal justice? How does literature do justice to the trauma in a way the law does not, or cannot?

Literature is a dimension of concrete embodiment and a language of infinitude that, in contrast to the language of the law, encapsulates not closure but precisely what in a given legal case refuses to be closed and cannot be closed. It is to this refusal of the trauma to be closed that literature does justice. The literary writers in this book thus stand beyond or in the margin of the legal closure, on the brink of the abyss that underlies the law, on whose profundity they fix their vision and through whose bottomlessness they reopen the closed legal case.

But the literary writers in this book are not outside the trials. They are inside.

Tolstoy precociously bears witness to the O. J. Simpson trial. Zola (and in a different way, Celan) precociously bears witness to the Eichmann trial. Both K-Zetnik and Zola find themselves literally convoked to court. But whereas the literary talents of Zola win for posterity a judgment and a truth that the writer fails to win from the French court, the literary talents of K-Zetnik, inevitably introduced into his testimony in the Eichmann trial, predictably meet only with the censure and with the juridical impatience of the Israeli court. The bench authoritatively instructs the witness to restrict himself to courtroom protocol and only to answer the prosecutor's questions. The writer in response dramatically and unpredictably faints on the witness stand before the audience and before the judge. The Eichmann trial thus inadvertently illustrates at once the tension between law and trauma and the tension between law and literature.

One could read this dramatic moment of the Eichmann trial as a profound allegory of the relationship between legal consciousness and the juridical unconscious in traumatic trials. The writer's collapse can be read as a parable of the collapse of language in the encounter between law and trauma. It reveals the literary as a dimension of silence in the courtroom, a dimension of speechless embodiment, which brings to the fore through the very failure of words the importance of the witness's body in the courtroom. Thus, the Eichmann trial includes this dimension of the body's collapse as a legally meaningful dimension.

The unpredictable moment of the writer's collapse has remained the most memorable moment of the Eichmann trial. It encapsulates the quintessence of the trial as a site of memory to the trauma of extermination, dramatized in the sudden image of the witness as a collapsed corpse. The trial articulates its legal meaning through this unforgettable interruption of consciousness: through the unconscious body of the witness, history within the courtroom speaks beyond the limits of speech. It is because the body of the witness is the ultimate site of memory of individual and collective trauma—because trauma makes the body matter, and because the body testifying to the trauma *matters in the courtroom* in new ways—that these trials have become not only memorable discursive scenes, but dramatically physical theaters of justice.

1

The Storyteller's Silence:
Walter Benjamin's Dilemma of Justice

One can ask oneself whether the relationship of the storyteller to his material, human life, is not itself a craftsman's relationship . . . exemplified by
the proverb, if one thinks of it as an ideogram of a story.
—Water Benjamin, "The Storyteller"

Death is the sanction of everything that the storyteller has to tell. He has
borrowed his authority from death.
—Walter Benjamin, "The Storyteller"

No justice . . . seems possible without the principle of some responsibility,
beyond all living present, before the ghosts of those who are not yet born or
who are already dead, be they victims of wars, political or other kinds of violence, nationalist, racist, colonialist, sexist or other kinds of extermination.
—Jacques Derrida, *Specters of Marx*

Why start a book on trials with the story of the life and of the thought of
Walter Benjamin? The story, I would argue, is a parable for the twentieth
century, a parable that a sophisticated literary author could perhaps enti-
tle "Before the Law": before the law both in the temporal and in the
spatial sense.[1]

"Kafka does not use the word 'justice,'" writes Walter Benjamin, "yet
it is justice which is the point of departure of his critique."[2] In the same
way, one could say: Benjamin seldom uses the word "justice," yet it is
justice that is the point of departure for his critique. The story of the life
and of the work of Walter Benjamin (the only chapter in this book that is
not about a trial) is, I would propose, a story about the relation between
silence and justice. It is a story that achieves the status of what Benjamin
will call "a proverb": "A proverb, one might say, is a ruin which stands
on the site of an old story and in which a moral twines about a happening like ivy around a wall."[3]

Part One: Benjamin's Justice

— I —

Two stories here will therefore intersect and, through their intersection, shed light on each other: the story of the life of Walter Benjamin and the story of his writing.

Although Benjamin does not write about trials, he does write about history as the arena of a constant struggle between justice and injustice. He does write about the relation between history and justice. In the wake of Benjamin, this chapter is dedicated to an exploration and (after Benjamin) an attempt at conceptualization of this central relation, which, as I will later show, similarly governs trials. The chapters that follow illustrate concretely how the questions Benjamin identified as central (as constitutive within the relation between history and justice) nowadays emerge as haunting questions at the center of contemporary trials.

History, Justice, and the Law

Trials have always been contextualized in—and affected by—a general relation between history and justice. But they have not always been judicially concerned with this relationship. Until the middle of the twentieth century, a radical division between history and justice was in principle maintained. The law perceived itself either as ahistorical or as expressing a specific stage in society's historical development. But law and history were separate. The courts sometimes acknowledged they were part of history, but they did not judge history as such. This state of affairs has changed since the constitution of the Nuremberg tribunal, which (through the trial of the Nazi leaders as representatives of the historical regime and the historical phenomenon of Nazism) for the first time called history itself into a court of justice.[4]

In the wake of Nuremberg, a displacement has occurred in the relationship between history and trials.[5] Not only has it become thinkable to put history on trial, it has become judicially necessary to do so. Nuremberg did not intend, but has in fact produced, this conceptual revolution that implicitly affects all later trials, and not only the tradition of war crimes and of international criminal law. In the second half of the twentieth century, it has become part of the function of trials to repair judicially not only private but also collective historical injustices.[6]

History on Trial

Thus, the Eichmann trial puts on trial the whole history of the Nazi persecution and genocide of the European Jews.[7] Decades later, the defense in the O. J. Simpson trial puts on trial the whole history of lynching and of the persecution of American blacks, while the prosecution puts concurrently on trial the historical injustices inflicted with impunity on battered women and on murdered wives. This book explores these two paradigmatic legal examples among the many other trials (civil as well as criminal) that judge history as such: the *Brown v. Board of Education* case in the United States; the *Irving v. Lipstadt* British libel case; the French Klaus Barbie trial; the trials of the officers and torturers of the "Dirty War" in Argentina; the Turkish trial of those accused of having committed genocide against the Armenians in 1921; the international ad hoc war crimes tribunals for Rwanda and for the former Yugoslavia. In this last case of Bosnia and the former Yugoslavia, the crime of history consists (again) both in human murder and in gendered murder, both in the crime of genocide itself and in the companion outrage targeted at women. What the war crimes tribunal in The Hague for the first time puts on trial as a crime against humanity is not just the ethnic crime (the genocidal history) of massacres and ethnic cleansing but also the sexual crime (the sexualized genocidal history) of systematic and collective rape.

The significance of all these legal cases that put history on trial—a significance this book proposes to extract and to explore—is not only that they are revolutionary in the sense that what they judge is both "the private" and "the public," but also, even more significantly, that in them the court provides a stage for the expression of the persecuted. The court allows (what Benjamin called) "the tradition of the oppressed"[8] to articulate its claim to justice in the name of a judgment—of an explicit or implicit prosecution—of history itself. *The court helps in the coming to expression of what historically has been "expressionless."*

In this chapter I will analyze how, *in anticipation of developments in law* and in advance of history, Benjamin gives voice precisely to this claim to justice in the name of the tradition of the oppressed. I argue that Benjamin is the philosopher and the conceptual precursor, the herald of this claim to justice. His theories are allegorical of the necessity of recovering the silence of the oppressed in the name of a judgment of history itself. In this he is inscribed prophetically in relation to contemporary trials. Benjamin's reflections on history predict, or at the very least anticipate, what will actually happen in the realm of the law in the second half of the twentieth century.

The Expressionless

The court, I claimed, gives a stage to "the tradition of the oppressed," in helping the "expressionless" of that tradition (the silence of the persecuted, the unspeakability of the trauma of oppression) to come into expression.

Walter Benjamin originally coined the term *expressionless (das Ausdruckslose)* as an innovative literary concept,[9] a concept that essentially links literature and art to the (mute yet powerful) communication of what cannot be said in words[10] but what makes art belong in "the true world," what "shatters" art, says Benjamin, into "the torso of a symbol," into a "fragment" of the real world (Benjamin, "GEA," 340). The expressionless in literature (and, I will later show, in law) is thus an utterance that signifies although and because it has no possibility of statement.

But in linking literature through the expressionless not only to a stillness and a speechlessness but also to a moment that connotes death, trauma, and petrification—"the moment in which life is petrified, as though spellbound in a single moment" ("GEA," 340)—Benjamin created, I will argue, a groundbreaking concept that can be applied as well to political phenomena, and that in particular sheds new light on twentieth-century *critiques of history*[11] and on contemporary historical developments, including late legal developments.[12]

I use the word *expressionless* throughout this book in Benjamin's pathbreaking sense,[13] but also in the sense of Levinas[14] (whose added resonance is here included in the Benjaminian sense):[15] expressionless *(das Ausdruckslose)* are those whom violence has deprived of expression; those who, on the one hand, have been historically reduced to silence, and who, on the other hand, have been historically made faceless, deprived of their *human* face—deprived, that is, not only of a language and a voice but even of the mute *expression* always present in a *living* human face.[16] Those whom violence has paralyzed, effaced, or deadened, those whom violence has treated in their lives as though they were *already dead*, those who have been made (in life) without expression, without a voice and without a face have become—much like the dead—historically (and philosophically) expressionless *(das Ausdruckslose)*.

This book proposes to explore precisely the status of the expression- less in court, and the legal modes by which the expressionless of history finds an expression in trials that judge history itself and in legal proceed- ings that deal with (and try to repair) the crimes of history.

In the cases that this book discusses and in others like them, the court either intentionally gives a stage to the expressionless of history or un- intentionally and unconsciously enacts that expressionlessness and is forced to witness it and to encounter it: legally to deal with it. Through the proceedings, the expressionless at least partially recovers the living humanity and the *expression* of a human face. In the courtroom (to put one against the other two key Benjaminian concepts), the *expressionless* turns into *storytelling*.

I argue that Benjamin claims in advance this type of exercise of justice and this court that judges history.

He grasps ahead of others the significance of the relationship between history (oppression, trauma, violence) and silence. He sees ahead of oth- ers the necessity for justice to repair this silence by dragging history itself to court.

Benjamin sees in advance, I argue (ahead of what will happen in the second half of the twentieth century) at once the urgent need for the re- pair of collective historical injustices, and the abhorrent acts of "barba- rism"—the barbaric *crimes*—that are constitutive of history as such.[17] He analyzes in advance at once the reasons for and the imperative historical necessity of putting history as such on trial, of bringing history as such— and most of all, contemporary history—into a court of justice.

— II —

"Hope in the Past," or Justice for the Dead

History in Benjamin's reflections is related not just to the structure of a trial but, more radically, to "Judgment Day": the day on which historical injustice will be cancelled out precisely through the act of judgment; the day on which justice and memory will coincide (perhaps the day on which the court will be redeemed from its inherent political *forgetful-*

ness). Only on Judgment Day will the meaning of history (a meaning that cannot be mastered or possessed by "man or men")[18] emerge from the political unconscious[19] and come to light. Only on Judgment Day will the past come into full possession of its meaning: a meaning in which even the expressionless of history (the silence of the victims, the muteness of the traumatized) will come into historical expression. "To be sure, only a redeemed mankind receives the fullness of its past—which is to say, only for a redeemed mankind has its past become [legally] citable in all its moments. Each moment it has lived becomes a *citation à l'ordre du jour*—and that day is Judgment Day" (Benjamin, "Theses," 254). The invocation of a Judgment Day to which history itself is destined is often read as testimony to Benjamin's involvement with—or act of faith in—a Messianic eschatology. I read it secularly as the (revolutionary, legal) day that will put history itself on trial, the day in which history will have to take stock of its own flagrant injustices.

Judgment Day implies a necessary reference of history and of historical justice to a reawakening of the dead;[20] and justice is, indeed, for Benjamin, above all justice (and, quite paradoxically, life) for the dead. Life for the dead resides in a remembrance (by the living) of their story; justice for the dead resides in a remembrance (by the living) of the injustice and the outrage done to them. History is thus, above and beyond official narratives, a haunting claim the dead have on the living, whose responsibility it is not only to remember but to protect the dead from being *misappropriated:* "Only that historian will have the gift of fanning the spark of hope in the past who is firmly convinced that even the dead will not be safe from the enemy if he wins" ("Theses," 255).

Critique of Violence

What the dead will one day put on trial is the violence of history: the violence of "the triumphal procession in which the present rulers step over those who are lying prostrate" ("Theses," 256); the violence by which the rulers institute their own rule (their own violence) as law: usurpers, they hold themselves to be proprietors of justice. "Walter Benjamin noted," writes Mariana Varverde, "that every philosophical reflection on justice can be recuperated by questionable political projects, as part of the bourgeois appropriation of all manner of 'cultural treasures' . . . The appropriation of philosophies of justice by the ruling classes of each generation was the greatest concern of Benjamin's thoughts on history."[21]

Only the dead can judge the sheer violence of the historical appropriation of philosophies of justice: only from the perspective of the dead can this violence disguised as justice and cloaked as law be seen in its nakedness and put on trial.

The law—and the court itself—are therefore not entirely (and not by definition) on the side of justice; they partake of the violence of history. The law must thus stand trial along with history itself. Like history, the law has an inherent relationship to death. It is precisely this constitutive relationship of law to violence and death that must be laid bare and in turn indicted. "The task of a critique of violence"—Benjamin observes—"can be summarized as that of expounding its relation to law and justice":[22]

> For if violence, violence crowned by fate, is the origin of law, then it may be readily supposed that where the highest violence, that over life and death, occurs in the legal system, the origins of law jut manifestly and fearsomely into existence . . . For in the exercise of violence over life and death more than in any other legal act, law reaffirms itself. But in this very violence something rotten in law is revealed . . . Law . . . appears . . . in so ambiguous a moral light that the question poses itself whether there are no other violent means for regulating conflicting human interests. (Benjamin, "Critique," 286–287)[23]

This radical critique of violence is born (Benjamin explains) from the unmatched catastrophe and the unparalleled ideological and technological violence of the First World War: a twentieth-century watershed event that encapsulates the undreamt of aggression and brutality revealed in the contemporary world. It is precisely this epiphany of violence which has deceptively paraded as civilization that it is urgent to unmask, demystify, and bring to trial. After the First World War, it is no longer possible to speak of violence naïvely.

> If in the last war the critique of military violence was the starting point for a passionate critique of violence in general—which taught at least one thing, *that violence is no longer exercised or tolerated naïvely*—nevertheless violence was not only subject to criticism for its lawmaking character, but was also judged, perhaps more annihilatingly, for another of its functions. For a duality in the function of violence is characteristic of militarism, which could only come into being through general conscription. Militarism is the compulsory, universal use of violence to the ends of the state . . . For the

subordination of citizens to laws—in the present case, to the law of general conscription—is a legal end. If that first function of violence [militarism] is called the lawmaking function, this second [conscription] will be called the law-preserving function. Since conscription is a case of law-preserving violence . . . , a really effective critique of it is far less easy than the declamations of pacifists and activists suggests. Rather, such a critique coincides with the *critique of all legal violence*—that is, with the critique of legal or executive force—and cannot be performed by any lesser program. ("Critique," 284, emphasis mine)

Violence is lawmaking when it institutes itself as law and creates new legal norms and new prescriptive standards. Such, for instance, was the case of the precedent-setting court of the victorious at Nuremberg:[24] it was the violence of victory that enabled the Nuremberg proceedings to take place and enabled the victorious Western Allies (and their tribunal) to set up a groundbreaking legal precedent and institute for the whole legal future the new justiciability and the new jurisprudential concept of "crimes against humanity." When violence is not at the origin of legitimation as lawmaking (when it does not institute a new law that legitimates it ex post facto), it is legitimated as law-preserving, it is in the service of a preexisting law. Such, as Benjamin points out, is the case of the institution of compulsory conscription in the First World War, or, to take a more extreme and more obvious example, the case of the Nazi violence deployed in the service of the Nuremberg laws. "All violence as a means is either lawmaking or law-preserving. If it lays claim to neither of these predicates, it forfeits all validity. It follows, however, that all violence as a means, even in the most favorable case, is implicated in the problematic nature of law itself" ("Critique," 287).

On Judgment Day, *the law will therefore judge the law:* the Western law (the International Military Tribunal) will judge the Nazi law; the Russian law will judge the Soviet law, and will free, amnesty, and rehabilitate the victims of the Moscow trials. In this respect, the most characteristic trial of history is the third of the Nuremberg trials, the so-called Justice Case, in which the Nazi judges (and civil servants) were put on trial and convicted.

Law itself is therefore both redemptive and oppressive; and so is in potential every trial. Every trial can be both at the same time, or it can be rather the one or the other. Benjamin's concern for justice derives precisely from this contradiction—from this suspension between redemption and oppression—inherent in the very nature of the law. It is because redemption is impossible that there is a demand for justice and an imperative of justice. One longs for justice and one hopes in legal justice because the only secular redemption comes from the law.[25] Yet, the law offers no ultimate redemption and no final day of judgment.[26] "Justice," writes Levinas, "is always a revision of justice and the expectation of a better justice."[27] Judgment Day is both concrete (particular, political, historical) and doomed to remain historically, eternally deferred.

— III —

Justice, Death, Silence, and the Unappropriated

When Benjamin claimed justice for the dead, he did not yet foresee himself as dead. Or did he? Did he know that he himself would one day be a victim of the violence of history exhibiting its mad injustices as law? Did he already know that, under such circumstances, he would rather take his own life than submit to the delusions and the distortions of such history? When this book will in its turn—after Benjamin—claim justice for the dead, it will claim it quite concretely first of all for Walter Benjamin himself: for the *private story* of his life and of his death, and for the *public story*—henceforth the collective legacy—of his reflective and imaginative work. To do justice to Benjamin, however, it will talk about his silence.

While Benjamin's philosophy of history incorporates a vision of redemptive justice that, in bringing the "expressionless" into expression, will recover and restore the missing, silenced history of the oppressed and of the disenfranchised, the life of Benjamin as an oppressed and disenfranchised German-Jewish refugee encapsulates, in contrast, a drama of *distorted justice* very similar (in its precise factual details) to the realities of Kafka's trial. If Kafka's apparently fantastic novel in effect prophetically depicts the future legal tragedy of Walter Benjamin and the array of possible and actual totalitarian *perversions* of the law, could it be said that Kafka's trial is, indeed—above all legal trials—the ultimate trial of the century (the one that truly puts the century on trial)? Like K. in Kafka's trial, Benjamin is harassed by the law. Like K., he is finally silenced by legal means. Indeed, the drama of his final fall to silence illustrates, in contrast to his hopes, at once the failure of civilization to redeem the silenced and the silencing capacity of law itself in its potential (and in its totalitarian reality) as civilization's most pernicious and most brutal tool of violence. Like K. in Kafka's trial, Benjamin ends up being himself a murdered victim of a persecutory culture that masquerades itself as trial and of a law that masquerades its crimes as questions of procedural legalities and legal technicalities.

"On September 26, 1940," writes Hannah Arendt, "Walter Benjamin, who was about to emigrate to America, took his life at the Franco-Spanish border":

There were various reasons for this. The Gestapo had confiscated his Paris apartment, which contained his library . . . and many of his manuscripts . . . Besides, nothing drew him to America, where, as he used to say, people would probably find no other use for him than to cart him up and down the country to exhibit him as 'the last European.' But the immediate occasion for Benjamin's suicide was an uncommon stroke of bad luck. Through the armistice agreement between Vichy France and the Third Reich, refugees from Hitler Germany . . . were in danger of being shipped back to Germany . . . To save this category of refugees . . . the United States had distributed a certain number of emergency visas through its consulates in unoccupied Europe . . . Benjamin was among the first to receive such a visa in Marseilles. Also, he quickly obtained a Spanish transit visa to enable him to get to Lisbon and board a ship there. However, he did not have a French exit visa . . . which the French government, eager to please the Gestapo, invariably denied the German refugees. In general this presented no great difficulty, since a relatively short and none too arduous road to be covered by foot over the mountains to Port Bou was well known and was not guarded by the French border police. Still, for Benjamin apparently suffering from a cardiac condition . . . even the shortest walk was a great exertion, and he must have arrived in a state of serious exhaustion. The small group of refugees that he had joined reached the Spanish border town only to learn that Spain had closed the border that same day and that the border officials did not honor visas made out in Marseilles. The refugees were supposed to return to France by the same route the next day. During the night Benjamin took his life, whereupon the border officials, upon whom this suicide had made an impression, allowed his companions to proceed to Portugal. A few weeks later the embargo on visas was lifted again. One day earlier Benjamin would have got through without any trouble; one day later the people in Marseilles would have known that for the time being it was impossible to pass through Spain. Only on that particular day was the catastrophe possible.[28]

"Before the Law," writes Kafka, "stands a doorkeeper. To this door-keeper there comes a man from the country who begs for admittance to the Law."

But the doorkeeper says that he cannot admit the man at the moment. The man, on reflection, asks if he will be allowed, then, to enter later. "It is possible," answers the doorkeeper, "but not at this moment." Since the door leading into the Law stands open as usual and the doorkeeper steps to one side, the man bends down to peer through the entrance. When the doorkeeper sees that, he laughs and says: "If you are so strongly tempted, try to get in without my permission. But note that I am powerful . . . this door was intended for you, and I am now going to shut it."[29]

The truth of Benjamin's life as a harassed German-Jewish refugee, as a running, stateless person, as an illegal border crosser, and as a would-be immigrant to the free world is the truth of Kafka's trial. Like K., Benjamin "has actually become a mute figure in the shape of the accused man, a figure (Benjamin insists) of the most striking intensity."[30] Like K., Benjamin is fundamentally and radically *a subject under a regime of trial.*

But in this era in which law becomes culture's most blatant tool of violence, in this totalitarian world of the Nuremberg laws and of the Moscow trials, Benjamin (like K. and unlike K.) does not even stand trial. He simply is excluded from the Law. He merely does not have an exit visa from the country (France) into which he fled from Nazi Germany and in which he took unwelcome refuge as a stateless, segregated, disenfranchised, and interned German refugee. Like K., Benjamin dies at the hands of officials, of representatives of the law: in the (Spanish) policemen that arrest him for his missing exit visa (from Occupied France), Benjamin confronts, like K., the guardians of procedures and the guardians of boundaries, the gatekeepers that deny admittance and forbid entrance to the Law. Benjamin's last moments, therefore, strikingly and eerily resemble K.'s last moments.

After an exchange of courteous formalities regarding which of them was to take precedence in the next task—these emissaries seemed to have been given no specific assignment in the charge laid jointly upon them . . . The two of them laid K. down on the ground, propped him against the boulder, and settled his head upon it. But in spite of the pains they took and all the willingness K. showed, his posture remained contorted and unnatural-looking . . . Once more the odious courtesies began, the first handed the knife across K. to the second, who handed it across K. back again to the first. *K. now perceived clearly that he was supposed to seize the knife himself, as it traveled from hand to hand above him, and plunge it into his own breast. . . . He could not completely rise to the occasion, he could not relieve the officials of their tasks* . . . His glance fell on the top story of the house . . . With a flicker of a light going up, the casements of a window there flew open; a human figure, faint and insubstantial at that distance and that height, leaned abruptly far forward and stretched both arms still farther. Who was it? A friend? A good man? Someone who sympathized? Someone who wanted help? Was it one person only? Or was it mankind? Was help at hand? Were there arguments in his favor that had been overlooked? Of course there must be. Logic is doubtless unshakeable, but it cannot withstand a man who wants to go on living. Where was the Judge whom he had never seen? Where was the high Court, to which he had never penetrated? He raised his hands and spread out his fingers.

But the hands of one of the partners were already at K.'s throat, while the other thrust the knife deep into his breast and turned it there twice. With failing eyes K. could still see the two of them immediately before him . . . watching the final act. "Like a dog!" he said; it was as if the shame of it must outlive him.[31]

There is, however, one essential difference between Benjamin and K.: K. submits himself to the "procedure" and collaborates with it. Benjamin, in contrast, makes good on what K. would like to do but fails to do: he dies by his own hand, he "relieves the officials of their tasks." He *sentences himself* to death in order to avoid precisely the execution of the verdict by officials—the (Nazi) officials of the era. In K. there is indeed a hidden element of *identification* with the law, and *with officials*—an element, thus, of collaboration with the executioners. It is precisely this "cooperation" between the victim and the executioner that Hannah Arendt will define years later, on the occasion of the Eichmann trial, as "the totality of the moral collapse the Nazis caused in respectable European society, not only in Germany but in almost all countries, not only among the persecutors but also among the victims."[32] K. knows that his murder by the law constitutes "a shame" that "will outlive him," but the shame is also his *distortion*—his "contortion"—by the law.[33] Benjamin says *no* to the distortion. He will not let history as violence appropriate him and appropriate his death. He will die not at the hands of others—of the officials of the law—but rather at his own hands. He will fall silent by his own decision.

Silence, Benjamin knows well, is the essence of oppression and traumatization, but it is also something that escapes (resists) the master. This mute refusal of cooperation (and of identification) with the master—this mute resistance to his own appropriation by the (fascist) forces of historical distortion—is the ultimate significance of Benjamin's own self-inflicted death. This death (to borrow words from Levinas) is "a breach made by the human in the barbarism of being."[34] Benjamin's creates this *breach*. He will not let history erase his final cry for justice, even if this cry must be "expressionless" and must remain forever a mute cry. Silenced by law, he will not let history appropriate the *meaning* of his silence.

"Conversation," Benjamin always remembered, "strives toward silence, and the listener is really the silent partner. The speaker receives meaning from him; the silent one is the unappropriated source of meaning."[35]

Through his choice of death and through his self-inflicted fall to silence, Benjamin remains, like justice, an unappropriated source of meaning. His life becomes a parable of the relation between history and silence.

Part Two: Benjamin's Silence

Nothing more desolating than his acolytes, nothing more godforsaken than his adversaries. No name that would be more fittingly honored by silence.
—Walter Benjamin, "Monument to a Warrior," *One-Way Street*

"Expect from me no word of my own. Nor should I be capable of saying anything new; for in the room where someone writes the noise is so great . . . Let him who has something to say step forward and be silent!"
—Karl Kraus, cited by Walter Benjamin

I propose now to address—and listen to—that element in Benjamin's own language and writing that specifically, decisively remains beyond appropriation and beyond communication. "In all language and linguistic creations," Benjamin has said, "there remains in addition to what can be conveyed something that cannot be communicated . . . It is the task of the translator to release in his own language that pure language which is exiled among alien tongues, to liberate the language imprisoned in a work."[36] In Benjamin's own work, in his abbreviated, cryptic style and in the essentially elliptical articulation of his thought, a surcharge of meaning is quite literally "imprisoned" in instances of silence. It is the task of the translator of Benjamin's own work to listen to these instances of silence, whose implications, I will show, are at once stylistic, philosophical, historical, and autobiographical. "Midway between poetry and theory,"[37] my critical amplification of this silence—my own translation of the language that is still imprisoned in Benjamin's work—will thus focus on what Benjamin himself has underscored but what remains unheard, unheeded in the critically repetitive mechanical reproduction of his work: "that element in a translation that goes beyond transmittal of subject-matter."[38]

— IV —

Wars and Revolutions

> Nothing is understood about this man until it has been perceived that, of necessity and without exception, everything—language and fact—falls for him within the sphere of justice . . . For him, too, justice and language remain founded in each other.
> —Walter Benjamin, "Karl Kraus"

It is customary to view Benjamin essentially as an abstract philosopher, a critic and a thinker of modernity (and/or of postmodernity) in culture and in art. In contradistinction to this dominant approach, I propose now to view Benjamin—far more specifically and more concretely—as a thinker, a philosopher, and a narrator of the wars and revolutions of the twentieth century. "Wars and revolutions," writes Hannah Arendt, "have thus far determined the physiognomy of the twentieth century. And as distinguished from the nineteenth century ideologies—such as nationalism and internationalism, capitalism and imperialism, socialism and communism—which, though still invoked by many as justifying causes, have lost contact with the major realities of our world, war and revolution . . . have outlived all their ideological justifications."[39]

[T]he seeds of total war developed as early as the First World War, when the distinction between soldiers and civilians was no longer respected because it was inconsistent with the new weapons then used . . . The magnitude of the violence let loose in the First World War might indeed have been enough to cause revolutions in its aftermath even without any revolutionary tradition and even if no revolution had ever occurred before.

To be sure, not even wars, let alone revolutions, are ever completely determined by violence. Where violence rules absolutely, . . . everything and everybody must fall silent.[40]

In my reading, Walter Benjamin's lifework bears witness to the ways in which events outlive their ideologies and consummate, dissolve, the grounding discourse of their nineteenth-century historic and utopian meanings. Benjamin's texts play out, thus, one against the other and one through the other, both the "constellation that poses the threat of total annihilation through war against the hope for the emancipation of all mankind through revolution,"[41] and the deadly succession of historical convulsions through which culture—in the voice of Benjamin, who is its most profound witness—must fall silent.

Theory and Autobiography

Silence can be either the outside of language or a position inside language, a state of noiselessness or wordlessness. Falling silent is, however, not a state but an event. It is the significance of the event that I will underscore and try to further understand in what will follow. What does it mean that culture—in the voice of its most profound witness—must fall silent? What does it mean for culture? What does it mean for Benjamin? How does Benjamin come to represent and to incorporate concretely, personally, the physiognomy of the twentieth century? And how in turn is this physiognomy reflected, concretized, in Benjamin's own face?

In searching for answers to these questions, I will juxtapose and grasp together theoretical and autobiographical texts. Benjamin's own work includes a singular record of an autobiographical event that, to my mind, is crucial to the author's theories as much as to his destiny (although critics usually neglect it). Benjamin narrates this event in one of his rare moments of personal directness, in the (lyrical) autobiographical text entitled, *A Berlin Chronicle*. I will interpret this event together with, and through, two central theoretical essays that constitute the cornerstones of Benjamin's late work: "The Storyteller" and "Theses on the Philosophy of History." In reading the most personal, the most idiosyncratic autobiographical notations through the most far-reaching, groundbreaking theoretical constructions, my effort is to give Benjamin's theory a face.[42] The conceptual question that will override and guide this effort will be: what is the relation between the theory and the event (and what, in general, is the relationship between events and theories)? How does the theory arise out of the concrete drama (and trauma) of an event? How does the concrete drama (and trauma) of an event become theory? And how do both event and theory relate to silence (and to Benjamin's embodiment of silence)?

— V —

Theories of Silence

Because my sense is that in Benjamin, the theory is (paradoxically) far less obscure than the autobiography, I will start my close reading of Benjamin by addressing first the two theoretical essays—perhaps the best known abstract texts of Benjamin—of which I propose to underscore the *common* theoretical stakes. I will argue that both "The Storyteller" and the "Theses on the Philosophy of History" can be construed as two theories of silence derived from, and related to, the two world wars: "the Storyteller," written in 1936, is retrospectively, explicitly connected with the First World War; "Theses on the Philosophy of History," written shortly before Benjamin's death in 1940, represents his ultimate rethinking of the nature of historical events and of the task of historiography in the face of the developments of the beginning of the Second World War.

I suggest that these two texts are in effect tied up together. I propose to read them one against the other and one through the other, as two stages in a larger philosophical and existential picture, and as two variations of a global Benjaminian theory of wars and silence. I argue therefore that "The Storyteller" and "Theses" can be viewed as two theoretical variations of the same profound underlying text. My methodology is here inspired by the way in which Benjamin himself discusses—in his youth—"Two Poems by Friedrich Hölderlin,"[43] in analyzing in the two texts (as he puts it) "not their likeness which is nonexistent" but their "comparability,"[44] and in treating them—despite their distance—as two "versions" (or two transformations) of the same profound text.

The End of Storytelling

"The Storyteller" is presented as a literary study of the nineteenth-century Russian writer Nikolai Leskov, and of his striking art of storytelling. But the essay's main concern is in depicting storytelling as a *lost art:* the achievements of the nineteenth-century model serve as the background for a differential diagnosis of the ways in which *storytelling is lost to the twentieth century.* Something happened, Benjamin suggests, that has brought about the death—the agony—of storytelling, both as a literary genre and as a discursive mode in daily life. Benjamin announces thus a historical drama of "the end of storytelling"—or an innovative cultural theory of the collapse of narration—as a critical and theoretical appraisal (through Leskov) of a general historical state of affairs.

The theory, thereby, is Benjamin's way of grasping and bringing into consciousness an unconscious cultural phenomenon and an imperceptible historical process that has taken place outside anyone's awareness and that can therefore be deciphered, understood, and noticed only retrospectively, in its effects (its symptoms). The effects, says Benjamin, are that today, quite symptomatically, *it has become impossible to tell a story.* The art of storytelling has been lost along with the ability to share experiences.

> Less and less frequently do we encounter people with the ability to tell a tale properly . . . It is as if something that seemed inalienable to us . . . were taken from us: the ability to exchange experiences.[45]

Among the reasons Benjamin gives for this loss—the rise of capitalism, the sterilization of life through bourgeois values, the decline of craftsmanship, the growing influence of the media and the press—the first and most dramatic is that people have been struck dumb by the First World War. From ravaged battlefields, they have returned mute to a wrecked world in which nothing has remained the same except the sky. This vivid and dramatic explanation is placed right away at the beginning of the text, like an explosive opening argument or an initial shock or blast inflicted on the reader, with whose shock the whole remainder of the text will have to cope and to catch up. The opening is, indeed, as forceful as it is ungraspable. The text itself does not quite process it, nor does it truly integrate it with the arguments that follow. And this ungraspability or unintegratability of the beginning is not a mere coincidence; it duplicates and illustrates the point of the text, that the war has left an impact that has struck dumb its survivors, with the effect of interrupting now the continuity of telling and of understanding. The utterance repeats in act the content of the statement: it must remain somewhat unassimilable.

In Benjamin, however, it is productive to retain what cannot be assimilated. And it is crucially important in my view that what cannot be assimilated crystallizes around a date. Before it can be understood, the loss of narrative is *dated*. Its process is traced back to the collective, massive trauma of the First World War.

> With the [First] World War a process began to become apparent which has not halted since then. Was it not noticeable at the end of the war that men returned from the battlefield grown silent—not richer, but poorer in communicable experience? What ten years later was poured out in the flood of war books was anything but experience that goes from mouth to mouth. And there was nothing remarkable about that. For never has experience been contradicted more thoroughly than strategic experience by tactical warfare, economic experience by inflation, bodily experience by mechanical warfare, moral experience by those in power. A generation that had gone to school on a horse-drawn streetcar now stood under the open sky in a countryside in which nothing remained unchanged but the clouds, and beneath these clouds, in a field of force of destructive torrents and explosions, was the tiny, fragile human body. ("St.," 84)

Thus, narration was reduced to silence by the First World War. What has emerged from the destructive torrents—from the noise of the explosions—was only the muteness of the body in its absolutely helpless, shelterless vulnerability. Resonating to this dumbness of the body is the storyteller's dumbness.

But this fall to silence of narration is contrasted with, and covered by, the new loudness, the emerging noise of information—"journalism being clearly . . . the expression of the changed function of language in the world of high capitalism."[46]

In a world in which public discourse is usurped by the commercial aims and by the noise of information, soldiers returning from the First World War can find no social or collective space in which to integrate their death experience. Their trauma must remain a private matter that cannot be symbolized collectively. It cannot be exchanged, it must fall silent.

The Unforgettable

Gone are the days when dying was "a public process in the life of an individual and a most exemplary one" ("St.," 93). Irrespective of the battlefield experience, mortality is self-deceptively denied in sterilized bourgeois life, which strives to keep death out of sight symbolically and literally.[47]

Narration was, however, born from the pathos of an ultimate exchange between the dying and the living. Medieval paintings represent the origin of storytelling: they show the archetypal or inaugural site of narration to be the deathbed, in which the dying man (or the original narrator) reviews his life (evokes his memories) and thus addresses the events and lessons of his past to those surrounding him. A dying speaker is a naturally authoritative storyteller: he borrows his authority from death.[48]

Today, however, agonizers die in private and without authority. They are attended by no listeners. They tell no stories. And there is no authority—and certainly no wisdom—that has survived the war. "We have no counsel either for ourselves or for others. After all, counsel is less an answer to a question than a proposal concerning the continuation of a story which is just unfolding" ("St.," 86).

It is not simply that there is no longer a proposal for historical or narrative continuation. The First World War is *the first war that can no longer be narrated.* Its witnesses and its participants have lost their stories. The sole signification that "The Storyteller" can henceforth articulate is that of mankind's double loss: a loss of the capacity to symbolize and a loss of the capacity to moralize.[49]

A Philosophy of History

The outbreak of the Second World War in 1939 (three years after the publication of "The Storyteller") brings Benjamin to write, in 1940—in the months that were to be the last ones of his life—what I have called his second theory of silence, entitled "Theses on the Philosophy of History." At first, this text seems altogether different from "The Storyteller." Its topic is not literature but history, of which the essay offers not a diagnosis but a theory. The theory is programmatic: its tone is not descriptive but prescriptive. The "theses" are audaciously abbreviated and provocatively dogmatized. They do not explicitly reflect on silence. The essay focuses rather on (scholarly and scientific) *discourses* on history. The word *silence* does not figure in the text.

And yet, speechlessness is at the very heart of the reflection, and of the situation of the writer. Like the storyteller who falls silent or returns mute from the First World War, the historian or the theorist of history facing the conflagration of the Second World War is equally *reduced to speechlessness:* no ready-made conceptual or discursive tool, no discourse about history turns out to be sufficient to explain the nature of this war; no available conceptual framework in which history is customarily perceived proves adequate or satisfactory to understand or to explain current historical developments. Vis-à-vis the undreamt of events, what is called for, Benjamin suggests, is a *radical displacement of our frames of reference,* a radical transvaluation of our methods and of our philosophies of history. "The current amazement that the things we are experiencing are 'still' possible in the twentieth century is *not* philosophical. This amazement is not the beginning of knowledge—unless it is the knowledge that the view of history which gives rise to it is untenable" (VIII, in Benjamin, *Ill.,* 257).

History is now the property and the propriety of Nazis (of those who can control it and manipulate its discourse). It is by virtue of a loyalty to history that Hitler is proposing to avenge Germany from its defeat and its humiliation in the First World War. All the existing discourses on history have proven ineffective either to predict or to counteract the regime and the phenomenon of Hitler.[50]

History in Nazi Germany is fascist. Fascism legitimates itself in the name of national identity on the basis of a unity and of a continuity of history. The philosophical tenets of this view are inherited from nineteenth-century historicism, which has equated temporality with progress, in presupposing time as an entity of natural development, progressively enhancing maturation and advancing toward a betterment as time (and history) go by. Benjamin rejects this view, which has become untenable vis-à-vis the traumas of the twentieth century.

It is the victor who forever represents the present conquest or the present victory as an improvement in relation to the past. But the reality of history is that of those traumatized by history, the materialist reality of those who are oppressed by the new victory. Historicism is, however, based on an unconscious identification with the discourse of the victor, and thus on an uncritical espousal of the victor's narrative perspective. "If one asks with whom the adherents of historicism actually empathize," Benjamin writes,

> The answer is inevitable: with the victor . . . Empathy with the victor inevitably benefits the ruler. Historical materialists know what that means. Whoever has emerged victorious participates to this day in the triumphal procession in which the present rulers step over those who are lying prostrate. According to traditional practice, the spoils are carried along in the procession. They are called cultural treasures, and a historical materialist views them with cautious detachment. For without exception the cultural treasures he surveys have an origin which he cannot contemplate without horror. They owe their existence not only to the efforts of the great minds and talents who have created them, but also to the anonymous toil of their contemporaries. There is no document of civilization which is not at the same time a document of barbarism. And just as a document is not free of barbarism, barbarism taints also the manner in which it was transmitted from one owner to another. (VII, *Ill.*, 256)

Historicism is thus based on a perception of history as victory. But it is blind to this presupposition. So blind that it does not see the irony with which this axiom has been borrowed—taken to extremes—by the discourses of fascism. Fascism is, indeed, quite literally, a *philosophy of history as victory.* Unlike historicism, it is not unconscious of this prejudice: it is grounded in a cynical and conscious *claim* of this philosophy of history.[51]

Historicism is thus based on a confusion between truth and power. Real history is, on the contrary, the ineluctable discrepancy between the two.[52] History is the perennial conflictual arena in which collective memory is named as a *constitutive dissociation* between truth and power.

What, then, is the relation between history and silence? In a (conscious or unconscious) historical philosophy of power, the powerless (the persecuted) are constitutionally deprived of voice.

Because official history is based on the perspective of the victor, the voice with which it speaks authoritatively is *deafening:* it makes us unaware of the fact that there remains in history a claim, a discourse, that we *do not hear.* And in relation to this deafening, the rulers of the moment are the heirs of the rulers of the past. History transmits, ironically enough, a legacy of deafness in which historicists unwittingly share. What is called progress, and what Benjamin sees only as a piling of catastrophe upon catastrophe, is therefore the transmission of historical discourse from ruler to ruler, from one historical instance of power to another. This transmission is constitutive of what is (misguidedly) perceived as continuity in history. "The continuum of history is that of the oppressors." "The history of the oppressed is a discontinuum."[53]

If history, despite its spectacular triumphal time, is thus barbarically, constitutively conflict ridden, the historian is not in possession of a space in which to be removed, detached, "objective"; the philosopher of history cannot be an outsider to the conflict. In the face of the deafening appropriation of historical philosophy by fascism, in the face of the Nazi use of the most *civilized* tools of technology and law for a most barbaric racist persecution, "objectivity" does not exist. A historical articulation proceeds not from an epistemological "detachment" but, on the contrary, from the historian's sense of urgency and of emergency.[54]

> The tradition of the oppressed teaches us that the "state of emergency" in which we live is not the exception but the rule. We must attain to a conception of history that is in keeping with this insight. Then we shall clearly realize that it is our task to bring about a real state of emergency, and this will improve our position in the struggle against Fascism. (VIII, *Ill.*, 257)

The theory of history is thus itself an *intervention in the conflict;* it is itself historical. In the middle of a cataclysmic world war that shifts the grounds from under our very feet, danger, Benjamin implies, is what triggers the most lucid and the most clairvoyant *grasp* of history. Historical insight strikes surprisingly and unexpectedly in "moments of sudden illumination" in which "we are beside ourselves."[55] Danger and emergency illuminate themselves as the conditions both of history (of life) and of its theory (its knowledge). New, innovative theories of history (such that enable a displacement of official history) come into being only under duress.

> To articulate the past historically does not mean to recognize it "the way it really was" (Ranke). It means to seize hold of a memory as it flashes up at a moment of danger. Historical materialism wishes to retain that image of the past which unexpectedly appears to man singled out by history at a moment of danger. (VI, *Ill.*, 255)

In Benjamin's own view, history—a line of catastrophe—is not a movement toward progress but a movement toward (what Benjamin calls enigmatically) redemption. Redemption—what historical struggles (and political revolutions) are about—should be understood as both materialist (Marxist, political, interhistorical) and theological (suprahistorical, transcendent). "Redemption" is discontinuity, disruption. It names the constant need to catch up with the hidden reality of history that always remains a debt to the oppressed, a debt to the dead of history, a claim the past has on the present.

Redemption is the allegory of a future state of freedom, justice, happiness, and recovery of meaning. History should be assessed only *in reference* to this state, which is its goal. Historical action should take place as though this goal were not utopian but pragmatic. Yet it can never be decided by a mortal if redemption, ultimately, can be immanent to history or if it is doomed to remain transcendental, beyond history. "This world," Benjamin has written elsewhere, "remains a mute world, from which music will never ring out. Yet to what is it dedicated if not redemption?"[56]

Dedicated to Redemption

When, therefore, will redemption come? Will there be a redemption after the Second World War? Will there ever be redemption *from* the Second World War? Benjamin foresees the task of the historian of the future. He will be sad. His history will be the product of his sadness.

Flaubert [Benjamin writes], who was familiar with [the cause of sadness], wrote: *"Peu de gens devineront combien il a fallu être triste pour ressusciter Carthage"* [Few will be able to guess how sad one had to be in order to resuscitate Carthage]. (VII, *Ill.*, 256)

Before the fact, Benjamin foresees that history will know a holocaust. After the war, the historian's task will be not only to "resuscitate Carthage" or to *narrate extermination* but, paradoxically, to *save the dead:*

Nothing that has ever happened should be regarded as lost to history. (III, *Ill.*, 254)

Only that historian will have the gift of fanning the spark of hope in the past who is firmly convinced that *even the dead* will not be safe from the enemy if he wins." (VI, *Ill.*, 255; Benjamin's italics)

Thus, the historian of the Second World War will be sad. Beyond sadness, he will have to be intently vigilant. In this war, particularly, the conceptual question of the historian's identification with the victor inadvertently evolves into a graver, far more serious question of political complicity.

The task of the historian of today is to *avoid collaboration* with a criminal regime and with the discourses of fascism. Similarly, the historian of tomorrow will have to be watchful to avoid complicity with history's barbarism and with culture's latent (and now patent) crimes. Benjamin's text, I argue, is the beginning of the critical awareness of the treacherous questions of collaboration that so obsessively preoccupy us to this day. It is still early in the war. Benjamin intuitively senses the importance of this question, as it will arise precisely, later, *out of* the Second World War. The historian, Benjamin suggests, must be revolutionary lest he be unwittingly complicit. And complicity, for Benjamin, is a graver danger, a worse punishment than death.

> Historical materialism wishes to retain the image of the past which unexpectedly appears to man singled out by history at a moment of danger. The danger affects both the content of the tradition and its receivers. The same threat hangs over both: that of becoming a tool of the ruling classes. In every era the attempt must be made to wrest tradition away from a conformism that is about to overpower it. (VI, *Ill.*, 255)

The historian, paradoxically, has no choice but to be a revolutionary if he does not want to be a collaborator.[57]

History and Speechlessness

Benjamin advances, thus, a theory of history as trauma—and a correlative theory of the historical conversion of trauma into insight. History consists in chains of traumatic interruptions rather than in sequences of rational causalities. But the traumatized—the subjects of history— are deprived of a language in which to speak of their victimization. The relation between history and trauma is speechless. Traditional theories of history tend to neglect this speechlessness of trauma: by definition, speechlessness is what remains out of the record. But it is specifically to this speechless connection between history and trauma that Benjamin's own theory of history intends now to give voice.

He does so by showing how the very discipline, the very "concept of history"[58] is constituted by what it excludes (and fails to grasp). History (to sum up) is thus inhabited by a historical unconscious related to—and founded on—a double silence: the silence of "the tradition of the oppressed," who are by definition deprived of voice and whose story (or whose narrative perspective) is always systematically reduced to silence; and the silence of official history—the victor's history—with respect to the tradition of the oppressed. According to Benjamin, the hidden theoretical centrality of this double silence defines historiography as such. This in general is the way in which history is told, or rather, this is in general the way in which history is silenced. The triumph of fascism and the outbreak of the Second World War constitute only the most climactic demonstration, the most aberrant materialization or realization of this historiography.

Whereas the task of the philosopher of history is thus to take apart "the concept of history" by showing its deceptive continuity to be in fact a process of silencing, the task of the historian is to reconstruct what history has silenced, to give voice to the dead and to the vanquished and to resuscitate the unrecorded, silenced, hidden story of the oppressed.

— VI —

The Event

I would like now to look backward from the theory to the autobiography, and to try to reach the roots of Benjamin's conceptual insights in an original event whose theoretical and autobiographical significance remains totally ungrasped in the voluminous critical literature on Benjamin. The event takes place at the outbreak of the First World War. It consists in the conjunction of the German invasion of Belgium on August 4, 1914, with the joint suicide, four days later, of Benjamin's best friend, Fritz Heinle, and of Heinle's girlfriend. A farewell express letter from the now dead friend informs Benjamin where to find the bodies. This shared readiness to die and this joint act of self-inflicted violence is interpreted by Benjamin and his friends as a symbolic gesture of protest against the war. For Benjamin, the event is therefore one of loss, of shock, of disillusionment, and of awakening to the reality of an inexorable, tragic, historical connection between youth and death. For the world, it is the outbreak of the First World War.

The impact of this event marks a dramatic turning point in Benjamin's life and in his thought. Before the event, Benjamin is involved in political activism in the youth movement, working to revolutionize German society and culture through a radical reform of education. In the youth groups supporting this reform, he holds a position of strong leadership as president of the Berlin Free Students' Union. After the event, he abdicates his leadership and turns away from political activity. He gives up any public role along with the belief that language can directly become action. He breaks with his admired teacher, Wyneken, of whose ideas he has been both the disciple and the ardent follower. Because his former mentor now guides youth toward the war, Benjamin realizes that philosophy has failed and that authority can no longer be relied on: "theoria in you has been blinded,"[59] he writes to Wyneken, in severing his links with him.

In the duplicity of governments, in the duplicity of teachers, and in the isolated words of the letter of a dead youth telling Benjamin—the friend, the leader, the collaborator—where to find the bodies, language has betrayed: but the betrayal constitutes precisely the event; the betrayal is precisely history. "Midway through its journey," Benjamin will write, "nature finds itself betrayed by language, and that powerful blocking of feeling turns to sorrow. Thus, with the ambiguity of the words, its signifying power, language falters . . . History becomes equal to signification in human language; this language is frozen in signification."[60]

Refusing to participate in the betrayal of language and in the madness of the war, Benjamin leaves Germany for Switzerland and resorts to a silence that will last six years, until 1920.[61] During these years, he does not publish anything. He writes and circulates among close friends a text on Hölderlin in which he meditates on the nature of the lyric and its relation to the poet's death.[62] The poet's death relates to Heinle's death. Heinle also has left poems, which Benjamin reads and rereads in an attempt to deepen his acquaintance with the dead. It is, indeed, as a dead poet that he now comes to know his friend. But Benjamin vows to give the dead poet immortality: to save Heinle from oblivion, to save the suicide from its meaninglessness, by publishing his friend's poetic work. This hope will never be relinquished. In the years of silence following the suicides, he edits Heinle's manuscripts. Benjamin's own text on Hölderlin and on the nature of the lyric is also an implicit dialogue with Heinle's work, a dialogue with Heinle's writing as well as with his life and with his death. Hence, Benjamin's specific interest in two poems by

Hölderlin, "The Poet's Courage" and "Timidity," which designate the difference between Heinle's (suicidal) "Courage" and the "Timidity" of Benjamin's own (condemnation to) survival: suicide or survival, two existential stances between which Benjamin no doubt has oscillated but that he declares to be, surprisingly and paradoxically, two "versions" of the same profound text, deeply "comparable" or similar despite their difference (Benjamin, *SWI*, 21, 33).

Belated Understanding

This drama and these suicides are narrated (among other things) in Benjamin's most personal autobiography, *A Berlin Chronicle*. I will argue that, for Benjamin, this autobiographical narrative becomes an allegory of the ungrasped impact of the First World War.

But the *Berlin Chronicle* is written eighteen years later, in 1932. The direct result of the events of the war at the time of their ungraspable occurrence is that Benjamin quite literally falls silent. And especially, quite literally and strictly silent, speechless about the subject of the war: as though by oath of loyalty to the dead friend; as though his own speech, or the language of youth they shared, had equally committed suicide. Something in himself has died as well. The traumatic (and belatedly, theoretical) significance of this silence remains equally ungrasped by critics, who keep expressing their politically correct critique of it and their amazement at this eccentricity of Benjamin. Nor does anybody grasp the profound connection of this early silence to the later, much admired classic essays "The Storyteller" and "Theses on the Philosophy of History." Benjamin's early experience is, thus, on the contrary, separated from his later theory and is at once dismissed and trivialized: "Silence as an expression of inner protest at contemporary events: little doubt was cast on the legitimacy of such a stance at the time,"[63] the latest biographer Momme Brodersen historicizes. The editors of Benjamin's *Selected Writings*, more tuned in, feel equally compelled to mark a pious reservation: "Remarkably enough, Benjamin's letters . . . focus exclusively on personal issues . . . There is rarely mention of the war, and no direct consideration of it or of his attitude toward it. It is as if Benjamin's injunction against political activity at the time also precluded cognizance of the most difficult events of the day" (*SWI*, 502). What critics fail to see is how Benjamin's own narration of his war experience in *A Berlin Chroni-*

cle is precisely, quintessentially, an autobiographical (and theoretical) *account of the meaning of his silence.*

— VII —

The Subject Represented by the "I"

> The death of the other man implicates and challenges me, as if, through its
> indifference, the *I* became the accomplice to, and had to answer for, this
> death of the other and not let him die alone . . . Responsibility here is not a
> cold juridical requirement. It is all the gravity of the love of one's fellowmen
> . . . which is presupposed by all literary culture.
> —Emmanuel Levinas, "The Philosophical Determination
>   of the Idea of Culture"

Eleven pages into *A Berlin Chronicle,* Benjamin begins the narration of his war experience by insisting on his reluctance to say "I": "If I write better German than most writers of my generation, it is thanks largely to twenty years' observance of one little rule: never use the word 'I' except in letters." (*BC,* 15). However, Benjamin adds ironically, in this solicited piece he has accepted not just to say "I" but to be paid for it; if, therefore, these subjective notes have become longer than he had intended, it is not only because the subject, "accustomed for years to waiting in the wings," would not so easily come to the limelight," but also because, metaphorically and literally, "the precaution of the subject represented by the 'I' . . . is entitled not to be sold cheap" (*BC,* 15–16).

The autobiographical impulse is therefore in conflict with a speechlessness, a muteness of the "I" that constantly defeats narration from inside. And yet, the text originates in an imperative to tell, in a symbolic debt that goes beyond the personal, and that makes narration unavoidable and indispensable. What is at stake, says Benjamin, are "deep and harrowing experiences" that constitute "the most important memories in one's life" (*BC,* 16). Of these experiences, all the other witnesses are now dead: "I alone remain" (*BC,* 17). The ethical impetus of the narration stems from this aloneness and from this necessity: since the narrator is the last surviving witness, history must be told despite the narrator's muteness. The narrator sees himself surrounded by dead doubles, younger than himself or of his age, dead witnesses who, had they been alive, might have helped him to cross the difficult thresholds of memory, but whose dead faces now appear to him "only as an answer to the question whether forty [Benjamin's age at the time of writing] is not too young an age at which to evoke the most important memories of one's life" (*BC*, 16). The *Chronicle* implicitly announces, thus, the author's forti-eth birthday, with which its writing coincides. The autobiographer cele-brates his birthday by mourning for the death of his contemporaries. From the start, death and birth are juxtaposed. "Berlin" is the name for this juxtaposition.

Prosopopeia

Longing for the complementary narration of his dead doubles and iden-tified with their eternal silence, the speaker in fact writes an epitaph much more than a biography. The *Chronicle* is an autobiography that is inherently, profoundly epitaphic, and that seeks, thus, not expression but precisely "the expressionless": the moment in which life is "petrified, as if spellbound in a single moment" (Benjamin, "GEA," 340). In line with Benjamin's analysis of "the expressionless," the writing possesses a "criti-cal violence" (ibid., 340) that interrupts expression, with which "every expression simultaneously comes to a standstill" (341) with the abrupt-ness of "a moral dictum" (340). "Only the expressionless completes the work by shattering it into a thing of shards, into a fragment of the true world, into the torso of a symbol" (340). To use the terminology of Paul de Man, we might say that in *A Berlin Chronicle* "autobiography veils a de-facement of the mind of which it is itself the cause."[64] De Man's rhe-torical analysis is here particularly pertinent: "the dominant figure of the epitaphic or autobiographical discourse is . . . the prosopopeia" (*RR*, 77), "the fiction of an apostrophe to an absent, deceased or voiceless en-tity, which posits the possibility of the latter's reply and confers upon it the power of speech" (*RR*, 75–76).

I would suggest, indeed, that an implicit figure of prosopopeia struc-tures not just Benjamin's autobiography but his entire work: the under-lying, understated evocation of the dead is present and can be deci-phered everywhere. Benjamin's whole writing could be read as work of mourning, structured by a mute address to the dead face and the lost voice of the young friend who took his own life in a desperate protest in the first days of the First World War. "In all mourning there is the deepest inclination to speechlessness, which is infinitely more than the inability or disinclination to communicate."[65] All of Benjamin's evolving subjects, I will argue, are implicitly determined by the conceptual implications of the underlying autobiographical prosopopeia, or the mute address to the dead friend: lyric ("Heinle was a poet," *BC*, 17), language ("Because she is mute, nature mourns," *SWI*, 73), *Trauerspiel* (the corpse is the sole bearer of signification), and, finally, history itself:

> In allegory the observer is confronted with the *facies hippocratica* [agonizer's face] of history as a petrified, primordial landscape. Everything about history that, from the very beginning, has been untimely, sorrowful, unsuccessful, is expressed in a face—or rather in a death's head.[66]

A Lecture on the Nature of the Lyric, or The Face of History (A Primal Scene)

> There arises, awakened by the silent and imperative language spoken by the face of the other, . . . the solicitude of responsibility . . . prior to deliberation . . .
> The response of responsibility that already lies dormant in a salutation, in the *hello*, in the *goodbye*. Such a language is prior to the statements of propositions communicating information and narrative.
> —Emmanuel Levinas, "Alterity and Diachrony"

It is precisely as a metaphor for his entire work as inarticulate prosopopeia that Benjamin describes the lecture on Hölderlin and on "the nature of the lyric" that, after Heinle's suicide, he struggled to articulate in memory of his deceased friend.

It is significant that the *Berlin Chronicle*'s narration of the war events and of its "harrowing experiences" starts (disorientingly, hermetically) by the description of this lecture—by the mediation, that is, of the trauma by the work, by the translation of the lived event into *a thought on literature*. The *Berlin Chronicle* cannot go directly either to the proper name of the dead friend or to the actual story of his death. Temporally as well as spatially, the story keeps moving in circles, as though around an empty, silent center. The word *suicide* does not figure in the text. Heinle's name is introduced as though in passing: it vanishes as soon as it is mentioned; and so does the event. Throughout the text, the name and the event keep vanishing.

It was in Heidelberg, during what was doubtless self-forgetful work that I tried to summon up, in a meditation on the nature of the lyric, the figure of my friend Fritz Heinle, around whom all the happenings in the Meeting House arrange themselves and with whom they vanish. Fritz Heinle was a poet, and the only one of them all whom I met not "in real life" but in his work. He died at nineteen, and could be known in no other way. All the same, this first attempt to evoke the sphere of his life through that of poetry was unsuccessful, and the immediacy of the experience that gave rise to my lecture asserted itself in the incomprehension and snobbery of the audience. (*BC*, 17)[67]

In a roundabout way, what Benjamin is trying to evoke is not Hölderlin but history: an original historical event that has remained completely untranslatable. History is "the original," the writings—its translations. The task of the translator is the witness's task. The lecture tried, but failed, to translate the impact of the event. Nevertheless, the lecture gives a sense of the remoteness, of the unapproachability of the historical event. Behind this failed translation of the lecture on Hölderlin and on the nature of the lyric, the untranslatable historical original—the lived experience of the outbreak of the war—constitutes for Benjamin a veritable intellectual and existential *primal scene*.

The Meeting House (Das Heim)

What, then, is the core of the historical event that cannot be approached but must be distanced even in the very act of bearing witness to it? What is the meaning of the story that the text cannot arrive at, cannot reach, cannot *begin* except through what has followed, the lecture that attempted to translate it—unsuccessfully?

It is the story of a death without signification, though pregnant with sense, with life, and with emotion. It is the story of a meeting and of a Meeting House that turns out to be, ironically, the house of an encounter with a corpse, the posthumous symbol of a lost community and of the loss of language as communal, and the empty center of the space of the remembrance of so many missed encounters: a missed encounter with the audience of the lecture; a missed encounter with the war; a missed encounter with the friend who, dying so young, dies before he could be truly met: "Fritz Heinle was a poet, and the only one of them all whom I met not 'in real life' but in his work. He died at nineteen, and could be known in no other way." It is the story of a war, and of its casualties that history does not narrate and does not count. It is the story of a letter doubled by a corpse that has become the bearer of a meaning it cannot deliver:

> No matter how much memory has subsequently paled, or how indistinctly I can now give an account of the rooms in the Meeting House, it nevertheless seems to me today more legitimate to delineate the outward space the dead man inhabited, indeed the rooms where he was "announced," than the inner space in which he created. But perhaps this is only because, in this last and most crucial year of his life, he traversed the space in which I was born. Heinle's Berlin was the Berlin of the Meeting House . . . I once visited him . . . after a long separation resulting from a serious dissention between us. But even today I remember the smile that lifted the whole weight of these weeks of separation, that turned a probably insignificant phrase into a magic formula that healed the wound. Later, after the morning when an express letter awoke me with the words, "You will find us lying in the Meeting House"—when Heinle and his girlfriend were dead—this district remained for a period the central meeting place of the living. (*BC,* 17–18)

The Letter and the Corpse

The unnamed suicide takes place in the blank, the interval between a future—"you will find us"—and a past: "were dead." The corpse has left an urgent letter that awakens Benjamin in shock. But the letter does not speak, it tells no story: it does not explain the motivation of the suicide or its grounds, it does not *narrate* anything other than the utter muteness of the body—of the corpse: "You will find us lying in the Meeting House." What remains of Heinle now are only words. Words of poetry, which Benjamin preserves and hopes to publish. Words of an unintelligible letter. "Just as a certain kind of significant dream—Benjamin writes—survives awakening in the form of words when all the rest of the dream content has vanished, here isolated words have remained in place as marks of catastrophic encounters" (*BC,* 14).

Heinle at nineteen, Benjamin at twenty-two have come to the end of the experience that enables telling, or that makes narration possible. In 1936, in "The Storyteller," Benjamin will write that people have returned mute from the battlefields of the First World War. Benjamin himself falls silent not at the war's end but before the war, at the beginning of the war, because he grasps before the others its significance in history and its senseless violence, because he sees ahead of time the consequences of the war. The meaning of the war reveals itself to him in one stroke, in an obscure illumination or in the shock of an epiphany of darkness, in the image of the suicide and in the vision of the combination of the private trauma and of the collective one.

> It was in this café that we sat together in those very first August days, choosing among the barracks that were being stormed by the onrush of volunteers. We decided on the cavalry of Belle-Alliance Strasse, where I duly appeared on one of the following days, no spark of martial fervor in my breast; yet however reserved I may have been in my thoughts, which were concerned only with securing a place among friends in the inevitable conscription, one of the bodies jammed in front of the barrack gates was mine. Admittedly only for two days: on August 8 came the event that was to banish for long after both the city and the war from my mind. (*BC*, 21)

"Autobiography"—said Paul de Man—"veils a de-facement of the mind of which it is itself the cause" (*RR*, 81). The "place among friends" Benjamin tries to "secure" in "the inevitable conscription" turns out to be a place among corpses. The *Chronicle* is an autobiography of trauma. The event consists in an erasure: an erasure of Berlin and of the war from the map of consciousness; an erasure of the self—its transformation into an automaton or a half-corpse, a body dispossessed of consciousness: "one of the bodies jammed in front of the barrack gates was mine," says Benjamin. The war, the shock against the mass of bodies replicated, two days later, by the shock of the discovery of two dead bodies, strips the self of "I": "It is to this immolation of our deepest self in shock that our memory owes its most indelible images" (*BC*, 57).

Unspeakable Youth, or Living Outside Experience

Benjamin mourns thus his own lost youthful self, for which Fritz Heinle has become the metaphor: he grieves at the same time over Heinle's and his own lost youth. "The Medium in which the pure melody of his youth would swell was stolen from him . . . In despair, he thus recalls his childhood. In those days there was time without flight and an 'I' without death . . . Finally, he is redeemed by losing his comprehension. Amid such obliviousness . . . he begins the diary. It is the unfathomable document of a life never lived" (Benjamin, "MY," 11).

The suicide represents, however, not simply death but a refusal to compromise with life. Benjamin loves deeply Heinle's absolute commitment to a youth that, unlike Benjamin, he refuses to survive. "Never in any other work," Benjamin will say of Goethe, "did he give to youth what he granted it in Ottilie: the whole of life, in the way that, from its own duration, it has its own death" ("GEA," 353). This description equally applies to Heinle. Paradoxically, Heinle's suicide comes to represent not death but, on the contrary, vitality of life: "The pure word for life in its immortality is 'youth,'" writes Benjamin, in analyzing how traumatized youth in Dostoevsky's *Idiot* comes to embody both a principle of life (an everlasting or fixed youth) and a concurrent principle of childish muteness:[68] "This young generation suffers from a damaged childhood" (*SWI*, 80–81).

Unexpectedly, trauma meets youth precisely in its absence—its erasure—of experience: "we have not yet experienced anything" (*SWI*, 3),[69] said Benjamin at twenty-one, speaking for youth. At twenty-two, the trauma as erasure—"the event that was to banish for long after both the city and the war from my mind"—equally remains outside experience.[70]

> In spite—or perhaps because—of this—. . . the city of Berlin was never again to impinge so forcefully on my existence as it did in that epoch when we believed we could leave it untouched, only improving its schools, only breaking the inhumanity of their inmates' parents, only making a place in it for the words of Hölderlin or George. It was a final, heroic attempt to change the attitudes of people without changing their circumstances. We did not know that it was bound to fail, but there was hardly one of us whose resolve such knowledge could have altered. And today, as clearly as at that time, even if on the basis of an entirely different reasoning, I understand that the "language of youth" had to stand at the center of our associations. (*BC*, 18)

Benjamin pledges fidelity to the "language of youth" the war has erased and that his subsequent work has struck dumb and reduced to silence. But *A Berlin Chronicle* narrates the way in which what is erased—the war, the corpse—remains precisely at the center. The center will thus be a silence. What is erased, what falls to silence at the outbreak of the war, is youth. But youth can have an unexpected afterlife. Heinle's youth lives on in Benjamin. And Benjamin's own silenced youth still speaks in interrupted lyric intervals that have become expressionless through Benjamin's own silence. "Fidelity shall be maintained, even if no one has done so yet" (*SWI*, 4), wrote Benjamin at twenty-one, signing "Ardor." Grown mute, the aged writer still asserts: "And today, as clearly as at that time . . . I understand that the language of youth had to stand at the center of our associations."

"Death," Benjamin discovers, "has the power to lay bare like love." "The human being appears to us as a corpse . . . the human body lays itself bare" ("GEA," 353). In a shocking, unnarratable epiphany of darkness, the war lays bare the body, in suddenly revealing youth as corpse.

The Burial

But the most traumatic memory that Benjamin keeps from the war is not simply this unnarratable epiphany—this sudden overwhelming revelation of youth as a corpse—but the added insult, the accompanying shame of the impossibility of giving the beloved corpse a proper burial, the shame of the incapability of taking leave of the dead bodies by giving them the final honor of a proper grave. It is because the bodies cannot be appropriately buried that the corpse of youth becomes a ghost that never will find peace. The grave, symbolically, cannot be closed. The event cannot be laid to rest.

And when, finally, after August 8, 1914, the days came when those among us who were closest to the dead couple did not want to part from them until they were buried, we felt the limits in the shame of being able to find refuge only in a seedy railway hotel on Stuttgart Square. Even the graveyard demonstrated the boundaries set by the city to all that filled our hearts: it was impossible to procure for the pair who died together graves in one and the same cemetery. But those were days that ripened a realization that was to come later, and that planted in me the conviction that the city of Berlin would also not be spared the scars of the struggle for a better order. If I chance today to pass through the streets of the quarter, I set foot in them with the same uneasiness that one feels when entering an attic unvisited for years. Valuable things may be lying around, but nobody remembers where. (*BC*, 20)

The graveyard stands for space in culture and in history: a grave materializes the survival of a name in the deterioration of the corpse. Symbolically, however, these casualties of war remain outside the map of history. The corpse of youth must remain nameless. "Valuable things may be lying around, but nobody remembers where."

The trauma, therefore, is not simply that a capitalist society and a capitalist war have killed youth and have taken *life* away. The real trauma is that they have taken *death* away, that they have robbed youth even of the possibility of mourning. In a world that has condemned youth to die at the war or from the war and in which even a burial is unaffordable; in a society in which even a grave is a commodity that needs to be bought and that can therefore be afforded only by the fortunate, youth, lacking proper funds, are subject—literally and metaphorically—to *a grief beyond their means:* "It was impossible to *procure* for the couple who died together graves in one and the same cemetery."[71]

The Lesson of the War

The mourning will thus be transformed into shame. And it is the lesson of this shame, the moral of this shame, that will enable the autobiographer to say "I" despite his reluctance, as long as he is sufficiently paid,[72] and that will, at the same time, give the narrator insight into the historical relation between war and revolution: "But those were days that ripened a realization that was to come later . . . that the city of Berlin would also not be spared the scars of the struggle for a better order." The lesson of the war is revolutionary, as history has demonstrated in effect in giving rise to the Russian Revolution in the wake, and as a major consequence, of the First World War. Benjamin will come both to endorse and to support this revolutionary logic that leads from war to revolution. If history has once revealed youth as a corpse, and if historically youth means "the existence of a beginning that is separated from everything following it as though by an unbridgeable chasm,"[73] only the new rupture of a revolution—only a new radical historical beginning—might perhaps one day redeem the corpse of youth or mean a possible return of youth in history. The loyalty to youth is henceforth revolutionary: it looks not to the past but to the future. "Fidelity shall be maintained." "And today, as clearly as at that time, *even if on the basis of an entirely different reasoning,* I understand that the language of youth had to stand at the center of our associations."[74]

Written for a Child

To whom, however, is this revolutionary lesson of a corpse passed on? To whom does Benjamin address the message of the "I," this tale of the divorce between words, deeds, motivation, understanding, that is called history? For whom does Benjamin defeat "the precaution of the 'I'" that is "entitled not to be sold cheap?" The dedication of *A Berlin Chronicle* reads: "For my dear Stephan" (*BC,* 3). Stephan is Benjamin's only son, then fourteen years old. This unnarratable narration of a war, this horrifying, baffling story of a suicide and of the absence of a grave is, paradoxically, surprisingly, itself *addressed precisely to a child*.[75]

What Benjamin attempts, in other words, is to *transmit* the story that cannot be told and to become himself the storyteller that cannot be one but that is one—the last narrator or the post-narrator. The trauma—or the breakdown of the story and of memory, the fragmentation of remembrance and the rupture of the chain or of the "web of stories"—is itself passed on to the next generation as a testament, a final gift. "*Memory* creates the chain of tradition which passes a happening on from generation to generation. . . . It starts the web which all stories form in the end. One ties on to the next, as the great storytellers . . . have always readily shown" (Benjamin, "St.," 98).

The *Berlin Chronicle,* much like "The Storyteller," is about transmission and about a breakdown of transmission. But this rupture is itself materialized now in the drama—in the image—of the suicide's corpse. What the corpse cannot tell will become the torso of a symbol.

> The images, severed from all earlier associations, . . . stand—like precious fragments or torsos in a collector's gallery—in the prosaic rooms of our later understanding. (*BC,* 26)

> Reminiscences . . . do not always amount to an autobiography. And these quite certainly do not . . . For autobiography has to do with time, with sequence and what makes up the continuous flow of life. Here, I am talking of a space, of moments and discontinuities. (*BC,* 28)

Benjamin knows that "the flood of war books" (*Ill.,* 84) published in the aftermath of the First World War cannot bridge this gap in experience. Like Freud, Benjamin has therefore understood that the impact of the break will be belated, and that the real problem of the trauma will be that of the second generation. This is why the post-narrator wants to re-establish the transmissibility of his experience, and to transmit the happening that cannot be told—to transmit the war, the corpse, the suicide—to his son.

> It is not the object of the story to convey a happening *per se,* which is the purpose of information; rather, it embeds it in the life of the storyteller in order to pass it on as experience to those listening. ("St.," 159)

> Where there is experience in the strict sense of the word, certain contents of the individual past combine with material from the collective past. (Ibid.)

"Seen in this way," Benjamin himself, much like the storyteller, "joins the ranks of the teachers and sages" (ibid., 108).[76]

— VIII —

The Angel of History

In *A Berlin Chronicle* (1932), Benjamin speaks of the First World War in facing Hitler's rise to power. In "The Storyteller" (1936), Benjamin speaks of the First World War because he foresees already the unavoidability of the outbreak of the Second World War. "At the door awaits the economic crisis, and the shadow of the next war is right behind," he writes in 1933. "In [the] buildings, in [the] paintings and in [the] stories [of those who have made the radically new their concern], humanity prepares itself to survive culture, if there is no choice."[77]

The traumatic repetition of the war will make Benjamin fall silent a second time, this time definitively.

Before this final fall to silence, in the second winter of the war, Benjamin will write, however, the "Theses on the Philosophy of History" (1940), in which the story of the silence of narration—the story of the First World War—is again narrated but this time interpreted as a theory of history. Again, Benjamin sees ahead of time the consequences of the war. The theory of history names the constellation of the two world wars—the past one and the present one—envisioned one against the other and one through the other. "One ought to speak of events that reach us like an echo awakened by a call," wrote Benjamin in *A*

Berlin Chronicle (*BC,* 59). It is therefore through the repetition of the trauma that the historian will read history and that the theorist will theorize it; it is from the repetition of the trauma that Benjamin derives his crucial insight into the "philosophy" of history as a constitutive process of silencing, a discourse covering the muteness of the victims and drowning in its own noise the real happenings of their repeated fall to silence.

Thus, the angel of history[78] is mute: his mouth is speechlessly open, as he is helplessly *pushed back toward the future,* pushed back from the Second World War to the speechless experience of the first. The invasion of France in May 1940 repeats the invasion of Belgium twenty-six years earlier, on August 4, 1914, an invasion that was to be followed, four days later, by the double suicide.

Benjamin is trapped in what has now become Occupied France. He plans to escape, to cross the Franco-Spanish border in the hope of ultimately reaching the United States, not so much because he wants to save his life as because he wishes to transmit a manuscript to the free world, because he wishes to *transmit,* that is, beyond the silence—and beyond the silencing—to the next generation. He carries this manuscript precisely on his body. Ironically, it is not known today what was this manuscript. Materially, the manuscript has not survived. It is presumed that this manuscript was indeed the very essay on History[79] of which copies were preserved elsewhere. But we cannot be sure. The title of the manuscript that Benjamin transported on his body will remain forever shrouded in silence.

"The Time of Death Is Our Own"

Arrested at the border and informed that he will be handed over, the next day, to the Gestapo, Benjamin will end his story by a final suicide. His own suicide will repeat, therefore, and mirror, the suicide of his younger friend, his alter ego, at the outbreak of the First World War.

What is highly ironic is that history repeats also the story of the absence of a grave—for lack of proper funds. The money left in Benjamin's pocket at his death turned out, apparently, to be sufficient only for the "rental" of a grave. After a while, the body was disinterred and the remains were moved to a nameless collective grave of those with no possessions. History repeats itself at once intentionally (suicide) and intentionlessly (absence of a burial). "The language of the intentionless truth

. . . possesses authority," Benjamin has written: "this authority stands in opposition to the conventional concept of objectivity because its validity, that of the intentionless truth, is historical."[80] After the fact, *A Berlin Chronicle* sounds almost like a prophecy: "Valuable things are lying around," Benjamin insisted, "but nobody remembers where." Benjamin, writes Demetz, "is buried in Port Bou, but nobody knows where, and when visitors come . . . , the guardians of the cemetery lead them to a place that they say is his grave, respectfully accepting a tip."[81] For a long time, there was in that Spanish cemetery "neither monument nor flower." In 1992, a monument was built.[82] But Benjamin's body is not in the grave where the monument now stands.

"For storytelling is always the art of repeating stories," Benjamin has written in "The Storyteller" ("St.," 91). Benjamin's own suicide will ironically and tragically repeat, thus, both the story of the suicide of his youth, and the shameful story of the absence of a burial. By asserting his own choice of death and by taking his own life, Benjamin repeats as well, from Heinle's story, *the message of the corpse:* the posthumous, mute message of the suicide as a symbolic gesture of protest against the war and as the autonomous assertion of an uncoerced and uncoercible will in the face of the overpowering spread of world violence. In repeating Heinle's suicide at the threshold of the First World War and in reactivating his symbolic message of resistance to the war, Benjamin's own rush to suicide in the early stages of the Second World War will achieve, thus, a definitive reunion with the cruelly lost friend. "It was after a long separation . . . But even today I remember the smile that lifted the whole weight of these weeks of separation" (*BC,* 17).

Benjamin had always known—since the trauma of the First World War and the example of the suicide of his friend—that "the cowardice of the living" (the survivor's "Timidity" that paralleled "The Poet's Courage" or the poet's death) "must ultimately become unbearable" (*SWI,* 14). Already at the age of twenty-one, he writes prophetically, as though in premonition of his future suicide:

The diary writes the story of our greatness from the vantage point of our death . . .
In death we befall ourselves. And the time of death is our own. Redeemed, we become aware of the fulfillment of the game . . . The vocation that we proudly dismissed in our youth takes us by surprise. Yet it is nothing but a call to immortality. (*SWI,* 15)

A Signature (A Call to Immortality)

Framed as it is by Benjamin's own texts, prefigured by his life and central to the processes of his entire thought, the suicide therefore is not just an act of weariness and abdication, a mere untimely gesture of fatigue and of despair—as Hannah Arendt has quite famously depicted it (and mourned it) in underscoring its essential feature as "bad luck."[83] Beyond the irony of fate, beyond misfortune, the suicide (as I have suggested earlier) makes of death a sign. In desperation, dying becomes a language. It makes a point. It is not only a decision to stop suffering and to lapse into protective and forgetful sleep. It is—across the gap of two world wars—a knocking at the doors of history. It is the punctuation of a life of writing which, by a final, willful act of silence, leaves behind *its signature:* a signature of desperate but absolutely *unconditional refusal of complicity and of collaboration* with the coercive tyranny of world wars.

> Yet tragic silence . . . must not be thought of as being dominated by defiance alone. Rather, this defiance is every bit as much a consequence of the experience of speechlessness as an experience which intensifies the condition. The content of the hero's achievements belongs to the community, as does speech. Since the community . . . denies these achievements, they remain unarticulated in the hero. And he must therefore all the more forcefully enclose within the confines of his physical self every action and every item of knowledge the greater and the more potentially effective it is. It is the achievement of his *physis* alone, not of language, if he is able to hold fast to his cause, and he must therefore do so in death.[84]

Projected into his own words, Benjamin's own suicide can be read as "the attempt of moral man, still dumb, still inarticulate . . . to raise himself up amid the agitation of that painful world" (ibid., 110). Benjamin himself embodies, thus, in his own concept but with "the authority of the intentionless truth," the "paradox of the birth of the genius in moral speechlessness" (ibid.). His death gives his posterity a language: it endows the future with a yet unborn word.

The repetition of the suicide recovers the collective meaning that was lost to death both in the battlefields—and in the suicide—of the First World War. "The voice of the anonymous storyteller" ("St.," 107) recovers "a collective experience to which even the deepest shock of every individual experience, death, constitutes no impediment or barrier" ("St.," 102).[85]

One can . . . ask oneself whether the relationship of the storyteller to his material, human life, his own and that of others, is not itself a craftsman's relationship, whether it is not his very task to fashion the raw material of experience, his own and that of others, in a solid, useful, and unique way . . . exemplified by the proverb, if one thinks of it as an ideogram of a story. A proverb, one might say, is a ruin which stands on the site of an old story and in which a moral twines about a happening like an ivy around a wall. ("St.," 108)

Through his death, Benjamin converts, thus, his own life into a proverb.

The Will (A Posthumous Narration)

> Death signifies in the concreteness of what for me is the impossibility of abandoning the other to his aloneness.
> —Emmanuel Levinas, "From the One to the Other: Transcendence and Time"

Scholem tells us that the idea of suicide was not new to Benjamin, who was close to suicide several times throughout his life. Particularly, Scholem has learned after the fact that, upon writing the *Berlin Chronicle,* Benjamin had an imminent suicide plan in mind, a plan that unpredictably was changed at the last moment. This is why, as a correlative or counterpart to the autobiographical *Chronicle,* Benjamin has also left a will, a will that he "did not destroy when his will to live gained the upper hand at the eleventh hour,"[86] and that after his death was found in his documents. The will reads:

All the manuscripts in my estate—both my own writings and those of others—shall go to Dr. Gerhard Scholem, Abyssinian Road, Jerusalem. My entire estate contains in addition to my own writings the works of the brothers Fritz and Wolf Heinle. It would be in accordance with my wishes if their writings could be preserved in the University Library in Jerusalem or in the Prussian State Library. These comprise not only Heinle's manuscripts but also my edited handwritten copies of their works. As regards my own works, it would be in accordance with my wishes if the University Library in Jerusalem provided space for some of them. Should Dr. Gerhard Scholem publish a posthumous selection of my writings . . . , it would be in accordance with my wishes if he sent a certain portion of the net profits from that edition—about 40–60 percent after deducting his expenses—to my son Stephan. (Scholem, 187–188)

In the enclosed farewell letter to his cousin Egon Wissing, the executor of his will, Benjamin declared: "I think it would be nice if the manuscript department of the library of the University of Jerusalem accepted the posthumous papers of two non-Jews from the hands of two Jews— Scholem's and mine" (Scholem, 188).

As posthumous narration, the will ensures transmission of the story of the other. Beyond its author's death, it must secure, safeguard, the other's immortality. It is in thus resisting another's loss of life and another's loss of meaning that Benjamin in death recovers, for himself and for his friend, what Heinle in his suicide lost precisely: "the narrator's stance." "With this comes to light the innermost basis for the 'narrator's stance.' *It is he alone who, in the feeling of hope, can fulfill the meaning of the event* . . . Thus, hope finally wrests itself from it . . . like a trembling question . . . This hope is the sole justification of the faith in immortality, which must never be kindled from one's own existence" (Benjamin, "GEA," 355; my emphasis).

Immortality takes from the other. Life can become immortal only insofar as it is linked to others' lives. What is immortal is the other, not the self. What is immortal is, in other words, not the narrator but the very story of the repetition, a story that, repeated at least twice, is not simply individual. And the transmission must go on.

In the "trembling question of a hope," Benjamin assigns to Scholem the task of continuing the story: the task of duplicating now, in Scholem's own life, the prosopopeia to the dead; the task of inheriting and of continuing the *Story of a Friendship*. Scholem will fulfill this task. Benjamin has proven thus that "not only a man's knowledge or wisdom,"

> but above all his real life—and this is the stuff that stories are made of—first assume transmissible form at the moment of his death. Just as a sequence of images is set in motion inside a man as his life comes to an end—unfolding the views of himself under which he has encountered himself without being aware of it—suddenly in his expressions and looks the unforgettable emerges and imparts to everything that concerned him that authority that even the poorest wretch in dying possesses for the living around him. This authority is at the very source of the story. ("St.," 94)

Textual Authority

Authority is what commends a text (a life) to memory, what makes it unforgettable. What Benjamin—prophetically again—says of Prince Myshkin, the protagonist of Dostoevsky's *Idiot*, can equally account for his own effect and for the literary impact of his own textual authority: "Immortal life is unforgettable. *It is the life that is not to be forgotten, even though it has no monument or memorial* . . . And 'unforgettable' does not just mean that we cannot forget it. It points to something in the nature of the unforgettable itself, something that makes it unforgettable" (*SW1,* 80; my emphasis). What is the secret of Myshkin's charisma? "His individuality," says Benjamin, "is secondary to his life" (ibid.). Like Myshkin, Benjamin is unforgettable because his individuality (including his own death, his suicide) is subordinated to his life.

Like the storyteller, Benjamin has "borrowed his authority from death" ("St.," 94). But the authority he has borrowed from death is none other than the storyteller's power to transmit, to *take across a limit,* the *uniqueness of a life.* It is life that, over and beyond the author's death, has been preserved in the texts of Benjamin. It is life that, over and beyond the Second World War, still reaches out to us and touches us and teaches us in the words of Benjamin and in his silence. It is the textual authority of Benjamin's life that has claimed Scholem and that has compelled him to repeat the story and to continue in his own way Benjamin's prosopopeia to the dead.

* * *

In "The Metaphysics of Youth," when he was still himself a very young man, Benjamin wrote:

> Conversation strives toward silence, and the listener is really the silent partner. The speaker receives meaning from him; the silent one is the unappropriated source of meaning. ("MY," 6)

Benjamin was a good listener, because he was always faithful to the silent one.

I would suggest that the task of criticism today is not to drown Benjamin's texts in an ever growing critical noise, but to return to Benjamin his silence.

2

Forms of Judicial Blindness, or the Evidence of What Cannot Be Seen: Traumatic Narratives and Legal Repetitions in the O. J. Simpson Case and in Tolstoy's *The Kreutzer Sonata*

> The camera introduces us to unconscious optics as does psychoanalysis to unconscious impulses.
> —Walter Benjamin, "The Work of Art in the Age of Mechanical Reproduction"

> The Real is that which always comes back to the same place.
> —Jacques Lacan, *The Four Fundamental Concepts of Psychoanalysis*

In this chapter I propose a theory of legal repetition, based on a comparative structural interpretation of a legal case and of a fictional, imaginary story written by one of the great writers of all times. I will attempt to integrate a literary vision with a legal vision, with the intention of confronting evidence in law and evidence in art. The case in the equation will be one that has impacted on our times—the notorious O. J. Simpson criminal trial, apparently an all-too-familiar legal case that will, however, be somewhat estranged by the analysis and sound less familiar through its unpredictable illumination by the literary case, equally a case of crime and trial. The literary text in the equation is a famous story by Tolstoy entitled *The Kreutzer Sonata*.

In both the legal drama of the case and the literary drama of the text, what is at issue is a marriage that ends up in murder. In both, a jealous husband is arrested and is put on trial for the murder of his wife—and is acquitted. A difference is, however, striking from the start: the husband in Tolstoy's work acknowledges his guilt, and is precisely telling us the story to explain not only why, but *how* he killed his wife.

A trial and a literary text do not aim at the same kind of conclusion, nor do they strive toward the same kind of effect. A trial is presumed to be a search for truth, but, technically, it is a search for a decision, and thus, in essence, it seeks not simply truth but a finality: a force of resolution. A literary text is, on the other hand, a search for meaning, for expression, for heightened significance, and for symbolic understanding. I propose to make use of this difference in literary and legal goals, by reading them *across* each other and against each other. I propose, in other words, to draw the questions of what was entitled at the time "the trial of the century" into Tolstoy's text, and even more importantly, to *draw out Tolstoy's insight*, so to speak, *into* the O. J. Simpson case in order to illuminate legal obscurities with literary insights and to reflect on ambiguities the trial has left by using textual issues that will turn out (surprisingly) to be quite relevant to them.

— I —

On the Separate Jurisdictions of Law and Literature

The dialogue between the disciplines of law and literature[1] has so far been primarily thematic (that is, essentially conservative of the integrity and of the stable epistemological boundaries of the two fields): when not borrowing the tools of literature to analyze (rhetorically) legal opinions, scholars in the field of law and literature most often deal with the explicit, thematized reflection (or "representation") of the institutions of the law in works of the imagination, focusing on the analysis of fictional trials in a literary plot and on the psychology or the sociology of literary characters whose fate or whose profession ties them to the law (lawyers, judges, or accused). My approach here will be different. I will compare a trial to a text. My starting point will be their comparably real and comparably astounding *impact*, the striking similarity of their historical reception. I will proceed, then, to compare the trial's and the text's narratives of crime and trial. This juxtaposition between legal facts and literary facts is, admittedly, quite bold. Its rewards will be assessed by the surprises it reserves.[2] The ground for juxtaposition will be, therefore, not just an analogy of theme (of meaning) but an analogy of impact. I read the impact (of the trial, of the text) as itself a *symptom* of the (unarticulated) meaning, or as itself part of the evidence presented by the case.

Part One: The Structural Unconscious of the Law
(A Theory of Legal Repetitions)

I will thus compare a work of fiction whose impact has generated passionate polemical reactions and a great deal of obsessional discussion with an actual criminal affair that has made legal history, and yet whose legal haunting has not stopped; a real case that had been legally decided and yet continued to translate itself obsessively into new legal and nonlegal channels.[3] The case (the trial and the text) is, quite significantly, *one in which the legal scene repeats itself.* My theoretical analysis will focus on the primal legal scene of the criminal trial. The civil trial in the Simpson case was act 2: it powerfully drew us *back* into the story's literary and dramatic spell and officially *authorized a legal repetition*—a reactivation of the judicial process. But the outcome of the civil trial was in turn incapable of truly closing this affair, which kept reclaiming our interest and our historical attention and thus presented itself, quite strictly (technically) as an interminable trial.[4]

This chapter will propose a theory of the phenomenality of structural juridical repetitions as internal to the logic of specific legal cases, or as a legal outcome of the (literary/psychoanalytic principle of the) traumatic narratives that constitute (as I will show) at once the literary story and the actual criminal case.

The dramatic mirroring between the hard facts of the law and the imaginary facts of literature will thus result in a far-reaching lesson consisting, among other things, in a new model of perception of legal events and in the conceptual articulation of a new analytic tool (focused on the relation between the traumatic nature of a case and its compulsive legal repetition), an analytic tool that will here help us not just to rethink the meaning of a legal case but to displace the very terms and the very questions through which we interpret cases,[5] both in fiction and in the reality of legal life. This lesson, based on the contaminating interpenetration of the story and the case, will in effect become compellingly informative and dramatically, surprisingly instructive only through a destabilization of the boundaries that epistemologically define and separate the territory of the Law from that of Literature. In actual life, the living entities of law and literature—trial and story—relate to each other not as reality to fiction or as empiricism to estheticism but as two narratives of trauma, two enigmas of emotional and physical destruction, two human responses to the shock of an unbearable reality of death and pain, and two linguistic acts of cultural and social intervention.

In reading law through literature, and in deciphering the meaning and the impact of the literary speech act though the meaning and the impact of "the trial of the century"; in asking how Tolstoy illuminates the O. J. Simpson case and how the real case speaks from inside Tolstoy's novella, my interest is not simply—not primarily—to add as yet another commentary to a much debated and much commented-on case, but to articulate—through the example of the case—an innovative theoretical perspective on the highly problematic and yet, in my view, absolutely fundamental relation of the law to the larger phenomenon of cultural or collective trauma. Through a philosophical analysis of the notorious criminal trial, I will demonstrate the ways in which the law remains professionally blind to this phenomenon with which it is nevertheless quite crucially and indissociably tied up. I argue that it is because of what the law cannot and does not see that a judicial case becomes a legal trauma in its own right and is therefore bound to repeat itself through a traumatic legal repetition. This compulsion to a legal repetition (like the one that is demonstrated through the O. J. Simpson case) is accounted for by narratives of trauma (Tolstoy's story will in turn address this issue and highlight it in its own specific literary way).

Legal memory is constituted, in effect, not just by the "chain of law" and by the conscious repetition of precedents but also by a forgotten chain of cultural wounds and by compulsive or unconscious legal repetitions of traumatic, wounding legal cases. My analysis will show how historically unconscious legal repetitions inadvertently play out in the historical arena the political unconscious of the law (the unconscious of past legal cases). These traumatic repetitions illustrate, therefore, in legal history, the Freudian notion of "a return of the repressed"; in the ghost of the return of a traumatizing legal case, what compulsively, historically returns from the forgotten legal past is the repressed of the judicial institution.

The relevance and the significance of this comprehensive theoretical perspective extend far beyond the limits of the O. J. Simpson case and its particular parameters. As a singularly eloquent example, the trial of the century becomes itself not just a vehicle, a leverage for this larger understanding, but an allegory of its need and of its urgency.

— II —

A Trial for Our Times

How does a trial come to claim the status of the trial of the century?[6] What was it in the O. J. Simpson case that has been grasped as so revealing, momentous, and uniquely symptomatic of the very nature of our times?

In a cover story that presented the case under the heading, "A Trial for Our Times," *Time* magazine suggested two definitions of the concept of legal event: "(1) what really happened, the facts, and (2) what people believe happened, the immense tapestry of folklore and conviction and myth that surrounds an event like the Simpson-Goldman murders. Category No. 1 addresses the needs of justice and history. But category No. 2 is important . . . in its own way." The purpose of a trial is, presumably, to transmute events from category No. 2 to category No. 1. But even if the legal process in this case has not achieved the transformation of the striking mythic images and witnessing beliefs into undoubted facts, the event behind the trial nonetheless remains sufficiently significant and sufficiently defined to *define the era* as a master-narrative, the key plot of "an unbeatably lurid end-of-the-millennium American" mixture of "race . . . , sex, celebrity, media hype, justice and injustice." "Sometimes," the essay goes on to reflect, "a trial plays out like a culture's collective dream," acting out "society's deepest passions: its fears, prejudices and desires."[7]

The dream, of course, is not just fantasy but is composed—like any dream—of fragments of reality. To render even more acute this reading of the O. J. Simpson trial as a cultural dream, I would add that a *collective* dream is, paradoxically enough, an unconscious and yet *public secret:* a secret that, while remaining unconscious, translates itself into a public spectacle—that of the courtroom ritual—which then becomes the ritual of an *obsession,* an obsessional dream. It was, then, as an acting out of society's unconscious and of culture's open or collective secrets that the brutal murders of Simpson's ex-wife, Nicole Brown, and her companion Ronald Goldman set the stage for "the defining trial of the 1990s."

An editorial in the *Boston Globe* entitled "Sad, But True: Titillating Case Defines Our Times" agreed emphatically, if with a different emphasis; it described the way in which the impact of the O. J. Simpson case overshadowed the more consequential impact of major political events.

"History textbooks of the future will make much of the Republican re-alignment . . . They will talk about the lightning victory in the Gulf War . . . They may even linger on the travails of Bill Clinton. But we will tell our children that, more than any of those things, our world . . . was shaped by the O. J. Simpson trial. Like it or not, it is the defining event of our time." "Many commentators are arguing that America, not simply Simpson, was on trial . . . That's too big a thought," the article concludes. "We know one thing, though: America, even if not on trial, was at the trial. And we will be there for a long time."[8]

In the *Los Angeles Times,* the trial as the event that marked the century was read not through the fascination of the crowd of its spectators, nor through the crime that the proceedings put on trial (Simpson's or America's), but through the very legal execution or performance of the trial: the way in which the diversity of race and sex defined not just the secret crime scene but the spectacular scene of the trial. Only in the twentieth century, indeed, could a trial take place with a woman at the head of the prosecution and a black attorney at the head of the defense.[9] The trial's definition of the century, in this view, proceeded not from its statements but from its utterance; what was distinctive in the trial was its *voice: "We heard the American voice* in so many registers and using so many different kinds of diction, sounding itself in so many accents . . . These days, both sexes and an astonishing cross-section of this country's ethnic resources are right in the middle of major events as significant players."[10]

Law and Trauma

I would suggest, for my part, that what gives a "trial of the century" its philosophical dimension (beyond its social meaning) and its historic depth (beyond the moment's fascination), what makes it a landmark trial of historical significance are three profound features: (1) its *complex traumatic structure;* (2) its *cross-legal nature,* or the repetition it enacts of another trial; and (3) its *attempt to define legally something that is not reducible to legal concepts.* I would suggest, moreover, that these three features are perhaps in general characteristic of every major trial with historical significance and certainly of major controversial trials that immediately grow into public or political "affairs" and whose symbolic impact is immediately perceived in the intensity with which they tend at once to *focus* public discourse and to *polarize* public opinion.

1. The Complex Traumatic Structure of the Trial (Race and Gender)

Every trial is related to an injury, a trauma for which it compensates and which it attempts to remedy and overcome. The three features I have mentioned (by which I define the archetypal theoretical significance of the trial of the century) are all related to the ostentatious way in which the structure of the trial, in this case, has revealed itself to be supported by the structure of a trauma. The trial has attempted to articulate the trauma so as to *control* its damage. But it is the structure of the trauma, I submit, that in the end controlled the trial. The trial has become itself a vehicle of trauma: a vehicle of aggravation of traumatic consequences rather than a means of their containment and of their legal resolution. I argue, therefore, that the case encapsulates the drama and the mystery, not simply of a link but of a real *parallel between traumatic structures and legal proceedings:* a parallel whose consequences are momentous, and yet which neither legal theory nor psychoanalytic theory has recognized, because they do not work together (and are, for the most part, completely unaware of each other).[11]

What makes the Simpson trial unforgettable, indeed, is the way in which the legal process followed a traumatic process and the proceedings paralleled traumatic structures. What makes the trial unforgettably complex, however, is the way in which *two* traumas—that of race and that of gender—have been set in competition with each other in the adversarial structure of the lawyers' arguments in such a way as to confuse and radically complicate both the perception of the trauma that the trial strove to remedy and the very question of who was the victim of the case: the abused and murdered wife or the wrongfully or hastily accused black husband? At the focus of the trial, therefore, *two* forms of victimization and abuse (race abuse and sex abuse) paradoxically enter into competition and mobilize their anger and their pain to dispute each other's claim for justice: two traumas paradoxically attempt to overpower one another and to silence each other's outcry.

But in these two competing narratives of trauma—in the conflicting stories of the prosecution (which blames an abusive husband for the murder of his wife) and of the defense (which blames the justice system for its racial bias and an abusive law enforcement body for a rush to an arrest and an unfounded inculpation of the husband)—there is an ironic symmetry: both the husband and the agents of the law are supposed to give protection but end up inflicting harm (confusingly, deceptively) precisely under their protective guise.

Civilization and Domesticated Violence, or History and Repetition at the End of the Millennium

It is perhaps not a coincidence if such a trial takes place at the close of the twentieth century, a century whose history of wars and violence has taught us how to recognize traumatic symptoms and events of trauma (that once seemed extraordinary) as part of *normal,* ordinary life; a century of civil rights but also of unprecedented *civilized abuses.* It is, thus, not by chance perhaps if the trial of the century comes up, in parallel, with two (contradictory) interpretations of *deceptive* violence and with two legal demystifications of the confusing, intimate, domestic, civilized kind of abuse that masks itself as closeness or protection.

What stands at the center of the trial, therefore, is not only the trauma but the blindness it induces, the radical confusion with which the trauma is tied up because of the deceptive package of the violence (marriage, love, police protection, justice). The trial strives to cancel out this blindness, to give the hidden trauma legal visibility. Yet, in the adversarial structure of the litigation, the two "domestic" traumas (gender, race) also dispute, deny each other's claim to visibility. Each trauma, in competing for exclusive visibility, at the same time *blinds* us to the other. The result is that the trial can by no means *totalize,* or give to see in its totality, the trauma underlying it. The complexity of the traumatic structure of the trial thus effectively prevented the trauma from becoming fully visible, in creating a specific form of judicial *blindness* that, paradoxically, was part of the legal achievement of the trial.[12]

2. The Cross-Legal Nature of the Trial

I forge the concept of "cross-legal" (on the model of cross-cultural) to designate a trial's reference to another trial, of which it recapitulates the memory, the themes, the legal questions or the arguments, and whose legal structure it repeats or reenacts—unwittingly or by deliberate design.

Indeed, in everyone's perception, black or white (although in different manners and with different readings), the Simpson trial looked like a return of the ghost of the Rodney King trial. For the defense, which underscored the repetition for its own strategic purpose through Mark Fuhrman's racist monologues, the O. J. Simpson trial was a confirmation of the same police corruption and brutality and of the same racist complicity (or white conspiracy) that King was the victim of. In spite of his assimilation with the white community, Simpson became a double of black motorist Rodney King, similarly chased or hunted on the highway and (presumably) equally indicted and scapegoated merely for the color of his skin. From the defense's point of view, the outline of this repetition gave to see or put in evidence the real subject of the trial, which was not so much the murder of the wife as the bitter conflict between so-called white justice and a persecuted black community. For the prosecution, on the other hand, and for those who found the evidence of Simpson's guilt incontrovertible, the trial was a repetition in a different sense: what was ironically here reenacted was the *first* King trial—the Simi Valley trial—*in reverse*, since the legal process, here as there, resulted similarly (though inversely) in a verdict influenced by a race bias and which similarly chose to disregard or nullify the overwhelming evidence. Whatever is the case, the Simpson trial claimed its status as the trial of the century—a trial that, in other words, can represent or sum up the significance of an entire history—because its structure was indeed susceptible to such a repetition.

I would suggest, moreover, that what distinguishes historic trials is, perhaps, in general, this tendency or this propensity to repetition or to legal duplication. In much the same way as Freud theorizes[13] that great historical events (especially events related to a murder) tend to repeat themselves and are inherently *dual* in nature, because their impact—as a consequence of trauma—takes effect and truly registers in history only through the gap of their traumatic repetition (or through their post-traumatic reenactment), great trials equally make history, I would suggest, in being not merely *about* a trauma but in constituting traumas in their own right; as such, they too are open to traumatic repetition; they too are often structured by *historical dualities,* in which a trial (or a major courtroom drama) unexpectedly reveals itself to be the post-traumatic legal reenactment, or the deliberate historical reopening, of a previous case or of a different, finished, previous trial.[14]

The O. J. Simpson trial, then, is structured like a trauma not simply in itself (in its own failure to provide a healing to the trauma it was meant to remedy) but *in its historical relation to other trials (and to other traumas)* on whose legal pathos it picks up and whose different claims to justice it repeats and, as it were, accumulates. What is traumatically conjured by the trial is, therefore, a (mostly unconscious) legal memory, the covered but unhealed wounds of a legal history. The trial inadvertently partakes of a trauma that is now not simply individual but is inscribed in the history of trials and whose individual complaint or grievance has now gained historical, collective, *cumulative legal meaning.* Hence, the enigmatic force, the impact of the trial; hence, the enigmatic historical momentum gained by a relatively simple (or reductive) legal argument.

The legal system, in such cases, is *cross-legally* traumatic, or is traumatic across different periods, across different legal situations, sometimes even across different legal cultures. I would suggest that the tremendous impact of the trial of the century comes not just from its immediate, conscious evocation of the Rodney King case (and of its relatively recent legal trauma) but, even more profoundly, from the way in which both Rodney King and O. J. Simpson, in their similar dramatic circumstances, may have conjured up a still less conscious echo of the Dred Scott case (1857), a case whose legal trauma, from a more remote past, still haunts American history and its history of trials, or its (changing) legal culture. As a possible unconscious echo of the Dred Scott case in its hauntingly inflammatory memory, the Simpson-King historical duality (or dual road hunt) may have unconsciously played out, replayed, issues belonging to a different period and to a slightly different legal culture, reopening old wounds of forced recaptures of alleged fugitives by a biased and committedly proslavery legal order. What the trial does, is, therefore, to repeat and to awaken, to *reopen* a traumatic history of trials.

3. The Trial's Excess of Its Legal Definitions

The last feature, which accounts for the privileged historical position of the trial of the century, and which defines its philosophical dimension, is related to the way in which the trial situates itself precisely at the juncture—at the very critical convergence—of the legal and of the political.

Can the political as such be analyzed, defined, or circumscribed in legal terms? The German philosopher Karl Jaspers thought that it could not because the two domains (legal, political) are qualitatively heterogeneous to each other and can by no means overlap.[15] Jaspers argued this opinion in a letter that he wrote in 1960 to his ex-student Hannah Arendt, on the occasion of her undertaking to review for the *New Yorker* the forthcoming Eichmann trial in Jerusalem:

> The political realm [Jaspers insisted] is of an importance that cannot be captured in legal terms (the attempt to do so is Anglo-Saxon and a self-deception that masks a basic fact in the functionings of political existence) . . . *A dimension that in being 'political' has, as it were, dignity, is larger than law, and is woven into the fabric of fate.*[16]

Larger than Law

It could certainly be claimed that this argument could equally apply to the O. J. Simpson case: both the fight of race (against racial prejudice) and the fight of gender (against domestic violence) involve, each in its turn, a political dimension that has "dignity." This double political dimension is, indeed, inherently "larger than law" and "is woven into the fabric of fate." This is where the trial's pathos comes from. But could the realm of the struggle for this dignity—this larger political dimension— be addressed in legal terms?

On this question, Arendt takes a different stand than Jaspers. In her answer to his letter, Arendt, who was to become herself a leading political theorist and thinker in America, takes issue with her former teacher's criticism of the "Anglo-Saxon" inclination and redefines in her own terms the way in which the Eichmann trial illustrates, indeed, the gap, the difference and the tension, but also, paradoxically, the juncture, the indispensable critical convergence, between the realm of the legal and the realm of the political:

> All this may strike you as though I too was attempting to circumscribe the political with legal concepts. And I even admit that as far as the role of the law is concerned, I have been infected by the Anglo-Saxon influence. But quite apart from that, it seems to me to be *in the nature of this case* that *we have no tools to hand except the legal ones* with which we have to judge and pass sentence on *something that cannot even be adequately represented either in legal terms or in political terms.* That is precisely what makes the process itself, namely, the trial, so exciting.[17]

This reflection holds and could equally account for the trial of the century: the O. J. Simpson case has gained both its unique position and its paradoxical symbolic representativity because it deals, profoundly and obscurely, with "something that cannot even be adequately represented either in legal terms or in political terms." It is, in other words, precisely the trial's irreducibility to the legal concepts that define it that has made it the trial of the century.

This final philosophical and analytic feature of the O. J. Simpson case could in its turn illustrate, perhaps, a general characteristic of important trials. It would be safe to say that every major trial essentially involves "something larger than law." In every major trial, and certainly in every trial of political or of historical significance, something other than law is addressed in legal terms and is submitted to the narrowness of legal definitions. And "that is precisely what makes the process itself, namely, the trial, so exciting."

Part Two: The Visible

— III —

The Murders of the Century (Which Century?), or from America to Russia

What can be, therefore, the relevance of literature to such an archetypal legal drama? Could a work of art offer a valid commentary on the real intricacies of a criminal hard case and on the real (philosophical and referential) understanding of the legal controversy of the century?

Since the O. J. Simpson case has been, indeed, collectively discussed and collectively experienced (lived) as a defining trial of our times, is it not surprising, in effect, to find the same case—or its duplicate (a wife's murder followed by the husband's trial)—in a literary text entitled *The Kreutzer Sonata* and written not by an American contemporary but by a Russian writer of the *nineteenth century*? If Tolstoy, the author of this text, seems to know so much about the O. J. Simpson case, could the trial of the century, after all, also paradoxically belong to the nineteenth century?[18]

Indeed, not only does Tolstoy, a century before us, write the story of the trial of the century; then as now, the writing and the publication of the story—(way before the media could be held responsible for its inflation)—win publicity that seems to be out of proportion to the value or to the importance of the case. Then as now, the drama of the case provokes the same excitement and the same heated division of opinions, the same intensity of controversy and of passionate debate.

The link between the trial and the times, moreover, is also at the center of Tolstoy's text. Having read the manuscript to one of his friends (Prince Urusov), Tolstoy records, in March 1889, the friend's responsiveness as proof of the subject's topicality: "He liked it very much. It is true that it is something new and powerful."[19] Tolstoy is interested, indeed, not just in the contemporary sensitivity of his new topic but also in its impact, in its practical effect: he knows that writing, in this case, writing *this* case, is making an effective *intervention* in the world—committing a didactically political act. "I almost finished *The Kreutzer Sonata* or *How a Husband Killed His Wife,*" he writes to his disciple and prospective publisher, Chertkov, in September 1889: "I am glad I wrote it. *I know that people need to be told what is written there.*"[20]

Censorship and Fame

Like the O. J. Simpson case, the story of *The Kreutzer Sonata* distinguishes itself, in its own century, by a particular relation to the law. In spite of the fictional character of this innovative literary case of murder of a wife, the publication of the text immediately provokes a scandal and becomes itself a legal case: the censor bans the text, the Russian church decries its immorality, the minister of the interior outlaws it and officially forbids its publication both as a separate volume and in Tolstoy's complete works. Ironically, it is only thanks to Tolstoy's wife, who, in a personal interview with the tsar, obtains permission partially to lift the ban (exclusively from the edition of Tolstoy's complete works), that the text can be published at all.

But even before its publication, the case of *The Kreutzer Sonata* becomes a compulsive topic of discussion in Russia's living rooms and in the streets—very like the O. J. Simpson trial in America. "As soon as it had been copied, the book was taken to Moscow . . . ; during the night, unpaid scribes made copies of the text and in less than a week nearly eight hundred lithographed copies were circulating in Saint Petersburg;

their numbers doubled, tripled, invaded the provinces. According to Strakhov, people no longer greeted each other in the street with 'How are you?' but with 'Have you read *The Kreutzer Sonata?*' Before the book was even printed, before the censor had given its decision, the case was being hotly debated all over Russia."[21] Tolstoy's daughter, Alexandra, writes in her memoirs:

> It is hard to convey now what took place when, for example, *The Kreutzer Sonata* . . . first appeared. Before [it] had been even passed for the press, hundreds, even thousands of copies [of it] were made, which went from hand to hand, were translated into every language and were read everywhere with incredible passion; it sometimes seemed that the public had forgotten all its personal concerns and was living exclusively for the sake of the works of Count Tolstoy . . . The most important political events were seldom the object of such overwhelming and universal attention.[22]

As in the O. J. Simpson case, what is particularly striking in the case of *The Kreutzer Sonata* is the outstanding contradiction between the seeming triviality of the private story and the impressive magnitude and scope of the community's emotional (and economical) investment in it, the utter political importance that the audience's response confirms to the drama of the crime and of the judgment, unaccountably magnified into a symbol of the times, and into a collective trial of the century.

What, then, does Tolstoy have to tell us, not merely about *The Kreutzer Sonata* but also about the O. J. Simpson case? What can the literary text teach us that can shed light on the trial of the century?

— IV —

Marriage and Violence

> A sexual trial is the deliberate development from an individual to a general immorality, against [whose] dark background the proven guilt of the accused stands out luminously.
> —Karl Kraus, cited by Walter Benjamin

The Kreutzer Sonata is the story of a husband who has killed his wife, was tried for murder, and was legally acquitted and set free. The story—about jealousy, hostility, sex, quarrels, murder, trial, and acquittal—is narrated to a stranger on a train by the now converted husband-murderer, as an unsolicited autobiographical confession.[23]

The confession, or the husband's retrospective testimony, is at the same time an *avowal* of his guilt and a *lesson* that he feels compelled to share about a retrospective insight he has gained—too late—into his tragedy: an insight into what he now believes to be a constitutional *relation between marriage and (domestic) violence*. Having thought about his case, he has come to be convinced that his outrageous, monstrous drama is in fact banal, ubiquitous; that violence, in other words, inhabits marriage as a rule and not as an exception or an accident (although everyone denies it). It is this unseen point about marriage, this blind spot of society, of men and women, and of culture, that his confession—his example—at the same time illustrates and puts on trial.[24]

> They asked me in court how I killed her, what I used to do it with. Imbeciles! They thought I killed her that day, the fifth of October, with a knife. It wasn't that day I killed her, it was much earlier. *Exactly in the same way as they're killing their wives now, all of them.* (60; emphasis mine)[25]

Addictions

The speaker and the story's hero, an aristocrat named Pozdnyshev, had led a promiscuous sexual life until his marriage at age thirty. This promiscuity—characteristic of most men in his social circle—evolved into what he himself now diagnoses as a genuine *sexual addiction:*[26]

> I had become what is known as a fornicator. Being a fornicator is a physical condition similar to that of a morphine addict, an alcoholic or a smoker of opium. Just as a morphine addict, an alcoholic or a smoker of opium is no longer a normal individual, so a man who has had several women for the sake of his pleasure is no longer a normal person but one who has been spoiled for all time—a fornicator. And just as an alcoholic or a morphine addict can immediately be recognized by his features and physical mannerisms, so can a fornicator. A fornicator may restrain himself, struggle for self-control, but never again will his relation to women be simple, clear . . . I, too, became a fornicator and remained one, and that was my undoing. (41)

Looking back at his own life before the marriage, he thus sees himself, along with all his male friends, "debauchees in our thirties with hundreds of the most varied and abominable crimes against women on our consciences" (41). These crimes against women do not derive from the physical act or from the sexual addiction in itself, but from the moral attitude that goes along with it:

> Debauchery isn't something physical. Not even the most outrageous physicality can be equated with debauchery. Debauchery— real debauchery—takes place when you free yourself from any moral regard for the woman you enter into physical relations with. But you see, I made the acquisition of that freedom into a matter of personal honor. (37)

This attitude, however, coexists in Pozdnyshev with the "intention of getting married and building for myself the most elevated and purest of family lives" (42), and with this plan in mind, he looks out for "a girl who might fill the bill" (42). He finds her, falls in love with her, gets married.

But from the start the marital intimacy turns into an abyss of estrangement, quarrels, jealousy, hostility, followed each time by a loving reconciliation. The sole common ground of the husband and the wife is sex— sex, pregnancies, breast-feeding, and five children in eight years, who, themselves, are a source of further disagreements, further worries, quarrels, and disgust.

Between Love and Rage

At first, Pozdnyshev believes that the quarrels are pure accidents and that his misery is an exception:

> I was tortured . . . by the fact that I was alone in having such a wretched relationship with my wife, and that everything was quite different in other people's marriages. At that stage I was still unaware that this is the common experience, that everyone believes, as I did, that theirs is an exceptional misfortune, and that everyone hides their shameful and exceptional misfortune not only from the eyes of others but also from themselves, and that they refuse to admit its existence. (58)

But later, he perceives a real pattern in the alternation of his married life between love and hate:

I didn't notice it then, but I was regularly affected by bouts of animosity that used to correspond to the bouts of what we called 'love.' A bout of 'love' would be followed by one of animosity; a vigorous bout of 'love' would be followed by a long bout of animosity, while a less intense bout of 'love' would be followed by a correspondingly shorter bout of animosity. We didn't realize it then, but this 'love' and animosity were just two sides of the same coin. (74)

(Whose portrait, in effect, does Tolstoy describe? Could not O. J. Simpson's life equally be understood, accounted for, by this analysis?[27] Would not the O. J. Simpson case in turn answer to, and quite precisely fit into, such a "portrait of a marriage?"

We were two convicts serving life sentences of hard labor welded to the same chain, we hated each other, we were making each other's lives hell, and trying all the time not to see it. At that time I had not yet learnt that this hell is the fate of ninety-nine per cent of all couples. (75)[28]

After the birth of the couple's fifth child, the doctors, for health reasons, advise the wife not to get pregnant any more, and she obeys them. Pozdnyshev, who was a jealous husband from the start, becomes even more jealous now, since his thirty-year-old wife—relieved from pregnancies and from childbearing—becomes more beautiful and more "coquettish."

"Yes, and then that man appeared," says Pozdnyshev (79).

The Triangle

One day, a violinist by the name of Trukhachevsky visits the couple, and the wife plays music with him at the piano. Pozdnyshev is immediately convinced that this common playing is the expression of a mutual attraction and a mutual seduction between the players. Yet instead of dismissing his guest, he extends an invitation to him to come again, to bring along his violin and give a true concert with his wife. The concert, in which Trukhachevsky and the wife—violin and piano—play together Beethoven's *Kreutzer Sonata,* takes place. In his obsessive jealousy, Pozdnyshev listens to the music like a voyeur: listening in on the musical harmony and the dramatic tension between the instruments, he furtively spies on the excitement of this common musical performance, as one would have spied on an actual intercourse or sexual performance between the two musicians. But Trukhachevsky soon leaves with the declared intention of not coming back, and Pozdnyshev himself goes away on a business trip, apparently calmed down. Yet on the train his jealousy, no longer a response to a real situation but only to potential ones, becomes a truly maddening obsession:

> As soon as I got into the railway coach [Pozdnyshev narrates] I lost all control over my imagination: I began to paint for me, in the most lurid fashion, a rapid sequence of pictures which inflamed my jealousy . . . They were all the same thing—of what was happening there, in my absence, of her being unfaithful to me. I was consumed with rage, indignation and a kind of strange, drunken enjoyment of my own hurt pride as I contemplated these pictures, and I couldn't tear myself away from them. I couldn't help looking at them, I couldn't erase them from my mind, and I couldn't stop myself dreaming them up. But that wasn't all: the more I contemplated these imaginary pictures, the more I believed they were real. The luridness with which they appeared before me seemed proof that what I was imagining was in fact reality. (103)

The Murder

Literally intoxicated with his own projected visual hallucinations of his wife's sexual betrayal, Pozdnyshev breaks off his trip and goes back home, unexpected, to surprise his wife and spy on her, with frenzied thoughts of punishing her guilt—which he no longer doubts—on the slightest (so-called) evidence. His fears are not dispelled upon arrival, since he finds the violinist, once again, at his home.

> For an instant I froze there in the doorway, clutching the poniard behind my back. At the same moment he smiled and started to say,
> . . . "Oh, we were just playing a little music together . . ."
> "Goodness, I wasn't expecting . . ." she began simultaneously . . .
> But neither of them managed to get to the end of their sentences. The same rabid frenzy I had experienced a week previously once more took possession of me. Once again I felt that compulsion to

destroy, to subjugate by force, to rejoice in the ecstasy of my furious rage, and I abandoned myself to it.

Neither of them managed to finish what they were saying . . . I rushed at her, still keeping the poniard hidden in case he tried to stop me plunging it into her side, under the breast. That was the spot I'd chosen right from the outset. In the very moment I attacked her, he saw what I was doing, and seized my arm—something I'd never expected he'd do . . .

I wrenched my arm free and went for him without a word . . .— he ducked under the piano and was out of the room in a flash . . . I was in a rabid frenzy, and I knew I must be a fearful sight, and was glad of it. I swung my left arm round as hard as I could, and my elbow struck her full in the face. She screamed and let go of my arm. Then, without letting go of the poniard, I gripped her throat in my left hand, threw her back and started to strangle her. How hard her neck was . . . She seized my hands in hers, trying to tear them free of her throat, and as if this was the signal for which I'd been waiting, I struck her with the poniard as hard as I could in her left side, beneath the ribs. (111–113)

The wife lies butchered in her blood. She agonizes. As the husband contemplates this bloody sight and absorbs the image of his wife, he is stunned and shocked by her bruised face; the swollen and unrecognizably disfigured face confronts him, as though from a picture.

The first thing that leapt to my gaze was her light gray dress . . . ; the dress was stained black all over with blood . . . What struck me most forcibly was her face: it was swollen, and along part of her nose and under one eye it was blue with bruises. This was the result of the blow I'd given her with my elbow when she'd been trying to hold me back. She had no beauty at all now, and I felt there was something repulsive about her. (116)

The Battered Face

It is here, when the intensity of the whole narrative translates itself into one striking visual image; here, when the story reaches its dramatic (visual) peak through this horrifying, graphic, cinematographic image of the battered face, that the narrative becomes dramatically evocative— feature by feature reminiscent—of the similarly horrifying picture of the battered face of Nicole Brown-Simpson: an equally bruised, swollen, and distorted face whose photographic image was projected, during the proceedings of the trial of the century, both on the courtroom monitor and on our television screens. Let me, thus, go back for a brief moment from the dying wife of Pozdnyshev to the murdered wife of O. J. Simpson, whose swollen and disfigured face we have all seen, eternalized precisely in those photographs kept in her safe and that have reached us, through the courtroom monitor, like an uncanny visual *communication* from beyond the grave, like an unsettling, voiceless testimony of a battered, murdered woman—the wordless and suppressed appeal of a mute body—now forever silenced. Like Pozdnyshev, we have eyewitnessed this disfigured face. Like Pozdnyshev, we can bear witness to its horrifying, haunting visual legacy.

But such a face is always seen (and recognized) too late. "We know now," wrote John Gregory Dunne in the *New York Review of Books,*

We know now, as we always do in the aftermath of bloodshed, that the marriage of Nicole and O. J. Simpson prior to their 1992 divorce had been volatile, and occasionally violent. There were frequent 911 calls to settle domestic disputes, and in 1989 the Los Angeles city attorney filed a spousal battery complaint against Simpson after a fight on New Year's eve. "He's going to kill me, he's going to kill me," she wept to the officers who answered her 911 call early that New Year's morning. They had found her hiding in the bushes outside her . . . house . . . wearing only sweatpants and a bra; her eye was blackened, her lips cut and swollen, there were scratches on her neck, and bruises on her cheek and forehead. Simpson shouted angrily at the police that it was a "family matter . . . why do you want to make a big deal out of it," and sped away in his Bentley. Cooling down, . . . Nicole refused to press charges . . . O. J. Simpson pleaded no contest to spousal battery and received the same light sentence that most first-time wife-beaters receive—a small fine, community service and mandatory counseling. After sentence was imposed, the couple issued a joint statement: "Our marriage is as strong today as the day we were married."[29]

Let me return, now, to Pozdnyshev's own wife, and to the husband's final contemplation of the image of her battered face.

What struck me most forcibly was her face: it was swollen, and along part of her nose and under one eye it was blue with bruises.

This was the result of the blow I'd given her with my elbow when she'd been trying to hold me back. She had no beauty at all now, and I felt there was something repulsive about her. (116)

She looked up at me with difficulty—she had a black eye—and she said, haltingly: "You've got what you wanted, you've killed me . . ." (117)

I looked at the children, at her battered face with its bruises, and for the first time I forgot about myself, about my marital rights and my injured pride; for the first time I saw her as a human being. And so insignificant did all that had hurt me and made me jealous appear, and so significant what I'd done, that I wanted to press my face to her hand and say: "Forgive me!"—but I didn't dare to. (117)

The Trial

The wife dies a few hours later. Pozdnyshev is arrested and is put on trial. He is acquitted, since his crime is deemed to be a crime of passion caused by the betrayal of his wife. His attempt to explain to the court that his wife may not have been unfaithful after all, that the murder was not truly motivated by the wife's betrayal, fails. He thinks the court has not truly understood his case.

At my trial the whole thing was made to look as though it had been caused by jealousy. Nothing could have been further from the truth. I'm not saying jealousy didn't play any part at all, mind you— it did, but it wasn't the most important thing. At my trial they decided I was a wronged husband who'd killed his wife in order to defend his outraged honour (that's the way they put it in their language). So I was acquitted. During the court hearings I tried to explain what was really at the bottom of it all, but they just thought I was trying to rehabilitate my wife's honour. (80–81)

In prison, while awaiting trial, Pozdnyshev had grasped a truth that has revolutionized his world. "My eyes," he tells us, "have been opened, and I've seen everything in a completely new light. Everything's been turned inside out. It's all inside out!" (38).

It is this obscure truth that he could not articulate during the trial (this truth that he could not bring to the knowledge of the court) that he is now trying to communicate in his confession.

— V —

Portrait of a Case, or the Profile of a Murderer

Let me now sum up and analyze the common points between this story and the O. J. Simpson case. We already know that both cases became vehicles for an enlarged political debate and for a broader cultural trial of the times—or of the century (although the times have changed and the century moves up toward us with the O. J. Simpson case). Both cases are composed of an identical chain of events consisting in two basic and defining episodes: (1) the murder of the wife; (2) the trial of the husband. I will distinguish, now, the analytical perspective of the murder from the analytical perspective of the trial, and will examine separately the areas of overlap and intersection of the cases, first in the story of the murder, and then in the story of the trial.

1. The Story of the Murder

Both murders are of an "unfaithful" wife. Both stories, therefore, are about a wife's unfaithfulness—and punishment. Whether the punishment should be attributed to a divine or human justice, to mere coincidence or to marital revenge, the punishment is death. Both stories are stories of jealousy, and their main character is a possessive husband. Both husbands practice stalking as a means of ascertaining the behavior of their wife. Both cases implicate a triangle, in that the crime scene implicates the unexpected presence or intrusion of a third participant—another man. Both stories dramatize a beating of the wife. Both are, thus, stories of domestic violence. Both cases sketch out the same "portrait of a marriage" in their repeated and compulsive switches between love and hate, desire and enraged hostility. The psychological makeup of the case is, thus, essentially the same. The husband in both cases is a sexual addict. Indeed, domestic violence could be itself another form of addiction—of sex addiction, since in both cases, the violence is sexual. After her 911 call, Nicole is found dressed only in a bra and sweatpants; and the stabbing is explicitly described in *The Kreutzer Sonata* as a destructive sexual act, a forced erotic penetration with a knife. The penetration of the knife is common to both stories; both murders are accomplished through a stabbing.

2. The Story of the Trial

If we consider, now, the functions and procedures of the trial, as distinct from the mere logic of the crime, the analogies between Tolstoy's case and the legal case are even more surprising and quite significantly systematic.

Indictments and Acquittals

(a) In both cases, the husband points an accusing finger toward the social order and the social institutions; the husband's case is argued, in both stories, not so much as a defense against the murder but as *a prosecution (and indictment) of society.*

(b) The *verdict*, in both cases, is the same: *acquittal.* This verdict is, however, rather enigmatic in the context of the literary text, since it stands in explicit contradiction to the husband's own confession that he did in fact commit the murder and is therefore unambiguously guilty. The question thus arises, Why does the literary text need to include at all a legal trial that acquits the husband in contradistinction to the facts? How is the acquittal necessary to the story? How does it partake of the writer's *literary* understanding (or interpretation) of the case? It seems to me that Tolstoy wants to suggest, precisely, by the introduction of the verdict a certain *complicity between the murder and the trial,* between the law and the transgression of the law—a secret but significant complicity between the crime and the society that judges it and puts the criminal on trial. Criminal proceedings are always instituted, in effect, not in the victim's name but in the name of the community whose law is broken. But the community, here, through the symbolism of a verdict that will not convict as its representative communal utterance, speaks in a voice that gives the husband's criminal offense a certain sanction of quasi-legitimacy. The murderer, in Tolstoy's text, implicitly acquires (or is legally granted by the court) a certain sort of communal amnesty, in resonance, indeed, with the communal absolution O. J. Simpson has received from his own community and with the communal sanction of legitimacy he

has been granted, as a man and as a husband, by the court's pronouncement in the trial of the century.

Messages

(c) A third common denominator between Tolstoy's case and the O. J.
Simpson case is that both cases illustrate what I would call *a pedagogical
use of the trial*. By his own explicit definition and avowed intention, Tolstoy is, at this point in life, a didactic writer and his art is a didactic art.
The Kreutzer Sonata is thus, paradoxically and quite provocatively, a *didactic* story about murder (the murder of a wife). A didactic story is, indeed, a narrative that is subordinated to a lesson, to a message it pur-
ports to illustrate or to exemplify.

Now, in the O. J. Simpson case the story of the trial has been equally
transformed into the medium of a message. In his closing argument, defense attorney Johnny Cochran thematized explicitly this function or didactic purpose of the trial, in conjuring the jurors to acquit so as to (in
his terms) "send a message" to society—about its racism, its corruption,
and the fundamental unreliability both of its justice system and of its police department. Since the jury has indeed acquitted Simpson, the trial
has been used to register and to convey this message.

But, in the literary case as in the legal one, I wish to underscore the
fact that it is not only the trial but also the very murder of the wife that
has become *a tool* for the transmission of the message. Cochran's proposition—or his message—in effect ignores, actively forgets, that the trial is
not simply about Simpson, but about a murder. What does it mean,
however, that a message about racism must be given through this trial
rather than through other channels? To the extent that the verdict in effect *erases* Simpson's murdered wife, or makes the murder—and the
murdered woman—totally irrelevant, precisely, to the message, the trial
in effect *repeats* the murder. The decision inadvertently reenacts the
crime in killing once again the victims.

The lesson that the trial in the end incorporates, the pedagogical use
of the proceedings, raises, therefore, serious questions about the moral
value (the ethical significance) of murder as an ideological tool. Since the
body of the message is a corpse, since the message must use a dead body
to promote and to legitimate itself, to what extent is such usage—such
abstraction of the body—in itself legitimate? This question can be asked

of both Tolstoy's text and the O. J. Simpson trial. Should the wife's corpse be the vehicle, moreover, of someone else's message?

The Failure of the Trial

(d) A fourth and final point of resemblance between Tolstoy's case and the O. J. Simpson case is that what is at the center of both stories is not just a trial but a *failure of the trial*. This failure of the legal framework, of the process, is what I take to be the most significant and most important common point. In Tolstoy's text, the confessing hero talks about this failure, this misfire of the trial, when he says to the narrator (his interlocutor on board the train) that the court has not really understood his case. He was acquitted on the understanding that the murder was a crime of passion, a case of jealousy and "outraged honor." But he himself has understood about the case something altogether different.[30] What it is precisely he has figured out remains obscure and is subject to the reader's own interpretation. But whatever it might be, the court has failed to understand it, in concluding—wrongly—that his protestations at the trial (his insistence that his wife may *not* have been unfaithful after all), his stuttering testimony, and his failed attempts at testifying to a different truth, were mere words of courtesy to his wife's memory, a charitable coverup or a rhetorical attempt to rehabilitate her name: "During the court hearings I *tried to explain what was really at the bottom of it all,* but they just thought I was trying to rehabilitate my wife's honour" (81). The court has failed, thus, both to understand and to translate into a legal language the hero's stuttering search for the truth.

I will argue that the O. J. Simpson case is similarly marked by a failure of the trial and that this failure is, in turn, equally essential to an understanding of the case. Indeed, the verdict that set free O. J. Simpson (like the one that acquitted Pozdnyshev) similarly did not *close* the case, or did not give the sense of closure that a verdict is designed precisely to provide. The verdict's effect was not that of an intellectual or an emotional catharsis but that of an anticlimax, which left large portions of the audience of the trial with a sort of emptiness.

Part Three: The Invisible

I would suggest that, as in Tolstoy's case, this failure of the trial had to do with something that, within the legal framework, could not be seen. *Something that could not be seen and that in fact was not seen by the court was at the center of the trial;* something that the trial could not see was at the story's heart. What is it that was not seen or could not be seen in the trial of the century?

Critical Episodes of Married Life

Part of what could not be seen in Simpson's trial has to do with what Tolstoy precisely points to as culture's *blind spot,* namely, the invisible relation between marriage and domestic violence. In a television interview given a day after the verdict, Brenda Moran, one of the jurors in the O. J. Simpson trial, referred to her juridical experience of looking at the evidence of the domestic violence as a sheer "waste of time." As a key witness to the trial, she therefore testified to the recalcitrant *invisibility of the domestic violence,* as well as to the jury's legal and judicial act of *looking through the beaten body* (of looking through and past the pictures of the battered face), in spite of the lawyers' endeavor to expose the evidence—the visual traces of the husband's blows—precisely to the jurors' *eyes* and thus to give the battered face a legal visibility. But in their verdict and, especially, in the absence of deliberation that preceded it, the jury did not so much "nullify the evidence" as it *nullified its visibility* and, in so doing, nullified the visibility of the face. In other words, the jury used the court's authority to ratify, indeed, the inherent cultural *invisibility* of the battered face.

The jury, therefore, *did not see the domestic violence.* And in line with Cochran's claim that Simpson had a normal marriage subject to "domestic discord," which merely proved that his client was "not perfect," juror Moran even insisted, in that interview, that Simpson was not even an abusive husband; all the trial proved, she said, was "one episode" of violence (or maybe two). One or two "episodes" of violence do not make out of someone an abuser.

Curiously enough, *The Kreutzer Sonata,* in its turn, opens with a conversation with a lawyer, who (like Cochran, like Moran) talks about *"the critical episodes" of "married life"* in defending marriage against

Pozdnyshev's denunciations of it. This polemical debate on the benign or nonbenign significance of marriage (that spontaneously evolves between passengers aboard a train) precedes and frames the story proper, the narrative of the confession. To Pozdnyshev's argument that "marriage nowadays is just a deception" that "usually ends either in infidelity, or violence" (35), the lawyer replies:

> "Yes, there's no doubt that married life has its critical episodes," said the lawyer, endeavouring to bring to an end a conversation that had grown more heated than was seemly. (35)

But rather than bringing an end to the conversation, this reference to "critical episodes" gives Pozdnyshev the opportunity to introduce himself by name (and introduce his story of the murder of the wife) both to the lawyer and to us. He introduces, thus, the fact or the reality of murder into its cultural invisibility and into its legal denial.

> "Yes, there's no doubt that married life has its critical episodes," said the lawyer . . .
> "I can see you've recognized me," said the gray-haired man quietly, trying to appear unruffled.
> "No, I don't think I have the pleasure . . ."
> "It's not much of a pleasure. Pozdnyshev's the name. I'm the fellow who had one of those critical episodes you were talking about. So critical was it, in fact, that I ended up murdering my wife." (35–36)

To go back now to O. J. Simpson in his relation to Tolstoy's text, it is quite interesting that in both cases the "critical episodes"—the story of the violence and the event of murder—are linked to something that essentially (in culture and in discourse) cannot be seen and that indeed fails to be seen within the framework of the trial.

Blind Justice (Seeing and Judging)

Could justice in effect be blind—in ways other than the ones in which it is normally expected to be?[31] Is not seeing crucial to the very practice and the very execution of the law,[32] because, as the saying has it, "justice must not only be done, but must be *seen* to be done?" A trial is, indeed, in its origin and in its essence, a theatrical event in that, by definition, it takes place upon a stage before an audience. The trial of the century was only more exemplary in that respect, since it had been from the beginning a *show trial,* a spectacularized case whose evolving courtroom drama was reproduced throughout the world, magnified and multiplied by millions of television screens. But any criminal proceedings implicate "the people" in whose name they are initiated as a community of viewers, a communal circle of social observers or of political (historical) spectators. Any court decision, in a way, is a historical decision about the significance, the meaning the community derives from its spectatorial stance with respect to various happenings[33] and, more generally, from its spectatorship of history. The rules of evidence, moreover, are in turn based on seeing. The strongest proof admitted by the court is proof corroborated by the eye: the most authoritative testimony in the courtroom is that of an eyewitness. Every trial, therefore, by its very nature as a trial, is contingent on the act of seeing.

Yet, in the case of the *People v. O. J. Simpson,* the jurors look but do not see. They do not see the beaten body. They look at pictures of Nicole's bruised countenance, but declare they cannot see either the husband's blows or the wife's (the victim's) battered face. The jurors in the O. J. Simpson case are thus themselves *the trial's failed eyewitnesses.* This failure of the court to see evokes, indeed, once more, Pozdnyshev's frustration with the court's shortsightedness or blindness and the parallel philosophical and legal failure of the trial in Tolstoy's case.

But in this sense, precisely, of the failure of the court to see (or of the *failure of the trial* to *eyewitness* its own evidence), the O. J. Simpson case repeats, indeed, with an ironic symmetry, the history, the trauma, and the structure of the Rodney King case or of the Simi Valley trial, which, in its turn, was precisely about *beating*—and about an *unseen* beating, about an inexplicable, recalcitrant relation between beating and blindness, beating and invisibility, an invisibility that cannot be dispelled in spite of the most probatory visual evidence. Indeed, quite similarly to the way in which Simpson's domestic violence was visually corroborated by the photos of Nicole's bruised face, Rodney King's beating by police was documented by a videotape. And yet the jurors in the Simi Valley trial (all white), *did not see the beating* (of the black). The jury watched the film but claimed it *did not see* police abuse and acquitted the four white policemen. Both decisions hinge, thus, on a failure to see beating. In both cases, what the jury *cannot see,* in other words, are (paradoxically) *the very blows that inflict trauma.* Both verdicts are in turn traumatic in that they *deny, in fact, the very trauma that the trial was supposed to remedy.* It is by virtue of this legal and historical resemblance of their basic structure in relation to the trauma (and the consequent trauma of the trial) that the Rodney King case and the O. J. Simpson case narrate together the story—and the trial—of the century.

Beating and Invisibility, or Hatred's Prohibited Sight

If the decision, in both cases, registers a legal failure to see trauma, this inherent failure is in turn reinforced, compounded, by an equal cultural failure to acknowledge hate.[34] It is significant indeed that, in both cases, what the jury fails to see—what cannot be seen precisely by the law— is *hate* (hate for women, hate for blacks) and that this secret, mute, insidious hate—this hate prohibited to sight—finds its expression, in both cases, in the graphic image—and in the physical translation—of a beating.

Beating is, indeed, a quintessential figure of *abuse of power* (physical and moral). As an emblem of oppression and humiliation, as a symbol of transgression of the other's property and of invasion of the other's body, beating is not just physiological but is inherently political. A radically offensive act, it is, I would suggest, the most rudimentary political offense and has the impact (physical and moral) of a political act par excellence.

But seeing—as the essence of the cognitive activity and as the foundation of both consciousness and memory—is in turn an act that is not simply physiological; it can in turn be inherently, unwittingly political. The French philosopher Louis Althusser[35] explains how seeing and not seeing are contingent on the limits (the ideological exclusions) of a frame of reference. "It is the whole field of a problematic," writes Althusser, "that defines and structures the invisible as its definite outside—*excluded* from the domain of visibility and *defined* as excluded by the existence and the structure of the problematic field itself":

> The invisible is defined by the visible as *its* invisible, *its* prohibited sight . . . To see this invisible . . . requires something quite different from a sharp or attentive eye, it takes an *educated eye*, a revised, renewed way of looking, itself produced by the effect of a 'change of terrain' reflected back upon the act of seeing.[36]

I would argue, in my turn, that the limitations of the possibilities of seeing, the structural exclusions from our factual frames of reference, are determined not only by (conscious or unconscious) ideology but by a built-in cultural *failure to see trauma*. As is evident from both the Rodney King case and the O. J. Simpson case, *the abuse of power* (beating) is *inscribed in culture as a trauma*. But, as we know from psychoanalytic studies[37] and as both cases demonstrate, trauma is precisely what cannot be seen; it is something that inherently, politically and psychoanalytically, defeats sight, even when it comes in contact with the rules of evidence and with the trial's legal search for visibility. The political is thus essentially tied up with the structure of the trauma. It is to the structure of the trauma, therefore (and not simply to a different ideology), that our "eyes" should be precisely *educated*.

To return, now, to the beatings that remain persistently unseen in both the Rodney King case and the O. J. Simpson case, to return, thus, to both juries' failure to act as eyewitness to the (physical and moral) violence whose literal invisibility cannot be dispelled in court, in spite of the most probatory visual evidence, in both cases, in effect, the photographic image (photos or videotape) turns out to be incapable of lifting out or canceling the cultural blind spot, or the political prescription not to see.[38] The century might well be, in Walter Benjamin's acute terms, "the age of mechanical reproduction" or the legal century of videotapes. But in spite of the advances in the technological methods of recording or of memorizing visual evidence, the trial of the century remains *a story of the century's blind spots*.

As Tolstoy's text shows, however, concerning gender, the legal story of the century is essentially the same as that of the preceding one. As regards marriage and violence, it seems we have made little progress and have not truly come out of the nineteenth century.[39] In any case, we have not yet entirely emerged from a traumatic story (or from a trauma) whose very pattern is characteristic of the previous century. As the coincidence between the literary text and the contemporary trial shows, so far as women are concerned as targets of abusive or appropriative violence, we seem to have inherited, quite strictly and specifically, the nineteenth century's blind spots. The murders and acquittals of the nineteenth century are still with us as our tragically intact inheritance.[40]

Law and History: Inheritance of Trauma

What have we done, thus, in a hundred years? Has history not taken place to register at least a legal difference? Or is it law itself that is responsible not just for the recording but for the censorship of history? Could the voluminous *legal recording* of the O. J. Simpson trial be itself merely the witness of the way in which history is paradoxically deprived of memory? How do verdicts (the acquittal, in the O. J. Simpson case) mark at once what history *remembers* and what history *forgets*, at once what is pragmatically included in and what is programmatically excluded from collective memory?

In their arbitrating function between contradictory facts and between conflicting versions of the truth, verdicts are decisions about what to admit into and what to transmit of collective memory. Law is, in this way, an organizing force of the significance of history.[41] But law relates to history through trauma.[42] What should have been historically remembered, in effect, is not only the trial but also the trauma that made the trial necessary, the individual and social trauma that the trial was supposed to remedy, to solve or to resolve. Yet a trauma cannot simply be remembered when, in the first place, it cannot be grasped—when, as these trials show, it cannot even be seen. Rather than memory, it compels a traumatic reenactment.[43]

I would argue, therefore, that a legal case truly becomes a locus of embodied history, a "site of memory" or a material, literal "lieu de mémoire" in Pierre Nora's sense,[44] only when it is spontaneously endowed with what Freud calls a "historical duality,"[45] when it reverberates, in other words, with what I have defined as a *cross-legal* resonance, or triggers inadvertently the movement of a repetition or the dynamics of a *legal recall*. In its simultaneous gesture of commemoration and of forgetfulness of what it in effect repeats, the O. J. Simpson trial constitutes precisely such a site of memory ("lieu de mémoire") because it constitutes a "site" (a locus, a location, an abyss) of traumatic repetition.[46]

The O. J. Simpson case unwittingly repeats, thus, both the twentieth-century traumatic legal narrative of Rodney King and the nineteenth-century traumatic legal story of Tolstoy. But Tolstoy's own literary, legal case consists already in a repetition, since its very starting point is the hero's *reenactment of the legal trial* (his reopening of the criminal proceedings' failed search for the truth) through the narrative of the confession, which, in turn, undertakes to repeat or to narrate again (to recapitulate, once more) the story that could not be heard in the proceedings and that failed to be communicated, or transmitted, to the court. The trial of the century repeats, then, all these repetitions—legal, literary, psychoanalytical, historical—by which the trial tries, and retries, to resolve the trauma and by which the trauma inadvertently repeats itself as an unconscious legal memory under the conscious legal process. The O. J. Simpson case, in summary, is the defining trial of our times because it recapitulates, precisely, all these repetitions. It is the trial of the century because it reenacts the Rodney King case; but this defining trial of the twentieth century turns out to be itself a repetition of the trial (of the trauma) of the nineteenth century.

I would suggest, indeed, that the main difference in this century's trials and acquittals is that history enables us, today, at least to catch up with Tolstoy—at least *to see that we do not see*—and thus historically to raise these questions: to ask about *the meaning of the repetition*. If history, indeed, repeats itself, and if events must happen at least twice to be perceived, might the repetition in itself, some day, help bring about (help train) "an educated eye?"

Eyes and Education, or Beating and Seeing

All three cases, therefore—Pozdnyshev's or Tolstoy's case, the Rodney King case, and the O. J. Simpson case—resonate with one another in similarly dramatizing, in the courtroom, a striking and misunderstood *relation between seeing and beating*, between *a violence that harms* or that seeks to hurt or kill and *a violence that blinds* or seeks to prohibit sight. In the literary scene as in the legal one, in their fictions and in their realities, all three cases (Simpson, King, Tolstoy) similarly concretize a failure of the trial through the story of the legal implications, on the one hand, of hatred as prohibited to sight and, on the other hand, of suffering or of trauma as *the structure of a blow* (or of an injury) *that cannot be seen*. All the trial can prove, therefore, is the trauma's *unlocatability*, the injury's constitutive invisibility, the blow's traumatic *nonjusticiability*. All the trial does is, therefore, to *repeat the trauma* in enacting, once more, its recalcitrant invisibility and in showing how the *trauma's power to defeat sight* infiltrates the very workings of the legal process and insidiously takes over the very structure of the trial. It is precisely this complex political and epistemological *relation of the beating to the seeing*, and this profound human and political enigma of a trauma that cannot be seen and cannot be located or translated into seeing (into seeability) even at the level of the trial, that seems to be at the center of Tolstoy's text and at the center of the story Pozdnyshev cannot quite bring to the knowledge of the court. But this is what, for him and for Tolstoy, the trial—and the story—are really all about.

Part Four: The Abyss

— VI —

The Explosion of the Legal Framework

What is it, then, that Pozdnyshev has failed to articulate and to transmit about his story (or about the real nature of his case) during the trial? What is this insight he tries desperately to articulate, but which remains deprived of legal language, this speechless, inarticulate, unheard, excessive truth, which remains outside the hearing of the court, which exceeds both what is said and what is heard in the proceedings, and which is defined, in Tolstoy's text, precisely—only—as *an excess of the narrative (of literature) over the trial?* What legal event is it, that is defined—or that can only be accounted for—by an excessive literary truth?

This question can be asked from two opposed perspectives: (1) What sort of paradoxical event creates a crisis that exceeds what can be legally articulated, but that nonetheless necessitates a trial for its very definition? (2) What is, on the other hand, this crisis or this paradoxical event that cannot do without a legal process, but that, literarily and philosophically, can be transmitted only through a failure of the trial—through an explosion of the legal framework? Such is the murder of the wife in Tolstoy's text (in its relation to the trial). And such is, similarly, the paradoxical relation of the murder of Nicole Brown-Simpson to the O. J. Simpson trial, to which Tolstoy might be, indeed, a literary key. Philosophically, Tolstoy seems to be asking, not by chance, perhaps, a question that applies both to his fiction and to the intricate legal reality of the contemporary trial: What is the story that can be told only through an *unpaid debt* of the decision to the truth, or of the verdict to the facts? What is this (literary, psychological, political, historical) *debt* that the decision, the acquittal, still holds with respect to the full legal truth, but which a conviction (as the mixed reactions to the civil verdict proved) could not in its turn possibly reduce, resolve, or fully pay?

What is it we can therefore understand, with Tolstoy's help, about the real nature of the (fictional and real) murder case? What can we ultimately understand or learn from the text—from the confession—of *The Kreutzer Sonata?* And how can what we understand illuminate the riddle of the legal case? How can the perspective of the literary text (and of a literary understanding) shed light on the overall historical performance of "the trial of the century"? What is it that Tolstoy is struggling, in conclusion, to communicate?

Let us listen, one last time, to Pozdnyshev's testimony, in its effort to convey the story that the court has missed:

> At my trial the whole thing was made to look as though it had been caused by jealousy. Nothing could have been further from the truth. I'm not saying jealousy didn't play any part—mind you—it did, but it wasn't the most important thing. At my trial they decided I was a wronged husband who'd killed his wife in order to defend his outraged honor (that's the way they put it in their language). So I was acquitted. During the court hearings I tried to explain what was really at the bottom of it all, but they just thought I was trying to rehabilitate my wife's honour. (80–81)

Jealousy was just a pretext, Pozdnyshev insists, almost an indifferent pretext:

> If it hadn't been him, it would have been some other man. If jealousy wasn't the *pretext,* some other one would have been found . . . (81)

> Whatever her relationship with that musician was, it wasn't important to me, any more than it was to her. What was important was what I've been telling you about—my pigsty existence. *It all happened because of that terrible abyss there was between us,* the one I've been talking about, the terrible stress of our mutual hatred for each other, that made the first *pretext* that came along sufficient to cause a *crisis.* (81)

Chasm

The case, then, is about the relation of the (private, sexual, trivial) *pretext* to the (social, legal) *crisis* of the violence and of the murder: "It all happened because of that terrible *abyss* there was between us." The real motivation of the story derives, thus, neither from the wife's (real or fantasized) unfaithfulness nor from the jealousy that this presumed unfaithfulness provokes, but from the very existence of "that terrible abyss." The story, then, is not the story that we thought; it is not the banal case of adultery (of jealousy) we had at first believed that we were reading.

What is it, then? I would argue that what we discover in Tolstoy's text is, far less predictably, the narrative of an abyss, a case, precisely, of the unexpected revelation of a hidden and profound chasm.

The metaphor of the abyss repeats itself throughout the text of *The Kreutzer Sonata.* Although Tolstoy's Russian uses several different words to concretize and to nuance this image of a precipice *(propast, puchina, bezdnia),* all these words depict the same experience of a break (a loss) of contact and of ground; all these figures point to the same insistent image of a fissure, a dividing gulf, a bottomless ocean, or a terrifying, gaping wound within the ground:

> *It all happened because of that terrible abyss there was between us,* the one I've been talking about, the terrible stress of our mutual hatred for each other, that made the first pretext that came along sufficient to cause a crisis. (81)

> It's horrible, horrible, horrible . . . the *abyss of error* [misunderstanding] we live in regarding women and our relations with them. (38)

> And so we continued to live, in a perpetual fog, without ever being aware of the situation we were in. If what finally happened hadn't happened, and I'd go on living like that until my old age, I think that even when I was dying I'd have thought I had a good life . . . ; *I would never have come to perceive the abyss of unhappiness,* the loathsome falsehood in which I was wallowing. (75)

> The first quarrel had a terrible effect on me. I call it a quarrel, but it wasn't really a quarrel, it was just the *revelation of the abyss that actually separated us.* (57)

An Abyss of Sexuality: An Abyss of Difference

What is this precipice that Tolstoy so insistently returns to?

In its most obvious significance, the metaphor of the abyss in *The Kreutzer Sonata* seems to be linked to the space of sexuality as a frightening enigma. But what is sexuality, precisely? Sexuality is, first and foremost, in this story (as it is, indeed, in O. J. Simpson's story) an *abyss between the sexes.* And this gulf between the sexes, this ill-understood abyss that so radically and so incurably separates the woman from the man and estranges the husband from the wife, refers in turn not just to the unfathomable abyss of sexuality and sexual desire (as the story's obscure origin) but, more specifically, to a fissure or a split *within* sexuality itself, to an inner schism or a chasm not just *between the narrator and his wife* but *within the narrator's own sexual desire;* there is an abyss, precisely, that inhabits human sexuality, like an internal hollowness at the bottom of a whirling chaos of attractions and repulsions, of rivalries and of conflicting, secret sexual ambiguities. This abyss of difference (internal and external) cannot but become an abyss of conflict. The relative positions in the story of the jealousy—in the triangle of the sexual competition—can change dynamically and secretly: desire for the wife and jealousy toward the male rival; attraction for (or fascination with) the rival and a secret sexual competition with the wife;[47] love-hate for the wife; love-hate for the would-be lover; jealousy, respectively, of both; a maze of attractions and repulsions; an abyss that inhabits sexuality like a chaotic whirlpool or an internal hollowness that constantly sucks it, splits it from inside itself; an abyss that fatally and radically divides sexuality from itself, makes it different from itself.

But what is even more important than the sexual significance of the abyss, what is even more significant than its (split) sexual nature, is the relation of the split—the precipice—to its *obscure depth* or to its abyssal, enigmatic core of darkness. This concrete obscurity (of the abyss) is recapitulated by a metaphor of darkness that runs throughout the text[48] and that, in resonance with that of the abyss, dramatizes (concretizes) *a resistance from inside the story to what can be seen* (or to what can pierce into awareness).[49] "It all happened because of that terrible abyss there was between us." Resisting awareness,[50] the radical darkness inside the abyss, the (literal and metaphorical) obscurity inside the story, functions, therefore, like a *black hole* at the story's center. This narrative black hole (the dark abyss inside the story) dynamically resists the trial's search for legal visibility and undercuts the story's constant effort to obtain both light and sight.

The Trial's Central Darkness, or the Narrative Black Hole

Like the trauma, like the narrative black hole that is the story's center, the abyss, indeed, is something normally hidden from sight, something whose obscure depth (or whose end) cannot be fathomed and whose *bottom* (or whose starting point) *cannot be seen.* But when the bottom is touched through the murder, when the abyss can suddenly and unexpectedly be glimpsed, what can be seen is nothing but an emptiness and an obscurity. At the story's end (at the conclusion of the trial, and at the horizon of the text), what is dramatically revealed is not depth, but the unsuspected bottomlessness of a terrifying chasm.

And so it was, I would propose, precisely in the O. J. Simpson case. The performance of the trial of the century was nothing if not a historical encounter with the unexpected bottomlessness of a chasm. What was finally revealed at the trial's end was, similarly, not the curtain's fall, not the closure of the case or a catharsis finally obtained by a legal resolution, but here again only the terrifying opening, only the emptiness[51] of an ungraspable abyss: an *abyss between the sexes;* an *abyss between the races;* an abyss between legality and justice; a gap in perception between blacks and whites; an abyss between contradictory experiences of the significance of law enforcement and between conflicting views of the use or the abuse of the power yielded to the justice system and to the agents of the law; an abyss between conflicting views of the significance or the insignificance of domestic violence; an abyss between the rich, who can buy justice, and the poor, who cannot afford to pay its price; an abyss between conflicting views or contradictory emotional perceptions of the verdict as a victory or as an absolute defeat. "Yet there was no real victory, no real defeat," wrote Robert A. Jordan, "for blacks and whites who are on opposite sides of this verdict. Rather, there is the fresh realization that . . . the divide between blacks and whites, is still *very deep* in this country."[52] But the impact of the trial, and the schism suddenly uncovered by the shock of the verdict of the century, had to do with something *deeper* still and not quite so definable, something that escaped definition at the very heart of the abyss revealed by the conclusion of the trial. As in Tolstoy, the sudden opening of the abyss was linked to the emergence of a split in the very integrity of legal justice.

An Abyss of Trauma

"But will Americans even bother to wonder how racially cleft . . . the criminal justice system must have been long before this case?" asked Francis X. Clines. "Will whites—so shocked at the television scenes of some blacks triumphant at the verdict announcement—now be ready to believe blacks' first-hand tales of negative contacts with police?"[53] "The verdict," wrote Isabel Wilkerson, "exposed a chasm in place for generations."[54] I would argue that this broken integrity (the schism in society, the split in the integrity of justice) was tied up with a splitting that, itself, was (and *repeated*) the effect of a traumatic shock. The chasm between blacks and whites becomes, ironically, a dialogue of shocks. The shock was related to an "accidented" space through which culture as a whole suddenly revealed itself as nothing other than a *cultural gap,* an "accidented" and inherently dissociated space of cultural trauma, insofar as trauma (individual as well as social) is precisely constituted by a gap in consciousness.

What should have been perceived, at the conclusion of the O. J. Simpson trial, is, thus, the concrete reality of the traumatic gap—or the concreteness of the trauma. What was perceived, instead, was the abyss—the gap—between two traumas: that of race and that of gender. But race and gender differed, mainly, in this trial, in their relation to a third trauma: that of law itself.

In its prosecution of a husband's murderous abuse, the law has been appealed to, here, by gender as a guardian of the victims' rights and thus as a necessary ally and, possibly, as the only *vehicle of correction of the abuse.* But in the argument of the defense (and in the collective memory of race), law is invoked as part and parcel of the trauma, and its enforcement is remembered and historically commemorated (litigated) as the very source, *the very vehicle of the abuse.*[55] Race and gender differ, thus, in their thematized relation to the law and in their consequent legal perception of the trial as itself part of the problem (part of the abuse), or as its possible redress, its cure.

But it was for gender that the criminal trial was ironically destined to become a *legal trauma;* it was for gender that the verdict of the century turned out to be, precisely, *legally traumatic.*[56] And this pronouncement of the law, this tacit, indirect, seeming legitimation of gender abuse that aggravated, ratified the trauma through the channels of a vehicle of law in turn entailed further traumatic, splitting consequences. "The verdict exposed a chasm in place for generations . . . And nowhere was the divide more stark than it was between black women and white women," writes Isabel Wilkerson: "Pressed to choose between men with whom they share race experience . . . and white women with whom they share the experience of sexism," black women jurors had no choice but to "break ranks." In choosing race solidarity with men over (and against) gender solidarity with female victims of abuse, the women jurors could not but create a cleavage within the integrity (the unity) of gender itself and in effect revealed an abyss inside the community of women—a schism concretized in the televised images, after the acquittal, of "black women smiling to the heavens, thanking Jesus" and of "white women sobbing, unable to speak."[57]

Philosophically, indeed, the abyss revealed by the trial of the century has compromised not only the integrity of gender, and not only the integrity of the legal process, but also the integrity of truth itself. Or, rather, the conclusion of the trial showed truth as an abyss between incommensurate realities, a schism between different ways of seeing, between incommensurable ways of looking at the very same facts. "Nothing that happened in the O. J. Simpson trial was as awful as the way it ended," the *Economist* commented. "Was the Jury wrong? One cannot know . . . The distressing part was not the verdict itself; it was the proof thus confirmed that black and white America have been watching different trials . . . This verdict makes plain what so many Americans—and so many of their friends abroad—had not wanted to believe. Thirty-odd years after the civil-rights revolution, America is two countries, not one. And they are growing apart, not together."[58]

"It all happened," says Tolstoy, "because of that terrible abyss there was between us." "It wasn't really a quarrel, it was just a revelation of the abyss that actually separated us." "It's horrible, horrible, horrible . . . the abyss of misunderstanding we live in regarding women and our relations to them."

> To live like that would have been insufferable if we'd understood the situation we were in, but we didn't understand it—we weren't even aware of it. It's the salvation as well as the punishment of human beings that when they're living irregular lives, they're able to wrap themselves in a blanket of fog so that they can't see the wretchedness of their situation . . .
>
> And so we continued to live, in a perpetual fog, without ever being aware of the situation we were in. If what finally happened hadn't happened, and I'd go on living like that until my old age, I think that even when I was dying I'd have thought I had a good life . . . ; *I would never have come to perceive the abyss of unhappiness,* the *loathsome falsehood* in which I was wallowing. (74–75)

Seeing the Gap

Could *The Kreutzer Sonata* be the narrative of what it takes (in tragedy and in destruction) to make one *see* precisely the abyss? Is the O. J. Simpson case the story of the price to pay, in turn, for the revelation of this chasm that had been there all along but that, like the protagonists of *The Kreutzer Sonata,* we in turn *could not see* or *did not want to see?* Could the trial of the century be, in other words, the legal drama or the case of law that historically sums up the century as a century that, blindly, has lived on the brink of an ungrasped historical abyss, an amnesiac century that needed, paradoxically, a defining trial to *discover* (suddenly to see) *its own history (its memory) as an abyss*—an essentially ungraspable, and still essentially *invisible* "abyss of unhappiness and loathsome falsehood"? And if the trial of the century is indeed the cultural story of our blindness, could this legal story of our blindness turn, like Tolstoy's, into the story of a revolutionary seeing?

> It's no good, I just can't talk calmly about it. It's not merely because of that episode, as that gentleman called it, but because ever since I went through it *my eyes have been opened* and I've seen everything in a completely new light. Everything's been turned inside out, *it's all inside out!* (38)

Suddenly, thus, the abyss was *inside out.*

I argue, in conclusion, that the O. J. Simpson trial *was* the trial of the century *because* it revealed precisely an abyss, or told the legal story of the century's severance in consciousness. The abyss might well be "inside out": insofar as it is not just an abyss of cultural hypocrisy but an abyss of cultural trauma, it remains the trial's secret. I argue that the case, in other words, has claimed its unique status as the trial of the century *because we still cannot decide*—and do not completely understand—*what the trial was about,* because we still do not know or cannot decide where exactly to locate the trauma, or what was really at the bottom of this (legal, cultural, and historical) abyss.

Between Law and Literature: Comparative Epistemologies

Thus it is that the comparison between the O. J. Simpson case and Tolstoy's text helps us to review and to rethink the implications—and the impact—of the contemporary trial.

I have examined factual and interpretive legal uncertainties in the instructively imaginative and dramatically suggestive light of literary facts whose narrative logic (whose own dramatic legal tale of murder and of trial) decisively resembles the contemporary case and whose intuitive, imaginative insight into criminal (human) behavior and into the enigma of the structure of the case and of the structure of the murder (as well as of the murder's paradoxical relation to the trial) turns out to be at once compelling and inspiring.

Thus it is that the comparison between the trial and the literary text, between the intricate legal reality and the imaginative literary vision of the case of the murder of the wife (and of the trial of the husband) cues us into the significance—and into the suggestive literary resonance—of the abyss.

I have proposed that the abyss is at the center—at the heart—of both the literary story and the contemporary trial, and that both the trial and the story of the text consisted in the unexpected revelation of the image—and of the ungraspable significance—of the abyss, both as an obscure original causality ("It all happened because of that terrible abyss there was between us") and as the fatal repetition, the unexpected and yet unavoidable return of a form of radical dispute ("I call it a quarrel, but it wasn't really a quarrel. It was just a revelation of the abyss that actually separated us").

Between Law and Literature (An Abyss)

He has seen through law as have few others. If he nevertheless invokes it, he does so precisely because his own demon is drawn so powerfully by the abyss it represents. By the abyss that, not without reason, he finds most gaping where mind and sexuality meet—in the trial for sexual offenses.
—Walter Benjamin, "Karl Kraus"

But the comparison between the legal drama and the literary drama has also shown that law and literature have radically different philosophies (different approaches) with respect to the abyss. Governed by their different goals, the legal practice and the literary practice embody, in effect, two different ways of *addressing* the abyss and *two ways of relating the significance of the abyss*, specifically, *to the significance and to the functions of the trial*.

As we have seen, in both the trial and the literary text, the abyss— an abyss of difference, hatred, racism, sexuality, "unhappiness," and trauma—a "quarrel" that "is not really a quarrel" but the "revelation" of a radically divisive inner breakdown, is above all something terrifying. But it is also what we cannot grasp and do not understand. It is something we can see only from outside. It is therefore what, essentially, *can-*

not be totalized, what a *closing argument* will of necessity fail to contain, to *close* or to enclose. By definition, an abyss is what escapes legal summation, what eludes reflective or conceptual totalization.

What, then, can a trial do with an abyss? The trial of the century sought (as the law always attempts to do) *to throw a bridge over the abyss,*[59] to stand in, or to step into, the breach by precisely filling in the gap, by closing the abyss or by enclosing it within the rationality of its legal categorizations (gender, race) in an attempt to cover or to *cover up its bottomlessness,* to integrate or to assimilate the gap within known categories of the social or political or legal order. In its pragmatic role as guardian of society against irregularity, derangement, disorganization, unpredictability, or any form of irrational or uncontrollable disorder, the law, indeed, has no choice but to guard against equivocations, ambiguities, obscurities, confusions, and loose ends. All these the abyss embodies, in the image of a danger the law fears above all: that of a failure of accountability (or of a breakdown in foundation and in foundational stability); that of a *loss,* of a *collapse* (absence) *of grounds.* Under the practical constraints of having to ensure accountability and to bring justice, the law tries to *make sense of the abyss* or to reduce its threat (its senselessness, its unintelligible chaos) by giving it a name, by codifying it or by subsuming its reality (which is inherently nameless and unclassifiable) into the classifying logic and into the technical, procedural coherence of the trial. But in so doing, the law (the trial or the litigation) inadvertently denies the abyssal nature of the abyss in pretending, or in misguidedly assuming, the abyss is something else, something that can be assimilated to known rules or precedents, something that can be enclosed, contained within the recognizability of known (stereotypical) legal agendas.

But the purpose of the literary text is, on the contrary, to show or to expose again the severance and the schism, to reveal once more the opening, the hollowness of the abyss, *to wrench apart what was precisely covered over, closed or covered up by the legal trial.* The literary text casts open the abyss so as to let us look, once more, into its depth and see its bottomlessness.[60]

And in so doing, in *reopening the case* and in revealing, once more, the obscurity, the empty opening of the abyss, the literary text enacts (or carries out through its own narrative, through its confession) a *repetition of the story* that the court has missed or has misunderstood, and that the trial could not tell. Literature enacts, thus, an artistic recapitulation of the dynamics of the trial and of the trial's search (and re-search) for the truth. By its own specific means, by its literary power or by the acuteness of its own search (struggle) for expression, the artistic trial strives to *transmit the force of the story that could not be told* (or that failed to be transmitted or articulated) in the legal trial.

What Tolstoy's text, in this way, inquires into is not just the meaning of the case, nor even simply the enigma of the case's force, but *the general significance of failed attempts (in law, in history) to close abysses,* the meaning of repeated yet impossible historical attempts to use the vehicles of law to cover over great collective traumas by the rationality and by the technicality of legal trials, by accounts of the law and by the settlements of courts.

In repeating, thus, both the story of the trauma and the dynamics of the trial, literature explains why and how the trial (like the trauma) is not closed, but partakes of a traumatic memory and of an unfinished business that is bound to receive a future legal sequence. Literature explains, in other words, why the trial, like the trauma, will (historically, traumatically) repeat itself.

Part Five: The Authority of Literature

— VII —

Beyond the Law or Before the Law: Writers as Precocious Witnesses

"Literature," writes Paul Celan, "often shoots ahead of us."[61] Literature is ahead of us. I have suggested elsewhere[62] that literature can be defined (accounted for, and understood) as a specific mode of testimony, and that writers often feel compelled to testify through literary or artistic channels precisely when they know, or feel intuitively, that in the court of history (and, I will now add, in a court of law) *evidence will fail* or will *fall short;* when they know that other sorts of testimonies will, for different reasons, not come through or that events have taken place that will, for different reasons, not be evidenced. Writers testify not simply when they know that knowledge cannot be obtained through other channels but, more profoundly, when they know or feel that knowledge, though available, cannot become eloquent, that *information cannot become consequential.*[63] I have argued that such writers can be understood (defined) as *precocious witnesses*[64] ("literature often shoots ahead of us") and that their art, their narrative, their literary style, or their artistic rhetoric is a precocious mode of bearing witness and of accessing reality when all other modes of knowledge are precluded or are rendered ineffectual. Tolstoy's literary text—I now propose—is, in effect, such a *precocious testimony* in (and to) the O. J. Simpson trial.

"I almost finished *The Kreutzer Sonata* or *How a Husband Killed His Wife*," Tolstoy announced in September 1889; "I am glad I wrote it: *I know that people need to be told what is written there.*"[65] A century later, they still do (as the obsession with the murder story of the century has once more shown). "I've only got one thing," says Pozdnyshev: "It's *what I know. Yes, I know something it will take other people quite a while to find out about* . . . No, people aren't going to find out what I know for quite a while to come" (68). What knowledge (what secret knowledge about murder, what secret knowledge about death, what secret knowledge about life) does the confessant feel he has that, unless he shares it, people are not likely to find out about? What does the husband-murderer know? And what does Tolstoy know? How does he know, why does he know? *For whom has Tolstoy confessed?*

And why was this confession of the husband—a confession that the O. J. Simpson trial could not get—in turn censored by the law? Why was there a conflict, in Tolstoy's day, between the confession and the law? Why did the Russian law try to reduce to silence the confession? What does Tolstoy know that can be confessed only *outside the law?* And why did the confessant, even in the fiction, in the literary story of *The Kreutzer Sonata*, feel that his confession could not be transformed into evidence in court, inside a trial? What sort of knowledge guided both Tolstoy and Pozdnyshev precisely as excluded from the trial? What sort of confession was it that had to be confessed not *to* the law but *despite* the law? And why does the master writer treat the law itself as yet another subterfuge, another misrepresentation with respect to the truth of the confession?

The Confession and the Law (Between Violence and Speech)

While Simpson goes to Oxford, England, to complain about the prejudices of the legal system and about the inequities of American justice,[66] Tolstoy writes a confession that declares the law incompetent to truly comprehend the crime or to address the real nature of the case. But the legal flaws do not become his alibi. He speaks not to evade responsibility but to testify: he speaks to *plead responsible*. While Simpson feels accomplished for the fact that he has been "convicted," as he says, "of nothing,"[67] and, within the trial, denies guilt and denies his presence at the crime scene irrespective of the evidence, Tolstoy pleads guilty irrespective of the verdict. Outside the trial, inside the confession, inside literature, he assumes the burden of a crime that is not literally his own but which he nonetheless profoundly acknowledges as his, and for which he assumes an exemplary personal (and cultural) responsibility. The confession does not ask, How can the law prevail? The confession asks, *What does speech mean in relation to an act of violence?* How can we recognize, how can we expiate a violence that is inscribed in culture as invisible, and that cannot be rendered visible in court? How can speech *make visible* a violence whose very nature is to blind? How can we *see* this blinding violence? How can we use speech to *see hate*, to look at our own hatred, when hatred (and especially our own) is normally prohibited to sight?

The confession wishes to confer on speech the highest moral value and the highest epistemological responsibility: that of accessing the truth; that of truly looking at what has been accessed, no matter how unbearable or how incriminating; that of sacrificing alibis and of acknowledging reality, for whatever price.

The discourse of the alibi speaks, on the other hand, precisely *not to know* and especially *not to acknowledge*. "On the night of the murder, I was asleep." You will understand that, asleep, I was not a witness to myself. How can I know where I was? Even were I to be a somnambulist, I wouldn't know. Has there been a murder? Who was murdered? I cannot be cross-examined, since I have no answers. But I can be interviewed—I love to be interviewed—since I do have lots and lots of replies. "At the night of the murder, I was playing golf; I was playing games with myself." The discourse of the alibi speaks to continue to play games with itself, to maintain both consciousness and conscience in a state of numbness, to remain asleep. The confession speaks to wake up.

Inside literature, outside the trial and despite the law, the confession speaks to turn away from subterfuge. Ordinary people—like Simpson, like ourselves—do not speak to turn away from subterfuge. We speak to avoid guilt. We speak to avoid pain. We use speech to protect ourselves. Profoundly, we speak to hope. "White America is still with me,"[68] insists Simpson to his British hosts. "I'm more popular with women now than I was before."[69] "Our marriage," said Nicole and O. J. Simpson after the police had intervened on the issue of domestic violence, "our marriage is as strong today as it was on the day we married."[70] Only master writers are prepared to say, like Kafka, "There is hope, but not for us." Only a Camus can write, "Hope is not our business. Our business is to turn away from subterfuge."[71] Only a Tolstoy can have, indeed, the strength, the courage, the integrity, the moral readiness to pay the price of this confession (a price of guilt, of cruelty, of suffering, of loneliness, of death; a legal price: a price of censorship, of legal prohibition, of exclusion from the law), to dispossess himself (and us) of all emotional illusions, to sacrifice all self-deceptions so as to unmask lies at all costs and, at all costs, to destroy—to take apart—all social, all emotional, all cultural alibis. What does Tolstoy know, to feel so compelled to give life to this brutal legal case and publicly to bare the husband's guilt? What moves the master writer, in assuming thus responsibility for a crime he did not in fact commit, to shock the world, to shake up his readership, to challenge and to tease the public's incredulity and scandalized amazement, to provoke the censor's ban, to defy the rage, the outrage of the church and the state (not to speak of that, more private, of his own wife); all the while declaring (implying by the story) that no court of law can bring this case to justice, that the law is not equipped to understand the nature of the crime or to address the nature of the case. Could Tolstoy be right?

In the twentieth century, the law attempts, but fails, to solve or to resolve the case—to bring truth to the light or bring the murderer to a confession. In the nineteenth century, the law attempts, but fails, to silence the confession's truth. It tries to outlaw the confession's publication, but it cannot arrest the case. Even censored, the text spreads. The handwritten manuscript is secretly read and, swiftly copied by thousands of hands, is reproduced, handwritten, by the thousands and, despite the censor, is made public and immediately distributed throughout the world, translated into many languages. "According to Strakhov, people no longer greeted each other in the street with 'How are you?' but with 'Have you read *The Kreutzer Sonata?*"[72] A century later, it is the same kind of obsession that propels the eager public toward the murder story of the O. J. Simpson case. "This has been a walking Rorschach test," says Medria Williams, a Los Angeles psychologist, of the fascination with the O. J. Simpson trial: "People are reacting as if it's O. J. when it's really about themselves."[73] To whom, then, has Tolstoy confessed? Why have people been so interested at once in the *confession* and in the *absence of confession* that has marked the trial of the century? Why have people been so drawn both to the fiction and to the reality of this case? For whom has Tolstoy confessed?

> I'd been taken to the local police station and from there to prison. And there I remained for eleven months awaiting trial. During that time I thought a great deal about myself and my past life, and I grasped what it had all been about.

The Secrets of the Case

> "I only began to grasp it when I saw her in her coffin . . ." He gave a sob, but continued hastily, at once: "It was only when I saw her dead face that I realized what I'd done. I realized that I'd killed her, that it was all my doing and that from a warm, moving, living creature she'd been transformed into a cold, immobile, waxen one, and that there was no way of setting this to rights, not ever, not anywhere, not by any means. If you've never experienced that, you can't possibly understand . . ." (117–118)

"There was no way of setting this to rights, not ever, not anywhere, not by any means." Does Pozdnyshev narrate the out-of-court truth of the O. J. Simpson trial? Can literature be viewed precisely as the *record* of what has remained *out of the legal records*? What does Tolstoy know? And, having read Tolstoy, having watched the trial of the century, what do we in our turn know?

Of course, we cannot say we know—we do not know—whether Simpson did or did not in effect murder his wife. We *do* know that, like Pozdnyshev, he treated her with cruelty and brutal violence. We *do* know, therefore, that the nature of his love was murderous. And this he probably in turn did not grasp and did not realize until it had become too late. Whether or not he killed Nicole, the overwhelming terror of his own brutality Simpson must have faced only when, like Pozdnyshev, he suddenly saw his ex-wife dead.

We also do know that, whereas Tolstoy confesses to a murder he did not empirically commit, the double murderer, whoever he might be, walks free and has not confessed to a crime he did most certainly commit.

* * *

Pozdnyshev was tried and acquitted, but the acquittal has not managed to redeem, to fix, or to restore his shattered life. The havoc that the murder has caused in his soul does not cease with the execution of the crime, nor do its repercussions in his life stop with the resolution of the trial.

Having been pronounced "not guilty," freed, he nonetheless remains chained to the bloody murder that no washing will erase, eradicate, or cleanse out of his life. He thus becomes the haunted captive of the bloody saga of which he has become the bearer and whose guilty secrets he will try, but will remain inherently unable, to divulge.

His destiny henceforth is to remain a hostage to the story of his violence: a (willing or unwilling) medium to the transformation of his case into a legend.

Pozdnyshev is willing. But he cannot acquit himself from this Sisyphean, endless task that goes against the grain of culture. He convicts himself. Culture acquits him. He cannot, in confessing, completely overcome the cultural taboos. But this is also his Sisyphean punishment—the testimonial or discursive punishment he takes upon himself. The haunted captive of a guilt that culture will not recognize, he will remain forever the life-prisoner of a confession that he still (as in the trial) feels he cannot quite *transmit* (pass to the other's comprehension, *transform into evidence* on which a consensus can be reached), and that he therefore cannot quite unload and cannot fully *terminate.*

A Confession without End

Pozdnyshev can close the narrative of the confession only with the outside interruption of the train's (interminal) arrest. The narrator quits confessing since he has to get off, go outside the train. Tolstoy himself will die in a train station, in the middle of the route and of a life itinerary that was not as yet exhausted, terminated.

But Pozdnyshev has not quite finished. He will certainly repeat again the story to some other passenger aboard some other train, on his way to a final destination that has not yet been—perhaps cannot be—reached. In the meantime, as the writer takes a (temporary) leave by bringing the last sentence to a close and by repeating (with a difference, with a double meaning) a last word that signals a departure and an ending (*"proschayte,* goodbye"), the confessant punctuates his exit from the train—and the story's open-endedness—only with the stated knowledge that his confession has not reached (or will not reach) its end, that it is bound to remain misunderstood:

> There was no way of setting that to rights, not ever, not anywhere, not by any means. *If you've never experienced that, you can't possibly understand* . . . (118)

(In Tolstoy's own terms, Simpson might be the one reader who will understand Tolstoy; but of course, if only for this very reason, he wouldn't read.) The confession thus remains, despite all the publicity that the confessant gives it and despite himself, his secret, a secret he cannot communicate. And this guilty secret, which the court will never understand, remains, at the same time, the case's and the trial's secret.

> They asked me in court how I killed her, what I used to do it with. Imbeciles! They thought I killed her that day, the fifth of October, with a knife. It wasn't that day I killed her, it was much earlier. Exactly in the same way as they're killing their wives now, all of them. (60)

Recapitulations

It is because what "they have asked in court" cannot receive a simple answer—cannot be answered in effect except by *recapitulating* the whole story from the start; because the knife (the murder weapon or the signifier of the trauma) is unlocatable (unfindable) except in the life story as a whole, and in the marriage story as a whole—that the confession has to renarrate not just the murder but the failure of the marriage of which it reiterates again the violence, in showing how this unseen violence, of which the unseen knife was just the final signifier, inhabited the marriage from the start: a figure in the carpet.

Trying to make visible this figure in the carpet; trying to narrate again the story that could not be told in court, the confession in its turn cannot but *repeat* the trial and once more *relive* (retell) the horror of the crime. But it cannot divulge the trial's secret. It cannot *locate* the starting point of the trauma or fully translate the trauma's origin into articulateness, into evidence or into seeability. And it cannot convert the blindness of the court and the misunderstanding of the trial into a transparent meaning or into a fully formulated and exhausted intelligibility. The confession, therefore, cannot end. It is a discourse and a speech act that goes on, and that will continue to go on, for as long as Pozdnyshev lives, for as long as Tolstoy lives; a speech performance—a confession—whose assumed responsibility of renunciation of all alibis, whose cultural insight into the ungraspability of gender traumas, and whose burden of traumatic understanding will continue to reverberate forever, beyond the end of Tolstoy's text and beyond the confessant's—and the author's—life or death.

I only began to grasp it when I saw her in her coffin . . . It was only when I saw her dead face that I realized what I'd done. I realized that I'd killed her . . . , and that there was no way of setting this to rights, not ever, not anywhere, not by any means. If you've never experienced that, you can't possibly understand . . .

Conclusion, or Justice and Mercy

Like Pozdnyshev, O. J. Simpson has (purportedly) shared with the public his life story, under the teasingly confessional title, *I Want to Tell You.* Like Tolstoy, he has published this life story as a book and has made a celebrated publication of a celebrated autobiography. Unlike Pozdnyshev, O. J. Simpson has claimed he is innocent and has no murder story to confess to. Unlike Tolstoy, he has chosen (in his right as a criminal defendant) *not to testify.*[74]

It is, however, for a different kind of court and for a different kind of justice that Tolstoy has testified, and has left a confession that has, perhaps, confessed for many others and that speaks, perhaps, for all of us: a confession that may well include, in Camus's terms, "a portrait of no one and of everyone";[75] a confession that (not by coincidence) no censor could stop yet that no trial could contain; a confession that no legal argument could summarize, that no court could translate into coherent legal language, that no jury could hear, yet that no legal prohibition could reduce to silence; a confession that has spoken, and still speaks, outside the trial and despite the law to turn away from subterfuge; a confession that in fact has never ended and still does not end but begins again the endless trial; a confession that continues endlessly into the night of our culture, of our history.

> "Well, *prostite,* forgive me . . ."
> He turned away from me . . . I went over to him in order to say goodbye . . .
> "*Proschayte,* goodbye," I said, offering my hand . . .
> "Yes, *prostite,* forgive me . . . ," he said, repeating the word with which he had brought his story to an end. (118)

"By nightfall on judgment day," wrote Francis X. Clines, "the national throng of juror-voyeurs was discovering that justice can be tempered with mercy, for it looked, at long last, as if the end of the O. J. spectacle was in sight."

Such mercy was to be hoped for as the white minivan [in which O. J. Simpson was released from jail after the acquittal] returned the football star free and clear to his home, and *dragged an old image back* across the national memoryscape. Its fleet *recapitulation* of the white Bronco's via doloroso crawl, the van speeding along the L.A. freeways was *as inarticulate an attempt at closing a story cycle* as might have been scripted in the film factories beyond the California hills.[76]

Stories like the O. J. Simpson trial, or the story of the murder of the wife of *The Kreutzer Sonata,* do not end. Their not ending is, perhaps, in some way, part of their poetic justice. They survive as narratives the life and death of their narrators and the convictions or acquittals of their perpetrators.

*   *   *

The questions that Tolstoy's confession poses to our culture have outlived Tolstoy, as they will outlive the murderer of Nicole Brown-Simpson and of Ronald Goldman. The significance of the confession will survive the repercussions of the known and unknown stories of the double murder and its transformation into the spectacular court version of the trial of the century. "The verdict has exposed a chasm in place for generations . . . People are reacting as if it's O. J. when it's really about themselves."[77] "People no longer greeted each other in the street with 'How are you?' but with 'Have you read *The Kreutzer Sonata?*'"

*   *   *

"The definition of a writer," says Kafka, "of such a writer, and the explanation of his effectiveness, to the extent that he has any":

He is the scapegoat of mankind. He makes it possible for men to enjoy sin without guilt, *almost without guilt.*[78]

Have you read *The Kreutzer Sonata?*

*   *   *

In a situation in which justice is impossible, in a culture that does not forgive, a literary story puts the century on trial and begs for mercy that it cannot receive.

I looked at the children, at her battered face with its bruises, and for the first time I forgot about myself, about my marital rights and my injured pride; for the first time I saw her as a human being. And so insignificant did all that had hurt me and made me jealous appear, and so significant what I'd done, that I wanted to press my face to her hand and say: "Forgive me!"—but I didn't dare to. (117)

"Well, *prostite*, forgive me . . ."

He turned away from me . . . I went over to him in order to say goodbye . . .

"*Proschayte*, goodbye," I said, offering my hand . . .

"Yes, *prostite*, forgive me . . . ," he said, repeating the word with which he had brought his story to an end. (118)

3

Theaters of Justice: Arendt in Jerusalem, the Eichmann Trial, and the Redefinition of Legal Meaning in the Wake of the Holocaust

"All sorrows can be borne if you put them into a story or tell a story about them." The story reveals the meaning of what otherwise would remain an unbearable sequence of sheer happenings . . . All her stories are actually "Anecdotes of destiny," they tell again and again how at the end we shall be privileged to judge.
—Hannah Arendt, "Isak Dinesen"

In the past half-century, two works have marked what can be called *conceptual breakthroughs* in our apprehension of the Holocaust. The first was Hannah Arendt's *Eichmann in Jerusalem,* which appeared in the United States in 1963 as a report on the Eichmann trial held in Israel in 1961. The second was the film *Shoah* by Claude Lanzmann, which first appeared in France in 1985. Twenty-two years apart and several decades after the Second World War, both works revealed the Holocaust in a completely new and unexpected light. Historical research, of course, existed both before these works and after them, but it did not displace collective frameworks of perception, and it did not change the vocabulary of collective memory. These two works did. Acceptable or unacceptable, they added *a new idiom* to the discourse on the Holocaust, which after them did not remain the same as it had been before them.

When they appeared, both works were in effect received as totally surprising, and the surprise was to some shocking and to all, impressive and unsettling in profound conscious and unconscious ways. Both works were seen as controversial. Both works were argued with, challenged both substantively and procedurally. Particularly Arendt's book provoked, immediately upon its publication and long after, a wave of controversy and responses that in fact has not yet been exhausted and whose energy continues up until this very day.

It is not a coincidence that the two works that have forced us to rethink the Holocaust in modifying our *vocabularies of remembrance* were, on the one hand, a trial report and, on the other hand, a work of art. We needed trials and trial reports to bring a conscious closure to the trauma of the war, to separate ourselves from the atrocities and to restrict, to demarcate and draw a boundary around, a suffering that seemed both unending and unbearable. Law is a discipline of limits and of consciousness. We needed limits to be able both to close the case and to enclose it in the past. Law distances the Holocaust. Art brings it closer. We needed art—the language of infinity—to mourn the losses and to face up to what in traumatic memory is not closed and cannot be closed. Historically, we needed law to totalize the evidence, to *totalize* the Holocaust and, through totalization, to start to apprehend its contours and its magnitude. Historically, we needed art to start to apprehend and to retrieve what the totalization has left out. Between too much proximity and too much distance, the Holocaust becomes today accessible, I will propose, precisely in this space of *slippage between law and art.* But it is also in this space of slippage that its full grasp continues to elude us.

Part One: The Banality of Evil

When I speak of justice, I speak of the idea of the struggle with evil.
—Emmanuel Levinas, "Philosophy, Justice and Love"

— I —

Law and Language

Although we have become familiar with its idiom, which we have debated now for four decades, *Eichmann in Jerusalem* remains today as baffling as it was in 1963.[1] The book has given rise to many misconceptions. It is remembered mostly by the catchword of its title—*A Report on the Banality of Evil*—as an argument about the moral nature of the world and as a proposition about evil.[2] Arendt's irony in coining her conceptual paradox is frequently misunderstood to mean, straightforwardly, a psychological description of the Nazi Perpetrator, and it is precisely this "psychology of evil" that becomes a subject of the controversy. Were the Nazis truly monstrous, or merely banal? Both sides of the controversy, I will argue, miss the point. The "banality of evil" is not psychological but rather legal and political.[3] In describing Eichmann's borrowed (Nazi) language and his all-too-credible self-justification by the total absence of motives for the mass murder that he passionately carried out (lack of mens rea),[4] Arendt's question is not, How can evil (Eichmann) be so banal? but, How can the banality of evil be addressed in legal terms[5] and by legal means? On what new legal grounds can the law mete out the utmost punishment precisely to banality or to the lack of mens rea? How can the absence of mens rea in the execution of a genocide become itself the highest—and not just the newest—crime against humanity?[6]

"We have to combat all impulses to mythologize the horrible," writes Arendt:

> Perhaps what is behind it all is that individual human beings did not kill other individual human beings for human reasons, but that an organized attempt was made to eradicate the concept of the human being.[7]

If evil is linguistically and legally banal (devoid of human motivations and occurring through clichés that screen human reality and actuality), in what ways, Arendt asks, can the law become an anchor and a guarantee, a guardian of humanity? How can the law *fight over language* with this radical banality (the total identification with a borrowed language)? When language itself becomes subsumed by the banality of evil, *how can the law keep meaning to the word "humanity"*? The crux of Arendt's book, I will thus argue, is not to define evil but to reflect on the significance of legal meaning in the wake of the Holocaust.

If the banality of evil designates a gap between event and explanations, how can the law deal with this gap? The Eichmann trial must decide not just the guilt of the defendant but how these questions can be answered. How, moreover, can a crime that is historically unprecedented be litigated, understood, and judged in a discipline of precedents? When precedents fall short, Arendt will ask, what is the role of legal history and legal memory? How can memory be used for the redefinition of a legal meaning that will be remembered in its turn, in such a way that the unprecedented can become a precedent in its own right—a precedent that might prevent an all-too-likely future repetition? What is the redefined legal relation between repetition and the new, and how does this relation affect the re-creation of authoritative legal meaning for the future? These are, I will propose, the restless questions that bring Arendt to Jerusalem.

"Israel has the right to speak for the victims," writes Arendt to her German friend and mentor, Karl Jaspers, "because the large majority of them are living in Israel now as citizens":

The trial will take place in the country in which the injured parties and those who happen to survive are. You say that Israel didn't even exist then. But one could say that it was for the sake of these victims that Palestine became Israel . . . In addition, Eichmann was responsible for Jews and Jews only . . . The country or state to which the victims belong has jurisdiction . . .

All this may strike you as though I too was attempting to circumscribe the political with legal concepts. And I even admit that as far as the law is concerned, I have been infected by the Anglo-Saxon influence. But quite apart from that, it seems to me to be in the nature of this case that we have no tools to hand except legal ones with which we have to judge and pass sentence on something that cannot even be adequately represented either in legal terms or in political terms. That is precisely what makes the process itself, namely the trial, so exciting.[8]

A Dissident Legal Perspective

Among the common misconceptions to which Arendt's legal stance has given rise, the most prevalent is that the book is "anti-Zionist."[9] According to Arendt's own testimony, she is pro-Zionist[10]—but at the outset critical of Israeli law[11] and critical of the Israeli government. Arendt perceives the trial as the space of a dramatic confrontation between the claims of justice and the competing claims of government and power. It is as though the courtroom were itself claimed simultaneously by *two competing masters:* justice on one side, and on the other side the incarnation of political power, embodied in the far too charismatic head of state, who has precisely planned the trial for his own political, didactic, and essentially nonlegal ends.[12] Arendt in this way sets up a secondary courtroom drama and a secondary case for arbitration and adjudication: not just *Attorney General v. Eichmann* but also, simultaneously, the drama of the confrontation between Justice and the State: *Justice v. the State,* or rather, as she sees it, *the State v. Justice.*[13]

And Ben Gurion, rightly called the "architect of the state," remains the invisible stage manager of the proceedings. Not once does he attend a session; in the courtroom he speaks with the voice of Gideon Hausner, the Attorney General, who, representing the government, does his best, his very best, to *obey his master.* And if, fortunately, his best often turns out not to be good enough, the reason is that the trial is presided over by *someone who serves Justice as faithfully as Mr. Hausner serves the State of Israel.*[14] Justice demands that the accused be prosecuted, defended, and judged, and that all the other questions of seemingly greater import . . . be left in abeyance.

And *Justice,* though perhaps an "abstraction" for those of Mr. Ben Gurion's turn of mind, proves to be a *much sterner master* than the Prime Minister with all his power.[15] (*EiJ,* 5)

In this dramatic confrontation between Justice and the State, Arendt sees her role as that of serving, in her turn, the "much sterner master." It is against the more "permissive" rule of the competing master—the prime minister—that she enlists at once her analytic skills, her legal erudition, and her most biting sense of irony. She thus proceeds from the determination to speak truth to power. Standing up against the state, she mobilizes law in an attempt to build a *dissident legal perspective.* Rather than call her "anti-Zionist," we may want to propose that, with respect to the legal position of the state prosecuting the accused (with respect, that is, to the official Zionist legal position), she is performing what might be called (somewhat metaphorically) "critical legal studies" before its time.[16]

The Critical Consciousness of the Event

Arendt's critique has had its own historical momentum; its dissenting legal force has paradoxically become today not only part of the event in history but part of its notorious legal historiography. This historiography in turn was part of the legacy of the event. Whether we choose to accept or to reject its controversial premises, Arendt's trial report, I will here argue, at once proves and seals the impact of the trial as a true event.[17] "Like truth," writes the historian Pierre Nora, "the event is always revolutionary, the grain of sand in the machine, the accident that shakes us up and takes us by surprise . . . It is best circumscribed from the outside: what is the event and for whom? For if there is no event without critical consciousness, there is an event only when, offered to everybody, it is not the same for all."[18]

I view Arendt, in Nora's words, as "the critical consciousness of the event," "the grain of sand in the machine." This chapter will explore the Eichmann trial quite precisely in its dimension as a living, powerful *event*—an event whose impact is defined and measured by the fact that it is "not the same for all."

It is not the same for Arendt as for me. I respect this fact as illustrating not just the significance but the "eventness" of the trial. I will try to look at the event from both perspectives: Arendt's and my own. I will try to hold both viewpoints in sight of each other's critical awareness. In what follows, I will pledge my reading against Arendt's, in espousing the state's vision of the trial and in highlighting differently than Arendt what I take to be the deeper meaning of the trial and, beyond its meaning, its far-reaching repercussions as event: an event that *includes Arendt* and of which Arendt remains, to this day, the most memorable and the most lucid critical consciousness.

— II —

History for Life

In *The Use and Abuse of History for Life*, Nietzsche analyzes different kinds of history (different relations to the past) that are all useful, relevant to life, and whose opposing insights in fact complement each other and define each other. There is what Nietzsche calls "monumental history," consisting in an aggrandizement, a magnification of the high points of the past as they relate to man's "struggle and action"; in contrast to this history that magnifies the past and seeks in it an inspiration, a "great impulse" for a future action, there is what Nietzsche calls "critical history"—a history "that judges and condemns" and that undercuts illusions and enthusiasms. "Critical history" derives, says Nietzsche, from man's "suffering and his desire for deliverance."

> If the man who will produce something great has need of the past, he makes himself its master by means of monumental history; . . . and only he whose heart is oppressed by an instant need and who will cast the burden off at any price feels the need of "critical history," the history that judges and condemns.[19]

I will suggest that Arendt is, in Nietzsche's precise terms, a critical historian of the trial. She casts aside the version of the trial presented by the state, in an attempt to free the present from the oppressive inheritances of the past. She seeks not *inspiration* from the past but *liberation* from the past. She strives not to erect past models but to define a purer justice. "That virtue," Nietzsche writes, "never has a pleasing quality. It never charms; it is harsh and strident" (*UAH, 36*). Whereas the official state vision of the Eichmann trial is, I would propose, precisely one of monumental history, Arendt's vision offers a substitutive critical (legal) history. Scholem, therefore, is quite right in pointing out that Arendt's "version of events" often "seems to come between us and the events."[20] Monumental history is inspirational, emotional, constructive. Critical history is often destructive and always deconstructive. I propose to analyze here one against the other what I call the monumental legal vision of the Eichmann trial[21] and the critical vision (or the critical version of events) offered by Arendt.

Part Two: Monumental Legal History

"For it was history," writes Arendt, "that, as far as the prosecution was concerned, stood in the center of the trial" (*EiJ*, 19). What makes of a legal case a monumental historical case is the dramatic, totalizing way in which the legal institutions undertake to put on trial history itself, thereby setting the whole world as the stage and as the audience of the trial. Nuremberg was such a case: a legal process mastering a monumental mass of evidence, and technically supported by a battery of earphones and interpreters through whose performance justice was enacted as a constant process of translation and transmission between different languages. The Eichmann trial follows the tradition set up by the Nuremberg tribunal, but with a crucial difference of perspective. Whereas the Nuremberg trials view murderous political regimes and their aggressive warfare as the center of the trial and as the center of what constitutes a monumental history, the Eichmann trial views the victims as the center of what gives history its monumental dimensions and what endows the trial with its monumental significance as an act of historic justice.[22]

The philosophy of history and law that sees the victims as the narrative center of history and that insists on this memorial relation between law and history was best expounded by the then prime minister of Israel, David Ben Gurion.[23]

American journalists, who have not suffered from the Nazi atrocities, may be "objective" and deny Israel's right to try one of the greatest Nazi murderers. But the calamity inflicted on the Jewish people is not merely one part of the atrocities the Nazis committed against the world. It is a specific and unparalleled act, an act designed for the complete extermination of the Jewish people, which Hitler and his collaborators did not dare commit against any other people. It is therefore the duty of the State of Israel, the only sovereign authority in Jewry, to see that the whole of this story, in all its horror, is fully exposed—without in any way ignoring the Nazi regime's other crimes against humanity, but as a unique crime without precedent or parallel in the annals of mankind.

. . . It is not the penalty to be inflicted on the criminal that is the main thing—no penalty can match the magnitude of the offense— but the full exposure of the Nazi regime's infamous crimes against our people. Eichmann's acts alone are not the main point in this trial. Historic justice and the honor of the Jewish people demand this trial. Historic justice and the honor of the Jewish people demand that this should be done only by an Israeli court in the sovereign Jewish State.[24]

Criminal proceedings are therefore initiated by the State of Israel in unique representation of the victims' previously unheard, unknown, and unnarrated narrative. The exposure of this unknown, unarticulated, and thus *secret monumental narrative* is the trial's goal. In the Nazi scheme, this narrative was meant to be erased as part of the erasure of the Jewish people. The articulation of this narrative as a living, active historical and legal force is therefore in itself an unprecedented act of historic (and not just of legal) justice. By the mere existence of the trial, genocide is countered, vanquished by an act of historical survival. Unaccountable genocidal injustice is countervailed by a rigorously applied procedure of restoration of strict legal accountability and of meticulous justice. "Adolph Eichmann," says the prosecutor at the end of his opening argument, "will enjoy a privilege that he did not accord to even a single one of his victims. He will be able to defend himself before the court. His fate will be decided according to law and according to the evidence, with the burden of proof resting upon the prosecution. And the judges of Israel will pronounce true and righteous judgment."[25] Thus it is that Gideon Hausner, Israel's attorney general and the chief prosecutor in this trial, literally frames the accusation in the victims' name,[26] as though speaking

for the dead and giving voice, materially, to the six million Jews exterminated by the Nazis:

> When I stand before you here, judges of Israel, in this court, to ac-
> cuse Adolph Eichmann, I do not stand alone. With me at this mo-
> ment stand six million prosecutors. But alas, they cannot rise to
> level the finger of accusation in the direction of the glass dock and
> cry out *J'accuse* against the man who sits there. For their ashes are
> piled in the hills of Auschwitz and the fields of Treblinka . . . Their
> graves are scattered throughout the length and breadth of Europe.
> Their blood cries to Heaven, but their voice cannot be heard. Thus
> it falls to me to be their mouthpiece and to deliver the awesome in-
> dictment in their name.[27]

Thus the Eichmann trial sets out to perform what I call, in using
Nietzsche's term, "monumental history": it sets out to present a "'monumental' contemplation of the past" that will provide an impulse for a future action and that will analyze events through their effects rather than
through their causes, as "events that will have an effect on all ages"
(*UAH*, 14–15).[28]

I am borrowing, however, Nietzsche's concept of "monumentality"
and of a monumentalized historical perception in displacement of this
concept. In Nietzsche, monumental history records the deeds and actions of great men. Monumentality (endurance of historical effects) consists, in other words, of the generic way in which history is written
by great men. In the Eichmann trial, in contrast, as the prosecutor's
monumentalizing opening address dramatically makes clear, monumental history consists not of the *writing of the great* but of *the writing of the
dead;* the monument the trial seeks to build in judging Eichmann is
erected not to romantic greatness (not to those who make or *have made*
history) but to the dead (a monument to those who *were subject to* history).

It is striking that the prosecutor's monumentalized indictment starts
with a historical citation. Monumental history is not only the trial's
theme and legal subject. History inhabits here the legal utterance stylis-
tically from its first word. In a unique dramatic and rhetorical self-
definition, the prosecutor's opening argument initiates itself through the
quotation and the recapitulation of another historical speech act of accusation.[29]

The six million dead, says the prosecutor, can no longer speak in their own name and formulate their own "J'accuse." It is therefore the indictment formulated by the state that will articulate for them their silenced accusation and will thus enable them not simply to accuse but to claim a legal subjectivity—to legally say "I" for the first time.

"J'accuse"

What would it mean for the dead to say "I" through the medium of the trial?[30] What is the significance—for those whom history deprived precisely of their "I"—of saying "I accuse" before a court of law and before the world? Why must the dead say "I" precisely in a foreign tongue, in borrowing a French expression? From whom do the dead borrow? What sort of foreign discourse, what legal/literary speech act do the dead quote to say "I accuse" for the first time?

"J'accuse"—"I accuse"—was the title of a famous text of vehement denunciation of racist injustice published in 1898 by the best-known French writer of the time, Emile Zola, as an explosive public letter to the president of France and as an artist's intervention in the legal controversy of the Dreyfus affair in France. In 1894, Captain Alfred Dreyfus, a Jewish officer in the French army, was convicted of betrayal of military secrets to Germany and sentenced to solitary life imprisonment in the penal colony called Devil's Island. When the fact of espionage was discovered and the military high command was pressured to supply the criminal's identity, it was natural for the army hurriedly to suspect and to scapegoat Dreyfus because he was a Jew. The conviction was obtained through an illegal secret process in a military court. Under the pretext of a threat to state security, the evidence was hidden not just from the public but also from the accused and from his lawyer. After the trial, it emerged that the incriminating piece of evidence was a forged document and that the real spy was another officer, Major Esterhazy. But Dreyfus's conviction as a traitor had meanwhile triggered throughout France and its colonies an outburst of anti-Semitic fury. In spite of the accumulating evidence confirming Dreyfus's innocence, the army and the politicians refused to admit their judicial error. A second military court judged Esterhazy only to acquit him and to ratify, thus, through a second trial, the authority of the closed case on Dreyfus's guilt. Appearing in a daily newspaper—with the effect of an exploding bomb—Emile Zola's pamphlet publicly accused the army and the government of a cover-up and a miscarriage of justice. It strongly proclaimed Dreyfus's innocence and advocated the necessity of reopening the case.

It should be noted that Emile Zola's act was historically unprecedented on three counts. (1) This was the first time that a non-Jew had spoken for Jews to publicly accuse—denounce—*legal* anti-Semitism or racist judicial injustice from the victim's point of view and in the victim's name. (2) In thus protesting for the victim, Zola broke in a revolutionary way with the prevailing Western or Platonic ethical and philosophical tradition, according to which a victim of judicial injustice had to *resign himself* on moral grounds to the legal authority of the decision wronging him, in order to safeguard the rule of law for culture's and civilization's sake.[31] (3) And most important: in an unprecedented manner, Zola mobilized art as the victim's ally in the victim's struggle against law and against his oppression by the law. It is not by chance that such an accusation against law required art (both marginality and power of expression) to articulate itself. Only an artist could indeed take up the challenge of arguing with the legitimacy of an act of state. For the first time, a literary writer understood his task as that of giving *legal* voice to those whom the law had deprived of voice. In identifying art's voice with the victim's voice, Zola universalized the victim.

The Truth Is on the March

Zola knew that, consequent to his audacious published accusations against the justice system, he himself would unavoidably be charged with libel and be prosecuted for slander of the army and the government. He deliberately put himself up for criminal trial in order to reopen Dreyfus's closed case. In joining thus the victim of the flagrant injustice and in taking in his turn the position and the role of the accused, Zola hoped to force the legal system to review the evidence of Dreyfus's case in a *nonmilitary* court: he wanted to initiate a legal repetition of Dreyfus's sealed trial through a public—as opposed to the old hidden, secret—legal process and thereby to bring to light the Jewish officer's innocence through his own trial. Thus the artist made—at his own cost—a revolutionary intervention in the legal process of the Dreyfus case. The writer chose politically to make creative use of the tool of law in order to break open the closed legal frame.[32]

But Zola was in turn convicted and had to flee from France to England. Finally, in 1899, after a change of governments and a long chain of legal twists, Dreyfus was pardoned and in 1906 fully exonerated and reinstated in his military rank. Zola was no longer alive to witness this longed for triumph. "Let us envy him," Anatole France said at Zola's funeral: "He has honored his country and the world with an immense body of work and a great deed . . . For a brief moment, he was the conscience of humanity."[33]

"The truth is on the march," Zola wrote in *J'accuse,* "and nothing shall stop it . . . the act that I hereby accomplish is but a revolutionary means to hasten the explosion of truth and justice."[34] In terms that reverberate into our century, Zola charged:

It is a crime to mislead public opinion, to manipulate it for a death-dealing purpose and to pervert it to the point of delirium. It is a crime . . . to whip reactionary and intolerant passions into a frenzy while sheltering behind the odious anti-Semitism, of which the great liberal France of the rights of man will die if it is not cured of it. It is a crime to exploit patriotism to further the aims of hatred. And it is a crime to worship the sword as the modern god. (51)

"I have but one goal," Zola said in very simple words at the conclusion of *J'accuse:* "I have but one concern: that light be shed, in the name of mankind which has suffered so much and has a right to happiness":

My ardent protest is but *a cry from my very soul.* Let them dare to summon me before a court of law. Let there be trial in the full light of day. I am waiting. (53, tm)

"France," Zola wrote in another publication just a week before *J'accuse,*

France, those are the people I appeal to! They must group together! They must write; they must speak up. They must work with us to enlighten the little people, the humble people who are being poisoned and forced into delirium.[35]

In his final "Statement to the Jury" at the closure of his trial, Zola said:

I did not want my country to remain plunged in lie and injustice. You can strike me here. One day, France will thank me for having helped to save her honor.[36]

Race Hatred, or the Monumental Repetition of a Primal Legal Scene

The pathos of Zola's historical denunciation of nationalistic racism had worked itself into the Eichmann trial, through the relation of the victim's silent, *unarticulated* cry to the *legal articulation* of the prosecutorial argument.

With me at this moment stand six million prosecutors. But alas, they cannot rise to level the finger of accusation in the direction of the glass dock and cry out "J'accuse" against the man who sits there. For their ashes are piled in the hills of Auschwitz and the fields of Treblinka . . . Their blood cries to Heaven, but their voice cannot be heard. Thus it falls to me to be their mouthpiece and to deliver the awesome indictment in their name.

It is not an accident that, in his opening argument against the Nazi criminal, the Israeli prosecutor picks up on the primal legal scene and on the primal soul cry of Zola's "J'accuse,"[37] trying to recapitulate at once the moral force of the historical denunciation and the subversive legal gesture, the revolutionary legal meaning of Zola's reversed speech act of accusation.

Monumental history, says Nietzsche, proceeds by analogy. The Dreyfus case in France was both a European trauma and a Jewish trauma. In parallel, the Holocaust in Germany was, on a different and undreamt of scale, a Jewish trauma that became a European trauma. But Germany, alas, had no Zola.

"While the Dreyfus Affair in its broader political aspects belongs to the twentieth century," writes Hannah Arendt, "the Dreyfus case [is] quite typical of the nineteenth century, when men followed legal proceedings so keenly because each instance afforded a test of the century's greatest achievement, the complete impartiality of the law . . . The doctrine of equality before the law was still so firmly implanted in the conscience of the civilized world that a single miscarriage of justice could provoke public indignation from Moscow to New York. The wrong done to a single Jewish officer in France was able to draw from the rest of the world a more vehement and united reaction than all the persecutions of German Jews a generation later."[38]

All this belongs typically to the nineteenth century and by itself would never have survived two World Wars . . . The Dreyfus affair in its political implications could survive because two of its elements grew in importance during the twentieth century. The first is hatred of the Jews. The second, suspicion of the republic itself, of parliament, and the state machine.[39]

The twentieth century repeats and takes to an undreamable extreme the structures of the nineteenth century. Behind the prosecutor's opening citation of Zola's protest, the shadow of Dreyfus stands at the threshold of the Eichmann trial for a whole historical *legal inheritance* in which the Jew is the perennial accused in a lynch justice. In twentieth-century Nazi Germany as in Dreyfus's nineteenth-century France, persecution ratifies itself as persecution in and through civilization—by the civilized means of the law. The Wannsee Conference legalizing genocide as a sweeping indictment and penalization of all Jews by virtue of their being Jews is but the crowning culmination of this history. As the secretary of that conference, who *transcribed* it while feeling not just innocent, but—so he testified, "like Pontius Pilate"—*innocented* by its verdict on the Jews,[40] as the ruthless agent of administrative genocide and as the Nazis' so-called "Jewish specialist," Eichmann is an emblem of this history. But this whole insidious framework of legal persecution and of *legalized abuse* can now for the first time be dismantled legally, since Zionism has provided a tribunal (a state justice) in which the Jew's victimization can be for the first time *legally articulated*. In doing justice and in exercising sovereign Israeli jurisdiction, the Eichmann trial tries to legally reverse the long tradition of traumatization of the Jew by means of law. The voiceless Jew or the perennial accused can for the first time speak, say "I" and voice his own "J'accuse." "This," Prime Minister Ben Gurion said, "is not an ordinary trial nor only a trial":

Here, for the first time in Jewish history, historical justice is being done by the sovereign Jewish people. For many generations it was we who suffered, who were tortured, were killed—and we who were judged. Our adversaries and our murderers were also our judges. For the first time Israel is judging the murderers of the Jewish people. It is not an individual that is at the dock at this historic trial, and not the Nazi regime alone, but anti-Semitism throughout history. The judges whose business is the law and who may be trusted to adhere to it will judge Eichmann the man for his horrible crimes, but responsible public opinion in the world will be judging anti-Semitism, which paved the way for this most atrocious crime in the history of mankind. And let us bear in mind that only the independence of Israel could create the necessary conditions for this historic act of justice.[41]

Part Three: Critical History

— III —

Arendt's Objections

Arendt disputes this vision of the trial and rejects the monumental history that it constructs on two conceptual grounds—the first juridical, linked to a different conception of the function of the trial (based on a different, more conservative philosophy of law), and the second epistemological, linked to a different historical perception of the Holocaust and amounting ultimately to a different philosophy of history. On both historical and legal grounds, Arendt takes issue with the very narrative perspective that puts the victims at the center of the trial. At odds with the narrative effort of the state, Arendt's competing effort is to *decenter* systematically the prosecution's story[42] and to focus the historical perception that transpires not on the victim but on the criminal and on the nature of the crime.

1. For a More Conservative Philosophy of Law: Arendt's Jurisprudential Argument

The prosecutor's grandiose rhetoric of speaking for the dead, the monumentalized indictment uttered in the name and in the voice of the deceased, undermines for Arendt the sobriety of the proceedings, since what is presented as the victims' outcry—the victims' search for justice and accountability—might be perceived as a desire for revenge. But if the prosecutor's public anger is what the cry of the deceased amounts to, Arendt would rather do without that cry. A courtroom is indeed no place for cries. Justice for Arendt is a thoroughly ascetic, disciplined, conceptual experience, not an emotional stage for spectacular public expression. "Justice"—Arendt protests—"does not permit anything of the sort; it demands seclusion, it permits sorrow rather than anger. And it prescribes the most careful abstention from all the nice pleasures of putting oneself in the limelight" (*EiJ*, 5).

> Justice demands that the accused be prosecuted, defended, and judged, and that all the other questions of seemingly greater import . . . be left in abeyance. Justice insists on the importance of Adolph Eichmann, . . . the man in the glass booth built for his protection . . . On trial are his deeds, not the sufferings of the Jews, not the German people or mankind, not even anti-Semitism or racism. (*EiJ*, 5)

The jurisprudential understanding of a crime cannot be focused on the victim. A criminal is tried not with the aim of vengeance on the part of those whom he has injured but in order to repair the community that he has endangered by his action. "Criminal proceedings," Arendt writes, "since they are mandatory and initiated even if the victim would prefer to forgive and forget, rest on laws whose 'essence' . . . is that a crime is not committed only against the victim but primarily against the community whose law is violated . . . it is the general public order that has been thrown out of gear and must be restored, as it were. It is, in other words, the law, not the plaintiff, that must prevail"[43] (*EiJ*, 261).

2. For a Less Conservative Philosophy of History: Arendt's Historiographical Argument

The second argument Arendt articulates as an objection to the trial's focus on the victims is historical and epistemological. The trial perceives Nazism as the monstrous culmination and as the traumatic *repetition* of a monumental history of anti-Semitism. But for Arendt this victim's perspective, this traumatized perception of history as the eternal repetition of catastrophe is *numbing*.[44] Arendt does not put it quite so literally: I am translating freely what I feel to be the intellectual and the emotional thrust of her argument. Repeated trauma causes numbness. But law cannot indulge in numbness. As a typical response to trauma, numbness may be a legitimate effect of history; it cannot be a legitimate effect of law, the language of sharpened awareness. A trial, Arendt deeply and intensely feels, is supposed to be precisely a translation of the trauma *into consciousness*. But here the numbing trauma is mixed into the form of the trial itself. In litigating and in arguing the charges on the basis of a numbing repetition of catastrophe, Jewish historical consciousness—and the trial as a whole—submits to the effects of trauma instead of remedying it. History becomes the illustration of what is already known. But the question is precisely how to learn something new from history. In the Israeli vision of the trial, the monumental, analogical perception of the repetition of the trauma of anti-Semitism *screens the new*—hides from view precisely the unprecedented nature of the Nazi crime, which is neither a development nor a culmination of what went before, but is separated from the history preceding it by an abyss. This abyss—this epistemological rupture—is what the Eichmann trial and its monumental history fail to perceive, in Arendt's eyes. This radical critique encapsulates Arendt's revolutionary concept of the Holocaust, as opposed to her conservative legal approach and to her conservative jurisprudential argument.

I will argue in what follows that the Eichmann trial is, at the antipodes of Arendt, historiographically conservative but jurisprudentially revolutionary. Arendt, on the contrary, is historiographically revolutionary but jurisprudentially conservative. I further argue that the paradox of *Eichmann in Jerusalem* proceeds from the creative tension between Arendt's philosophical, historiographical, and epistemological radicalism and her jurisprudential conservatism.

The Holocaust, Arendt contends, requires a historiographical radicalism. But the Eichmann trial is—quite disappointingly—not capable of such a radical historical approach. It fails to give a revolutionary lesson for the future because it is imprisoned in the endless repetition of a catastrophic past. It is locked up in trauma and in repetition as a construct, which prevents a grasp of the unprecedented. "I have insisted," Arendt writes, "on . . . how little Israel, and the Jewish people in general, was prepared to recognize, in the crimes that Eichmann was accused of, an unprecedented crime":

> In the eyes of the Jews, thinking exclusively in terms of their own history, the catastrophe that had befallen them under Hitler, in which a third of the people perished, appeared not as the most recent of crimes, the unprecedented crime of genocide, but on the contrary, as the oldest crime they knew and remembered. This mis-

understanding . . . is actually at the root of all the failures and the shortcomings of the Jerusalem trial. *None of the participants ever arrived at a clear understanding of the actual horror of Auschwitz, which is of a different nature from all the atrocities of the past* . . . Politically and legally, . . . these were "crimes" different not only in degree of seriousness but in essence. (267; emphasis added)

Part Four: Extending the Limits of Perception

Arendt thus situates the problematic of the Eichmann trial in a particularly meaningful relation between repetition and the new, between a memory of history and law as an experience and a discipline of precedents, and the necessity to break fresh ground, to project into the future and into the structure of the precedent the legal meaning of the unexampled and the unprecedented. I will argue in my turn that, in focusing on repetition and its limits in the Eichmann trial, Arendt fails to see the way in which the trial in effect does not *repeat* the victim's story, but historically creates it for the first time. I submit, in other words, that the Eichmann trial legally creates a radically original and new event: not a rehearsal of a given story, but a groundbreaking narrative event that is itself historically and legally unprecedented.

— IV —

"Universalist philosophers," writes Richard Rorty, "assume, with Kant, that all the logical space necessary for moral deliberation is now available—that all important truths about right and wrong can not only be stated, but be made plausible, in language already to hand."[45] As a believer in the universalist language of the law, Arendt makes such an assumption in coming to Jerusalem and in reporting as she does on the trial's shortcomings. But the Eichmann trial, I would argue, strives precisely to *expand* the space available for moral deliberation through law. The trial shows how the unprecedented nature of the injury inflicted on the victims cannot be simply stated in a language that is already at hand. I would argue that the trial struggles to create a new space, a language that is not yet in existence. This new legal language and this new space in which Western rationality as such shifts its horizon and extends its limits are created here perhaps for the first time in history precisely by the victims' firsthand narrative.

Private and Public

Over a hundred witnesses appear, with the determination to translate their private traumas to the public space. To her surprise, Arendt is so moved by some of the testimonies that she can uncharacteristically at moments think uncritically and, as she puts it, "foolishly: *'Everyone, everyone should have his day in court'*" (*EiJ*, 229). In general, however, Arendt has a hard time stomaching the testimonial exhibition of atrocities and finds the listening profoundly taxing.[46] She is embarrassed by the unreserved disclosures of human degradation and is deeply discomforted by what she experiences as an exposure of the private to the public ear:

> [T]his audience was filled with "survivors," . . . immigrants from Europe, like myself, who knew by heart all there was to know[47] . . .
> As witness followed witness and horror was piled on horror, they sat there and listened in public to stories they would hardly have been able to endure in private, when they would have had to face the storyteller. (*EiJ* 8)

In relegating the victim experience to the private realm and in expressing her discomfort at the mixture of the private and the public, Arendt fails to recognize, however, how the very essence of the trial consists in a juridical and social *reorganization* of the two spheres and in a restructuring of their jurisprudential and political relation to each other.[48] Beyond the incidental scope of Arendt's reservation and of her anger at what she experiences as an invasion of the public by the private, I argue that the trial is, primarily and centrally, a *legal process of translation* of thousands of private, secret traumas into one collective, public, and communally acknowledged one.

The Revolution in the Victim

But such translation is not given. The victim's story has to overcome not just the silence of the dead but the indelible coercive power of the oppressor's terrifying, brutal silencing of the surviving, and the inherent, speechless silence of the living in the face of an unthinkable, unknowable, ungraspable event. "Even those who were there don't know Auschwitz . . . For Auschwitz is another planet,"[49] testifies a writer named K-Zetnik, who cannot complete his testimony because he literally loses consciousness and faints on the witness stand. "That mute cry," he later will write, "was again trying to break loose, as it had every time death confronted me at Auschwitz; and, as always when I looked death in the eye, so now too the mute scream got no further than my clenched teeth that closed upon it and locked it inside me."[50]

> But what can I do when I'm struck mute? I have neither word nor name for it all. Genesis says: "And Adam gave names . . ." When God finished creating the earth and everything upon it, Adam was asked to give names to all that God had created. Till 1942 there was no Auschwitz in existence. For Auschwitz there is no name other than Auschwitz. My heart will be ripped to pieces if I say, "In Auschwitz they burned people alive!" Or "In Auschwitz people died of starvation." For that is not Auschwitz. People have died of starvation before, and people did burn alive before. But that is not Auschwitz. What, then, is Auschwitz? I have no words to express it; I don't have a name for it. Auschwitz is a primal phenomenon. I don't have the key to unlock it. But don't the tears of the mute speak his anguish? And don't his screams cry his distress? Don't his bulging eyes reveal the horror? I am that mute.[51]

In the film *Shoah*, two survivors of Vilna, Motke Zaidl and Itzhak Dugin, testify about the Nazi plan in 1944 to open the graves and to cremate the corpses, so as to literally erase all traces of the genocide:

> The last graves were the newest, and we started with the oldest, those of the first ghetto . . . The deeper you dug, the flatter the bodies were . . . When you tried to grasp a body, it crumbled, it was impossible to pick up. We had to open the graves, but without tools . . . Anyone who said 'corpse' or 'victim' was beaten. The Germans made us refer to the bodies as *Figuren*.[52]

A victim is by definition not only one who is oppressed but also one who has no language of his own, one who, quite precisely, is *robbed of a language* with which to articulate his or her victimization.[53] What is available to him as language is only the oppressor's language. But in the oppressor's language, the abused will sound crazy, even to himself, if he describes himself as abused.[54]

The Germans even forbade us to use the words 'corpse' or 'victim.' The dead were blocks of wood, shit. Anyone who uttered the word 'corpse' or 'victim' was beaten. The Germans made us refer to the bodies as *Figuren* [that is, as puppets, as dolls], or as *Schmattes* [which means 'rags'].⁵⁵

In the new language that it is the function of the Eichmann trial to invent and to articulate from scratch, the Jews have to emerge precisely from the "subhumanity" that has been linguistically impressed on them, even inside themselves, by the oppressor's language. "We were the bearers of the secret," says Philip Muller, ex-Sonderkommando member, in the film *Shoah:*

We were reprieved dead men. We weren't allowed to talk to anyone, or contact any prisoner, or even the SS. Only those in charge of the Aktion.⁵⁶

Because history by definition silences the victim, the reality of degradation and of suffering—the very facts of victimhood and of abuse—are intrinsically inaccessible to history. But the legally creative vision of the Eichmann trial consists in the undoing of this inaccessibility. The Eichmann trial is the victims' trial only insofar as it is now the victims who, against all odds, are precisely *writing their own history.*

To enable such a writing through which the mute bearers of a traumatizing destiny become the speaking subjects of a history, the Eichmann trial must enact not simply memory but *memory as change*. It must dramatize upon its legal stage, before the audience, nothing less than a *conceptual revolution in the victim*. And this, in fact, is what the trial does. In this sense, the Eichmann trial is, I would submit, a revolutionary trial.⁵⁷ It is this revolutionary transformation of the victim that makes the victim's story *happen* for the first time, and happen as a legal act of *authorship of history*. This historically unprecedented revolution in the victim that was operated in and by the Eichmann trial is, I would suggest, the trial's major contribution not only to Jews but to history, to law, to culture—to humanity at large. I further argue that, as a singular legal event, the Eichmann trial calls for a rethinking—and sets in motion a transvaluation—of the structures and the values of conventional criminal law.⁵⁸

It is a well-known fact that, prior to the Eichmann trial, the Holocaust was not discussed in Israel but was, rather, struck by shame, silence, and widespread denial.[59] Holocaust survivors did not talk about their past, and when they did, they were not listened to. Their memories were sealed in muteness and in silence. Their stories often were kept secret even from their families. The emotional explosion triggered by the Eichmann trial and by the revolution in the victims it dramatically and morally effected publicly unlocked this silence.

Now, for the first time, victims were legitimized and validated, and their newborn discourse was empowered by their new roles not as victims but as prosecution witnesses within the trial. I argue that a new moral perception was made possible precisely by this change of role and change of status. "Injustices," says Rorty in a different context,

Injustices may not be perceived as injustices, even by those who suffer them, until somebody invents a previously unplayed role. Only if somebody has a dream, and a voice to describe that dream, does what looked like nature begin to look like culture, what looked like fate begin to look like a moral abomination.[60]

The trial was thus a transforming act of law and justice: a Jewish past that formerly had meant only a crippling disability was now being reclaimed as an empowering and proudly shared political and moral identity. Living Israelis were connecting to the dead European Jews in the emerging need to share the Holocaust.[61] Broadcast live over the radio and passionately listened to, the trial was becoming the central event in the country's life. Victims were thus for the first time gaining what as victims they precisely could not have: authority—historical authority, that is to say, *semantic authority* over themselves and over others. Ultimately, the acquisition of semantic authority by victims is what the trial was about.

Part Five: The Web of Stories

Prior to the Eichmann trial, what we call the Holocaust did not exist as a collective story. It did not exist as a semantically authoritative story.[62]

"Where there is experience in the strict sense of the word," writes Walter Benjamin, "certain contents of the individual past combine with material from the collective past"[63] to form an "image of a collective experience to which even the deepest shock of every individual experience, death, constitutes no impediment or barrier"[64]:

> Memory creates the chain of experience which passes a happening from generation to generation. It starts the web which all stories together form in the end. One ties on to the next, as the great storytellers . . . have always readily known.[65]

It is this new collective story that did not exist prior to the trial—a story at the same time of the victims' suffering and of the victims' recovery of language—and the newly acquired semantic and historical authority of this revolutionary story, that for the first time create what we know today as the Holocaust: a theme of international discussion and of world conversation designating the experience of the victims and referring to the crime against the Jewish people independently from the political and military story of the Second World War.

— V —

Israel's claim to a law through Eichmann's judgment and the monumental legal history constructed by the trial have thus to some extent fulfilled the mission of the law to be, in Robert Cover's concept, "a bridge to the future." "Law"—writes the renowned American legal philosopher in his article "Folktales of Justice"—"Law is neither to be wholly identified with the understanding of the present state of affairs nor with the imagined alternatives. It is the bridge—. . . a bridge built out of committed social behavior."[66] Law ratifies an aspect of commitment in our lives, and the commitment obligates itself toward a future that we hope will be a better future. Our legal commitments are in turn formed by lessons and prescriptions we derive from narratives about the past and from our readings of these narratives. "No set of legal institutions exist apart from the narratives that locate it and give it meaning," Cover reminds us:

> For every constitution there is an epic, for every decalogue a scripture. Once understood in the context of the narratives that give it meaning, law becomes not merely a system of rules to be observed, but a world in which we live.[67]

For the world to be livable after the Holocaust, a human narrative of the past catastrophe and of the past devastation needed to be legally articulated and combined with future rules of law. The legal narrative of

Nuremberg did not suffice, since it did not articulate the victims' story but subsumed it in the general political and military story of the war.[68] What Nuremberg did do (and this was its unmatched juridical accomplishment) was to establish an unprecedented legal concept of "crimes against humanity," and to set up the death penalty against the Nazi perpetrators of these crimes as a new norm or new legal precedent. "We have also incorporated its principles into a judicial precedent," writes Justice Robert Jackson, the architect and the chief prosecutor of the Nuremberg trials:

"The power of the precedent," Mr. Justice Cardozo said, "is the power of the beaten path." One of the chief obstacles to this trial was the lack of a beaten path. A judgment such as has been rendered *shifts the power of the precedent* to the support of these rules of law. No one can hereafter deny or fail to know that the principles on which the Nazi leaders are adjudged to forfeit their lives constitute law—and law with a sanction.[69]

Arendt deplores the fact that, through its legal excesses and its conceptual failures, the Eichmann trial, unlike Nuremberg, has failed to project into the future an innovative legal norm or a valid (universal) legal precedent.[70] I have argued against Arendt that the function of the trial was not to create a legal precedent but to create a legal narrative, a legal language, and a legal culture that were not yet in existence, but that became essential for the articulation of the unprecedented nature of the genocidal crime.

"Each community," says Cover, "builds its bridges with the materials of sacred narrative that take as their subject much more than what is commonly conceived as 'legal.'"[71] The Eichmann trial, I submit, was a singular event of law that, through its monumental legal record and its monumental legal chorus of the testimonies of the persecuted, unwittingly became creative of a canonical or *sacred narrative*.[72] This newborn sacred narrative was, and could not but be, at once a tale of jurisdiction and a collective tale of mourning.

"One evening," writes the poet Paul Celan, "after the sun (and not only the sun) had gone down in the West,"

the Jew went for a walk, . . . the Jew, the son of a Jew, and his name went with him, his unspeakable name, as he walked and went on and went shuffling along, you could hear it, going with stick, going on stone . . .

And who do you think came towards him? His cousin, . . . his own first cousin came towards him, . . . he was tall, . . . Tall came to Small . . .

. . . and there was a stillness in the mountains where they went, he and the other . . .

"You came from far away, came here . . ."

"So I did. I came. I came, like you."

"I know that." . . .

"You do know. You know what you see: The earth has folded up here . . . and split open in the middle . . . —for I ask, for whom is it meant, this earth, for I say it is not meant for you or me—a language, to be sure, without I or Thou, merely He . . . , do you understand . . ."

"I understand, I do understand. Because I came, ah yes, from afar, ah yes, like you . . ."

". . . And nonetheless you came, . . . why, and whatever for?"

"Why and whatever for . . . Perhaps because I had to talk to myself or to you, because I had to talk with mouth and tongue, not only with stick. For to whom does he talk, the stick? He talks to stone, and the stone—to whom does he talk?"

"To whom does he talk, cousin? He doesn't talk, he speaks, and he who speaks, cousin, talks to no one, he speaks because no one hears him . . . Do you hear?"

"Do you hear, he says—I know, first cousin, I know . . . Do you hear, he says, here I am, I am, I am here, I have come. Come with my stick, I and no other, I and not he, I with my hour, appointed not deserved, I who was dealt the blow, I who was not, I with my memory, I, with my memory failing . . ."

"I here, I: I who could tell you all, who could have told you, . . . I perhaps accompanied—at last—by the love of those unloved, I on the way to myself, up here."[73]

*   *   *

It might well be precisely through its *legal inimitability* that the Eichmann trial, matching legal chronicle to legal parable, has succeeded in creating at the same time an unprecedented legal narrative of private and collective trauma and an unprecedented cultural and historical juridical citation for the future: the privileged text of a modern *folktale of justice*.

4

A Ghost in the House of Justice:
Death and the Language of the Law

Justice requires and establishes the state . . . But justice itself cannot make us forget the origin of the right or the uniqueness of the other, henceforth covered over by the particularity and the generality of the human. It cannot abandon that uniqueness to political history, which is engaged in the determinism of powers, reasons of state, totalitarian temptations and complacencies. It awaits the voices that will recall, to the judgments of the judges and statesmen, the human face.
—Emmanuel Levinas, "Uniqueness"

A witness faints on the stand during the Eichmann trial. This chapter will explore the meaning of this unexpected legal moment, and will ask: Is the witness's collapse relevant—and if so, in what sense—to the legal framework of the trial? How does this courtroom event affect the trial's definition of legal meaning in the wake of the Holocaust? Under what circumstances and in what ways can the legal default of a witness constitute a legal testimony in its own right?

I will present, first, Hannah Arendt's reading of this episode (in *Eichmann in Jerusalem*), and will then contrast her reading with my own interpretation of this courtroom scene. Next I will analyze the judges' reference to this scene in their opinion. I will return in the end to Walter Benjamin, with whom this book began, who will become relevant again at once as part of Arendt's story (as a subtext of Arendt's text: a hidden presence in *Eichmann in Jerusalem*) and as a guide for my own reading of the trial.

These different and successive analytical and textual vantage points will be systematically and commonly subordinated to the following three overriding theoretical inquiries:

1. What is the role of human fallibility in trials?

2. Can moments of disruption of convention and of discourse—moments of unpredictability that take the legal institution by surprise—nevertheless contribute to the formulation of a legal meaning?

3. How can such moments shed light on (what I set out to highlight as) the key structural relation between law and trauma? What tools does the law have—and what are the law's limits—in adjudicating massive death and in articulating legal meaning out of massive trauma?

Part One: Death and the Language of the Law

— I —

Two Visions of Historic Trial

In the postwar trials that attempted to judge history and to resolve the horrors of administrative massacre in the wake of the unprecedented trauma of the Second World War, two antithetic legal visions of historic trial have emerged: that of the Nuremberg trials in 1945–46, and that of the Eichmann trial in 1961. The difference between these two paradigms of historic trial derived from their divergent evidentiary approach: the Nuremberg prosecution made a decision to shun witnesses and base the case against the Nazi leaders exclusively on documents, whereas the prosecution in the Eichmann trial chose to rely extensively on witnesses as well as documents to substantiate its case. While both prosecutors similarly used the trial to establish what in Nietzsche's term can be called a "monumental [legal] history,"[1] Nuremberg was a monumental documentary case, whereas the Eichmann trial was a monumental testimonial case (despite its equally substantial use of documents). In 1954, the chief prosecutor and the architect of Nuremberg, Justice Robert Jackson, retrospectively explained the grounds for his choice of proof:

> The prosecution early was confronted with two vital decisions . . . One was whether chiefly to rely upon living witnesses or upon documents for proof of the case. The decision . . . was to use and rest on documentary evidence to prove every point possible. The argument against this was that documents are dull, the press would not report them, the trial would become wearisome and would not get across to the people. There was much truth in this position, I must admit. But it seemed to me that witnesses, many of them persecuted and hostile to the Nazis, would always be chargeable with bias, faulty recollection, and even perjury. The documents could not be

accused of partiality, forgetfulness, or invention, and would make the sounder foundation, not only for the immediate guidance of the tribunal, but for the ultimate verdict of history. The result was that the tribunal declared, in its judgment, "The case, therefore, against the defendants rests in a large measure on documents of their own making."[2]

Fragile Evidence

The documentary approach matched the bureaucracy of the Nazi regime and was particularly suitable to the exposure of the monstrous bureaucratic nature of the crime and of its alibis. The testimonial approach was necessary for the full disclosure of the thought-defying magnitude of the offense against the victims, and was particularly suitable to the valorization of the victims' narrative perspective.

The reason he decided to add living witnesses to documents, the Israeli prosecutor Gideon Hausner in his turn explained, was that the Nuremberg trials had *failed to transmit*,[3] or to impress on human memory and "on the hearts of men," the knowledge and the shock of what had happened. The Eichmann trial sought, in contrast, not only to establish facts but to transmit (transmit truth as event and as the shock of an *encounter* with events, transmit history as an experience). The tool of law was used not only as a tool of *proof* of unimaginable facts but, above all, as a compelling *medium of transmission*—as an effective tool of national and international *communication* of these thought-defying facts. In comparing thus the evidentiary approach of Nuremberg to his own legal choices, the Israeli prosecutor wrote:

> There is an obvious advantage in written proof; whatever it has to convey is there in black and white . . . Nor can a document be . . . broken down in cross-examination. It speaks in a steady voice; it may not cry out, but neither can it be silenced . . .
>
> This was the course adopted at the Nuremberg trials . . . It was . . . efficient . . . But it was also one of the reasons why the proceedings there failed to reach the hearts of men.
>
> In order merely to secure a conviction, it was obviously enough to let the archives speak . . . But I knew we needed more than a conviction; we needed a living record of a gigantic human and national disaster . . .
>
> In any criminal proceedings the proof of guilt and the imposition

of a penalty, though all-important, are not the exclusive objects. Every trial also . . . tells a story . . . Our perceptions and our senses are geared to limited experiences . . . We stop perceiving living creatures behind the mounting totals of victims; they turn into incomprehensible statistics.

It was beyond human powers to present the calamity in a way that would do justice to six million tragedies. The only way to concretize it was to call surviving witnesses, as many as the framework of the trial would allow, and to ask each of them to tell a tiny fragment of what he had seen and experienced . . . Put together, the various narratives of different people would be concrete enough to be apprehended. In this way I hoped to superimpose on a phantom a dimension of reality.[4]

Because of the difference in their evidentiary approach, the Nuremberg trials made a more solid contribution to international law, in setting up a binding legal precedent of "crimes against humanity"; the Eichmann trial made a greater impact on collective memory. The two trials dramatize the difference between human and nonhuman evidence. Jackson desires to exclude human vulnerability both from the process of the law and from the exercise of judgment. He thus protects the courtroom from the death it talks about. Because Jackson wants his legal evidence to be literally invulnerable, he has to give preference to nonhuman and nonliving evidence. "The documents could not be accused of partiality, forgetfulness, or invention." "Witnesses," on the other hand, "many of them persecuted," "would always be chargeable with bias, faulty recollection, and even perjury."

In choosing, on the contrary, to include as evidence the previously excluded, fragile testimony of the persecuted, the Eichmann trial quite specifically gives legal space to the potential legal failings and shortcomings Jackson fears. It consciously *embraces* the vulnerability, the legal fallibility, and the fragility of the human witness. It is precisely the witness's fragility that paradoxically is called upon to testify and to bear witness.[5]

An Oath to the Dead (A Pseudonym)

Nowhere was this fragile essence of the human testimony more dramatically exemplified and more acutely tested than when, in one of the most breathtaking moments of the trial, a witness fainted on the stand.

He was called to testify because he was a crucially relevant eyewitness: he had met Eichmann in Auschwitz.[6] But he collapsed before he could narrate this factual encounter. His testimony thus amounted to a legal failure, the kind of legal failure Jackson feared. And yet this legal moment of surprise, captured on film,[7] left an indelible mark on the trial and has impressed itself on visual and historic memory. This courtroom scene has since been broadcast many times on radio and television. Despite the repetition, the power of this legally compelling moment does not wane and its force of astonishment does not diminish and does not fade. It has remained a literally unforgettable key moment of the trial, a signal or a symbol of a constantly replayed and yet ungrasped, ungraspable kernel of collective memory.[8] I propose to try to probe here the significance of this mysteriously material kernel.

Who was this witness? He happened to be a writer. He was known under the pseudonym Ka-Tzetnik (K-Zetnik).[9] He saw himself as a messenger of the dead, a bearer of historical meaning he had the duty to preserve and to transmit. K-Zetnik is a slang word meaning a concentration camp inmate, one identified not by name but by the number the Nazis tattooed on each inmate's arm. "I must carry this name," K-Zetnik testified during the Eichmann trial, "as long as the world will not awaken after the crucifying of the nation . . . as humanity has risen after the crucifixion of one man."[10] K-Zetnik had published, prior to the Eichmann trial, several books that were translated into many languages and that had gained a celebrity on both sides of the Atlantic. Describing human existence in the extermination camps, they were all published as the successive volumes of what the author calls "the Chronicle of a Jewish Family in the Twentieth Century." The name K-Zetnik was selected almost automatically. The author began writing soon after he was liberated from Auschwitz, in a British army hospital in Italy. He asked the Israeli soldier who was taking care of him to bring him pen and paper: he had made an oath to the dead, he said, to be their voice and to chronicle their story; since he felt his days were numbered, he had to hurry up; his writing was from the beginning racing against death. For two and a half weeks he hardly got up, writing in one fit his first book. He asked the soldier who was taking care of him to transfer the finished manuscript to Israel. Reading the title "Salamandra" on the first page, the soldier whispered: "You forgot to write the name of the author." "The name of the author?" the surviving writer cried out in reply: "They who went to the crematories wrote this book; write their name: Ka-Tzetnik."[11] Thus the soldier added in his handwriting the name that soon was to acquire world fame.

— II —

The Collapse

"What is your full name?" asked the presiding judge.[12]

"Yehiel Dinoor,"[13] answered the witness. The prosecutor then proceeded.

"What is the reason that you took the pen name K-Zetnik, Mr. Dinoor?"

"It is not a pen name," the witness (now seated) began answering. "I do not regard myself as a writer who writes literature."

This is a chronicle from the planet of Auschwitz. I was there for about two years. Time there was different from what it is here on earth. Every split second ran on a different cycle of time. And the inhabitants of that planet had no names. They had neither parents nor children. They did not dress as we dress here. They were not born there nor did anyone give birth. Even their breathing was regulated by the laws of another nature. They did not live, nor did they die, in accordance with the laws of this world. Their names were the numbers 'K-Zetnik so and so' . . . They left me, they kept leaving me, left . . . for close to two years they left me and always left me behind . . . I see them, they are watching me, I see them—

At this point, the prosecutor gently interrupted: "Mr. Dinoor, could I perhaps put a few questions to you if you will consent?"

But Dinoor continued speaking in a hollow and tense voice, oblivious to the courtroom setting, as a man plunged in hallucination or in a hypnotic trance. "I see them . . . I saw them standing in the line . . ."

Thereupon the presiding judge matter-of-factly intervened: "Mr. Dinoor, please, please listen to Mr. Hausner; wait a minute, now you listen to me!"

The haggard witness vacantly got up and without a warning collapsed into a faint, slumping to the floor beside the witness stand.

Policemen ran toward Dinoor to lift his collapsed body, to support him and to carry him out of the courtroom.[14] The flabbergasted audience remained motionless, staring in disbelief. "Quiet, quiet, quiet!" ordered the presiding judge: "I am asking for silence." A woman's cry was heard from the direction of the audience. A woman wearing sunglasses was coming from the audience toward the unconscious human body held by the policemen, saying she was the witness's wife. "You may approach," the bench conceded. "I do not believe that we can go on." The witness was still limp and lifeless, plunged in a deep coma. "We shall take a recess now," declared the presiding judge. "Beth Hamishpat" ("the House of Justice") shouted the usher, as the audience rose to its feet and the three judges in their black robes were going out. An ambulance was called and rushed the witness to the hospital, where he spent two weeks between life and death in a paralytic stroke. In time, he would recover.

The Legal versus the Poetical

The Israeli poet Haim Gouri, who covered the trial, wrote:

> What happened here was the inevitable. [K-Zetnik's] desperate attempt to transgress the legal channel and to return to the planet of the ashes in order to bring it to us was too terrifying an experience for him. He broke down.
>
> Others spoke here for days and days, and told us each his story from the bottom up . . . He tried to depart from the quintessential generalization, tried to define, like a meteor, the essence of that world. He tried to find the shortest way between the two planets among which his life had passed . . .
>
> Or maybe he caught a glimpse of Eichmann all of a sudden and his soul was short-circuited into darkness, all the lights going out . . .
>
> *In a way he had said everything.* Whatever he was going to say later was, it turns out, superfluous detail.[15]

This empathetic description, which took the testimony on its terms and which, examining it from the vantage point of its own metaphors, poetically reflected back the shock and the emotion of the audience, was a poet's coverage of a fellow poet's testimony. The legal coverage of this episode that Hannah Arendt sent to the *New Yorker* and later published in *Eichmann in Jerusalem* was much harsher and much less forgiving.

Arendt disputed fundamentally the way in which the prosecution framed the trial, in narratively focusing it on the victims. The state sought to narrate a unique legal story that had never before been told and that had failed to be articulated by the Nuremberg trials. To do so, it sought to reconstruct the facts of the Nazi war against the Jews from the victims' point of view and to establish for the first time in legal history a "monumental history" not of the victors but of the victims. But Arendt argued that the trial should be focused on the criminal, not on the victim; she wanted it to be a cosmopolitan trial rather than a Jewish nationalist one; she wanted it to tell the story of totalitarianism and of totalitarian crimes against humanity, rather than the story of the Jewish tragedy and of the crime against the Jewish people. She thus felt impelled to fight Jewish self-centeredness on every point (and on every legal point), and systematically to deconstruct and to decenter the prosecution's monumentalizing victim narrative. In her role as legal reporter for the *New Yorker,* Arendt finds a stage for exercising her ironic talents not only to dispute the story of the prosecution but to narrate a contrapuntal legal narrative and to become in turn an ironic or a *contrapuntal prosecutor*—a prosecutor or (in Nietzsche's terms) a critical historian of the monumental trial.[16]

When she was first confronted with the Nazi crimes during the Nuremberg trials, Arendt believed the magnitude of the phenomenon and the abyss it opened in perception could not be apprehended by the law, except in rupturing its legal framework. She thus wrote in 1946 to Karl Jaspers, her ex-teacher and the continued German friend and interlocutor whom she refound at the end of the war and through whose sole agency she has now reconnected with her own disrupted German youth:

> Your definition of Nazi policy as a crime ("criminal guilt")[17] strikes me as questionable. The Nazi crimes, it seems to me, *explode the limits of the law;* and that is precisely what constitutes their monstrousness. For these crimes, no punishment is severe enough . . . That is, this guilt, in contrast to all criminal guilt, oversteps and shatters any and all legal systems. That is the reason why the Nazis in Nuremberg are so smug . . . And just as inhuman as their guilt is the innocence of the victims. Human beings simply can't be as innocent as they all were in the face of the gas chambers (the most repulsive usurer was as innocent as a newborn child because no crime deserves such a punishment). We are simply not equipped to deal, on a human, political level, with a guilt that is beyond crime and an innocence that is beyond goodness or virtue. This is *the abyss* that opened up before us as early as 1933 . . . and into which we have finally stumbled. I don't know how we will ever get out of it, for the Germans are burdened now with . . . hundreds of thousands of

people who cannot be adequately punished within the legal system; and we Jews are burdened with millions of innocents, by reason of which every Jew alive today can see himself as innocence personified.[18]

Jaspers does not agree with Arendt. Her attitude, he says, is *too poetical*. But poetry, he emphasizes, is a much more inadequate, a much less sober tool of apprehension than the law. Poetry by definition is misguided because, by its very nature, it is made to *miss the banality* of the phenomenon. And the banality, in Jaspers's eyes, is the constitutive feature of the Nazi horror, a feature that should not be mystified or mythified.

You say that what the Nazis did cannot be comprehended as "crime"—I'm not altogether comfortable with your view, because a guilt that goes beyond all criminal guilt inevitably takes on a streak of "greatness"—of satanic greatness—which is, for me, as inappropriate for the Nazis as all the talk about the "demonic" element in Hitler . . . It seems to me that *we have to see these things in their total banality*, in their prosaic triviality, because that's what truly characterizes them. . . . I regard any hint of myth and legend with horror . . . Your view is appealing—especially as contrasted with what I see as the false inhuman innocence of the victims. But all this would have to be expressed differently . . . The way you express it, *you've almost taken the path of poetry*. And a Shakespeare would never be able to give adequate form to this material—his instinctive aesthetic sense would lead to falsification of it . . . There is no idea and no essence here. Nazi crime is properly a subject for psychology and sociology, for psychopathology and jurisprudence only.[19]

From its inception, the future concept of the "banality of evil" emerges as a concept that defines itself by its methodological invalidation of the "the path of poetry," against which it sets up the purposely reductive terminology of "jurisprudence only" and the sobering path of the law (and of the social sciences). "I found what you say about my thoughts on 'beyond crime and innocence' half convincing," Arendt replies at first ambivalently, but she concedes: "We have to combat all impulses to mythologize the horrible."[20]

When the Eichmann trial is announced fifteen years later, Jaspers and Arendt switch positions. Jaspers maintains that Israel should not try Eichmann, because Eichmann's guilt—the subject of the trial—is "larger than law."[21] Arendt insists that only law can deal with it: "We have no tools to hand except legal ones," she says.[22] By now, the tool of law is in her hands, par excellence, *a tool of apprehension of banality,* a tool specifically of *demythologization* and of deliberate, sobering reduction. And if the perpetrator must be banalized and demythologized to be understood in his proper light, so does the victim. No longer can the victim's innocence be allowed to burst the legal frame or to explode the tool of law. No longer can the victim be spared the banality of innocence.

— III —

Arendt's Contrapuntal Tale

Arendt reserves some of her harshest language and some of her fiercest irony in *Eichmann in Jerusalem* for the description of K-Zetnik's unsuccessful court appearance. Indeed, nowhere is Arendt's role as contrapuntal, critical historian of the trial more clearly and more blatantly expressed than in her narration of this episode. Arendt views K-Zetnik's failure on the stand as symptomatic of the general misfire of the trial. She blames this general misfire on the misdirections and the blunders of the prosecution, whose witness has symbolically defaulted through its own fault.

Generally, Arendt makes three objections to the prosecution's choice of witnesses:

1. Contrary to legal rules of evidence, the witnesses are not selected for their relevance to Eichmann's acts but for the purposes of the depiction of a larger picture of the Nazi persecution of the Jews. "This case"—writes Arendt disapprovingly—"was built on what the Jews had suffered, not on what Eichmann had done" (*EiJ*, 6). This depiction by the victims of the persecution they had suffered and their reconstruction of the global history of their victimization is irrelevant in Arendt's eyes. K-Zetnik as a witness seems to Arendt to exemplify the witnesses' irrelevance.

2. Contrary to Arendt's judgment and to her taste, the prosecution prefers witnesses of prominence. It has a predilection, in particular, for famous writers, such as K-Zetnik and Abba Kovner. The former's testimony was a fiasco. The latter, Arendt caustically notes, "had not so much testified as addressed an audience with the ease of someone who is used to speaking in public and resents interruptions from the floor" (*EiJ*,

230). In Arendt's eyes, a witness's fame is a corrupting element of the judicial process. The writer's professional articulateness compromises the truth of the testimony in turning testimonies into speeches. Such is K-Zetnik's case.

3. The prosecution's choice of witnesses is guided—Arendt charges—by theatrical considerations. The witnesses are called for the sensational effects provided by their "tales of horror." K-Zetnik's breakdown is an accidental yet consistent illustration of this logic that transforms testimony into a theatrical event that parasitizes the trial.

> At no time [Arendt writes] is there anything theatrical in the conduct of the judges . . . Judge Landau . . . is doing his best, his very best to prevent this trial from becoming a show trial under the influence of the prosecutor's love of showmanship. Among the reasons he cannot always succeed is the simple fact that the proceedings happen on a stage before an audience, with the usher's marvelous shout at the beginning of each session producing the effect of the rising curtain. Whoever planned this auditorium . . . had a theater in mind . . . Clearly, this courtroom is not a bad place for the show trial David Ben Gurion, Prime Minister of Israel, had in mind when he decided to have Eichmann kidnapped in Argentina and brought to the district court of Jerusalem to stand trial for his role in "the final solution to the Jewish question . . ."
>
> Yet no matter how consistently the judges shunned the limelight, there they were, seated at the top of the raised platform, facing the audience as from the stage in a play . . . The audience was supposed to represent the whole world . . . They were to watch a spectacle as sensational as the Nuremberg Trials, only this time "the tragedy of Jewry as a whole was to be the central concern . . ."
>
> It was precisely the play aspect of the trial that collapsed under the weight of the hair-raising atrocities . . .
>
> Thus, the trial never became a play, but the show trial Ben Gurion had had in mind . . . did take place . . . (*EiJ*, 4–9)

Most of the witnesses, Arendt narrates, were Israeli citizens who "had been picked from hundreds and hundreds of applicants" (*EiJ*, 223). But Arendt is suspicious of witnesses who volunteer. She is allergic to the narcissism she keeps spying both in the legal actors (the chief prosecutor in particular) and in the witnesses whom she suspects of seeking or being complacent with the elements of spectacle that parasitize and compromise the trial. K-Zetnik is for her a case in point. The narrative of his collapse becomes, in Arendt's hands, not an emotional account of human testimonial pathos but a didactic tale that illustrates ironically what accidents can happen when a witness is, quite paradoxically, too eager to appear. It is thus with her most sarcastic, her most undercutting and most funny style that Arendt will approach this testimony.

> How much wiser it would have been to resist these pressures altogether . . . and to seek out those who had not volunteered! As though to prove the point, the prosecution called upon a writer, well known on both sides of the Atlantic under the name K-Zetnik . . . as the author of several books on Auschwitz which dealt with brothels, homosexuals, and other "human interest stories." He started off, as he had done at many of his public appearances, with an explanation of his adopted name . . . He continued with a little excursion into astrology: the star "influencing our fate in the same way as the star of ashes at Auschwitz is there facing our planet, radiating toward our planet." And when he had arrived at "the unnatural power above Nature" which had sustained him thus far, and now, for the first time, paused to catch his breath, even Mr. Hausner felt that something had to be done about this "testimony," and very timidly, very politely interrupted: "Could I perhaps put a few questions to you if you will consent?" Whereupon the presiding judge saw his chance as well: "Mr. Dinoor, please, please listen to Mr. Hausner and to me." In response, the disappointed witness, probably deeply wounded, fainted and answered no more questions. (*EiJ*, 223–224)

Even Mr. Hausner felt that something had to be done about this "testimony." For Arendt, this is a "testimony" only in quotation marks. It is an aberration of a testimony. Arendt's derision is, however, not directed personally at K-Zetnik but derives from an impersonal black-humorous perception of the ludicrous, hilarious way in which the courtroom as a whole could be mistaken, at this legally surprising moment, for a theater of the absurd. The buffoonery comes from the situation, not from the people: the farcical or comic element derives from the discrepancy and from the total incommensurability between the two dimensions that the testimony inadvertently brings into dialogue: the natural and the supernatural, the rationality and discipline of courtroom protocols and the irruption of irrationality through a delirious rambling or what Arendt calls an "astrological excursion" (the witness's voyage into "other planets"). I would argue differently than Arendt that the courtroom in its very legal essence here flirts with madness and with nonsense. For some, this courtroom drama and the suffering it unfolds both in the past and in the present of the courtroom constitute a tragedy, a shock. For Arendt, this is a comedy. Pain is translated into laughter. If this is theater, sometimes potentially sublime or tragic, it is a Brechtian theater. Keeping her distance is for Arendt key. The ludicrous example of K-Zetnik's fainting and his default as a witness illustrates, for Arendt, not the proximity uncannily revealed between madness and reason, not the profound pathos of a cognitive abyss abruptly opened up inside the courtroom and materialized in the unconscious body of the witness, but the folly of the prosecution in both its disrespect for legal relevance and in its narcissistic and misguided predilection for witnesses of prominence. This double folly of the prosecution gets both its poetic justice and its comic punishment when its own witness faints outside the witness stand and inadvertently becomes an inert, hostile witness who "answers no more questions."

Evidentiary Misunderstandings

Looking at the facts, Arendt's fierce irony, ironically, is based on two erroneous assumptions.

1. Contrary to what Arendt presumes, Dinoor did not volunteer to share his "tale of horror" on the witness stand but, on the contrary, was an involuntary and reluctant witness. As a writer, he had always shunned in principle public appearances. In consequence, he had at first refused to testify. He had to be pressured by the chief prosecutor to consent (reluctantly) to appear before the court.

2. Among the trial's testimonies, Arendt depicts K-Zetnik's as the one that is self-evidently the most crazily remote from facts.[23] She thus regards this testimony as the most grotesque and hyperbolic illustration of "the right of the witnesses to be irrelevant" (*EiJ*, 225) and presumes it could not possibly bear any legal relevance to Eichmann's case. What Arendt does not know and does not suspect is that Dinoor was one of the very few survivors known to have actually met Eichmann at Auschwitz.[24] Had he been able to complete his testimony, he would have turned out to be a material eyewitness.

Yet what K-Zetnik wants is not to prove but to transmit. The language of the lawyer and that of artist meet across the witness stand only to concretize within the trial their misunderstanding and their *missed encounter.*[25]

In what follows, I explore this "missed encounter" (the way in which K-Zetnik's language fails the prosecutor and the way in which the courtroom and the trial fail K-Zetnik). I will view this missed encounter as exemplary, on the one hand, of a dimension (of reality, of death, and of disaster) that the law has to confront but is structurally bound to miss. On the other hand, I will show how the very moment of incongruity—the enacted drama of the misunderstanding and of the missed encounter between the artist and the law—nevertheless impacts upon the structures of the law and in the end endows the Eichmann trial with an unprecedented jurisprudential dimension. The missed encounter allows for insights that an encounter, or a cohesive moment, might have foreclosed.

* * *

"When the prosecutor invited me to come and testify at the Eichmann trial," writes K-Zetnik more than twenty years after the trial,

> I begged him to release me of this testimony. The prosecutor then said to me: Mr. Dinoor, this is a trial whose protocol must put on record testimony proving that there was a place named Auschwitz and what happened there. The mere sound of these words made me sick to my stomach, and I said: Sir, describing Auschwitz is beyond me! Hearing me, his staff eyed me with suspicion. You, the man who wrote these books, you expect us to believe you can't explain to the judges what Auschwitz was? I fell silent. How could I tell them that I am consumed by the search for the word that will express the look in the eyes of those who headed toward the crematorium, when they passed me with their gaze inside my eyes? The prosecutor was not convinced, and I appeared at the Eichmann trial. Then came the judges' first question about Auschwitz and no sooner did I squeeze out a few miserable sentences than I dropped to the floor and was hospitalized half paralyzed and disfigured in my face.[26]

Trauma and the Language of the Law

"Mr. Dinoor," goes Arendt's contrapuntal narrative,

> "please, please listen to Mr. Hausner and to me."

In response, the disappointed witness, probably deeply wounded, fainted and answered no more questions. (*EiJ*, 224)

Follows Arendt's serious commentary on her own sarcastic and laughingly didactic tale:

This, to be sure, was an exception, but if it was an exception that proved the rule of normality, it did not prove the rule of simplicity or of ability to tell a story, let alone of the rare capacity for distinguishing between things that had happened to the storyteller more than sixteen, and sometimes twenty, years ago, and what he had read and heard and imagined in the meantime. (*EiJ*, 224)

For these very reasons, Nuremberg at the war's end excluded living witnesses and limited the evidence to documents, opting for a case of legal invulnerability that only the nonhuman and nonliving paper evidence could guarantee. "The documents," said Jackson, "could not be accused of partiality, forgetfulness, or invention"; "witnesses," on the other hand, "many of them persecuted and hostile to the Nazis, would always be chargeable with bias, faulty recollection, and even perjury." In a similar vein, Arendt disqualifies K-Zetnik as a witness because his testimony fails to meet legal criteria and fails to be contained by the authority of the restrictive safeguards of the legal rules. In Jackson's spirit, out of concern for the law as representative of culture and as the arbiter of truth in history, Arendt excludes K-Zetnik's discourse because it stands for the *contamination between facts and fiction*—for the confusion and the interpenetration between law and literature—that the law in principle cannot accept and has to resolutely, rigidly rule out.

By legal standards, K-Zetnik represents for Arendt a communicative failure. I will argue here that Arendt in her turn represents, in more than one sense, in her stance toward K-Zetnik, *the limits of the law* in its encounter with the phenomenon of *trauma*.

I would like now to contrast Arendt's interpretation of K-Zetnik's legal failure with my own reading of this courtroom scene.

— IV —

Intrusions

What Arendt's irony illuminates is how the law is used as a straightjacket to tame history as madness.

Arendt's sarcastically positivistic vision of K-Zetnik's failure makes a positivistic recourse to a summarily explanatory psychological vocabulary, through which the legal vision overrides (and Arendt condescendingly dismisses) the witness's (narcissistic) subjectivity. "In response, the disappointed witness, probably deeply wounded, fainted and answered no more questions" (*EiJ*, 224).

Against this oversimplifying psychological vocabulary, I propose to use a psychoanalytical vocabulary informed by jurisprudential trauma theory.[27] I will combine thereby a psychoanalytic reading with a philosophical and legal reading of this courtroom scene.

* * *

Out of the witness stand falls, in my vision, not a "disappointed witness" but a terrified one. The witness is not "deeply wounded" but is *re-traumatized*. The trial reenacts the trauma.

I have argued in Chapter 2 that the law is, so to speak, professionally blind to its constitutive and structural relation to (both private and collective, cultural) trauma, and that its "forms of judicial blindness" take shape wherever the structure of the trauma unwittingly takes over the structure of a trial and wherever the legal institution, unawares, triggers a legal repetition of the trauma that it puts on trial or attempts to cure. In K-Zetnik's case, this happens punctually.

When the judge admonishes Dinoor from the authoritarian position of the bench, coercing him into a legal mode of discourse and demanding his cooperation as a witness, K-Zetnik undergoes severe traumatic shock in reexperiencing the same terror and panic that dumbfounded him each time when, as an inmate, he was suddenly confronted by the inexorable Nazi authorities of Auschwitz. The judge's words are heard not as an utterance originating from the present of the courtroom situation but as a censure uttered from within "the other planet," as an intrusive threat articulated right out of the violence of the traumatic scene that is replaying in K-Zetnik's mind.[28] The call to order by the judge urging the witness to obey—strictly to answer questions and to follow legal rules—impacts the witness *physically* as an invasive call to order by an SS officer. Once more, the imposition of a heartless and unbending rule of order violently robs him of his words and, in reducing him to silence, once more threatens to annihilate him, to erase his essence as a *human* witness. Panicked, K-Zetnik loses consciousness.[29]

In a trembling [he will later write about his unrelenting Auschwitz nightmares] I lift my eyes to see the face of God in its letters, and see in front of me the face of an SS man.[30]

I grow terrified . . . The rules here are invisible . . . No telling what's permitted and what's prohibited.[31]

I was seized by fear and trembling. I am crying of dread. I want to hide my face and not be seen. But there is no escape from Auschwitz. There is no hiding place in Auschwitz.[32]

Between Life and Death: Frontier Evidence

> The objectivity of justice—whence its rigor—[is] offending the alterity of the face that originally signifies or commands outside the context of the world, and keeps on, in its enigma or ambiguity, tearing itself away from, and being an exception to, the plastic forms of the presence and objectivity that it nonetheless calls forth in demanding justice.
> —Emmanuel Levinas, "Alterity and Diachrony"

Prior to his fainting spell, at the point where the prosecutor interrupts him, K-Zetnik tries to define Auschwitz by re-envisaging the terrifying moment of Selection, of repeated weekly separation between inmates chosen for an imminent extermination and inmates arbitrarily selected for life. This moment is ungraspable, the witness tries to say.

And the inhabitants of that planet had no names. They had neither parents nor children . . . They did not live, nor did they die, in accordance with the laws of this world. Their names were the numbers . . . They left me, they kept leaving me, left . . . for close to two years they left me and always left me behind . . . I see them, they are watching me, I see them.

What K-Zetnik keeps reliving of the death camp is the moment of departure, the last gaze of the departed, the exchange of looks between the dying and the living at the very moment in which life and death are separating but are still tied up together and can for the last time see each other eye to eye.

Even those who were there don't know Auschwitz [writes K-Zetnik in a later memoir]. Not even someone who was there for two long years as I was. For Auschwitz is another planet, whereas we humankind, occupants of the planet Earth, we have no key to decipher the code-name Auschwitz. How could I dare defile the look in the eyes of those who head toward the crematorium? They passed me, they knew where they were going, and I knew where they were going. Their eyes are looking at me and my eyes are looking at them, the eyes of the going in the eyes of the remaining, under silent skies above the silent earth. Only that look in the eyes and the last silence . . .

For two years they passed me and their look was inside my eyes.[33]

A Community of Death, or Giving Voice to What Cannot Be Said

In constantly reliving through the moment of departure the repeated separation between life and death, what K-Zetnik testifies to is, however, not the separation or the difference between life and death but, on the contrary, their interpenetration, their ultimate resemblance. On the witness stand, he keeps reliving his connection to the dead, his bond to the exterminated. His loyalty to them is symbolized by his adopted name, K-Zetnik, with which he signs, he says, the stories that in fact are theirs:

> Since then this name testifies on all my books . . .
> I am a man! . . . A man who wants to live! . . .
> "You have forgotten to write your name on the manuscript . . ."
> "The nameless, they themselves! The anonymous! Write their name: K-Zetnik."[34]

> How could I explain that it was not me who wrote the book; they who went to the crematorium as anonymous, they wrote the book! They, the anonymous narrators . . . For two years they passed before me on their way to the crematorium and left me behind.[35]

> All of them are now buried in me and continue to live in me. I made an oath to them to be their voice, and when I got out of Auschwitz they went with me, they and the silent blocks, and the silent crematorium, and the silent horizons, and the mountain of ashes.[36]

In a way K-Zetnik on the witness stand is not alone. He is accompanied by those who left him but who live within him. "I made an oath to them to be their voice." The writer K-Zetnik therefore could symbolically be viewed as the most central witness to the trial's announced project to *give voice to the six million dead*. K-Zetnik's testimony and his literary project pick up on the prosecutor's legal project.

When I stand before you, Judges of Israel, in this court [the prosecutor said in his opening address] . . . I do not stand alone. With me . . . stand six million prosecutors. But alas, they cannot rise to level the finger of accusation in the direction of the glass dock and cry out "J'accuse" against the man who sits there. For their ashes are piled in the hills of Auschwitz . . . Their blood cries to Heaven, but their voice cannot be heard. Thus it falls to me to be their mouthpiece and to deliver the awesome indictment in their name.[37]

Between Two Names

Because he is in turn speaking for the dead, K-Zetnik must remain, like them, anonymous and nameless. He must testify, that is, under the name K-Zetnik.[38] His memory of Auschwitz is the oblivion of his name. But in a court of law, a witness cannot remain nameless and cannot testify anonymously. A witness is accountable precisely to his legal, given name.

"*Mr. Dinoor,* please, please listen to Mr. Hausner and to me," says the presiding judge impatiently, putting an end to the account that the witness gives of his adopted name.

K-Zetnik faints because he cannot be interpellated at this moment by his legal name, Dinoor: the dead still claim him as *their* witness, as K-Zetnik who belongs to them and is still one of them. The court reclaims him as *its* witness, as Dinoor. He cannot bridge the gap between the two names and the two claims. He plunges into the abyss between the different planets. On the frontier between the living and the dead, between the present and the past, he falls as though he were himself a corpse.

$$- \text{V} -$$

Unmastered Past

Having no interest in sociopsychological or psychoanalytical phenomena, Arendt has neither a profound insight into nor an interest in trauma. She has an interest, however, in its *legal remedy*—in the trial as a means to *overcome* and to subdue a traumatic past. But K-Zetnik does not seize his legal chance to overcome the trauma on the witness stand. He is, rather, once more overcome by it. What is worse, he makes a spectacle of his scandalous collapse within the legal forum. K-Zetnik thus defeats the purpose of the law, which is precisely to *translate the trauma into consciousness.* He loses consciousness and loses his self-mastery, whereas the purpose of the law is, on the contrary, to get under control and to regain a conscious mastery over the traumatic nightmare of a history whose impact, Arendt recognizes in her nonpathetic, understated style, continues to have repercussions in the world's consciousness and thus remains with all of us precisely as the world's, Israel's as well as Germany's, "unmastered past."[39]

At the heart of the unmastered past, the trial tries to master an abyss.[40]

Trials and Abysses

K-Zetnik's loss of consciousness materializes in the courtroom what the trial cannot master: at once an abyss of trauma and an epistemological abyss, a cognitive rupture that Arendt, unrelatedly, will theorize and underscore in her political and philosophical account of the Nazi genocide.[41] Arendt herself experienced this epistemological abyss when the news of Auschwitz reached her for the first time as a shock that could not be assimilated. "What was decisive," Arendt confides to Günter Gaus in a German radio interview in 1964,

> What was decisive was the day we learnt about Auschwitz. That was in 1943. And at first we didn't believe it . . . because militarily it was unnecessary and uncalled for. My husband . . . said don't be gullible, don't take these stories at face value. They can't go that far! And then a half-year later we believed it after all, because we had the proof. That was the real shock. Before that we said: Well one has enemies. That is entirely natural. Why shouldn't a people have enemies? But this was different. *It was really as if an abyss had opened.*[42]

But despite the shock, despite the cognitive rupture and the epistemological gap in history and in historical perception, Arendt's life consists in crossing the abyss and overstepping it, going beyond the rupture it has left. It later seems to Arendt, as she says to Günter Gaus, that "there should be a basis for communication precisely in the abyss of Auschwitz."[43] The law provides a forum and a language for such communication.

I would argue that the Eichmann trial is, for Arendt, quite precisely what she calls "the basis for communication" in and over the abyss of Auschwitz. But K-Zetnik's plunge into a coma interrupts the process of communication painstakingly established by the law. K-Zetnik has remained too close to the reality and to the shock of the event, perhaps too close for Arendt's comfort. He is still a captive of the planet of the ashes. He is still *in* the Holocaust, still on the brink of the abyss, which he unwittingly reopens in the courtroom when the law has barely started to construct its legal bridge.

The law requires that the witness should be able to narrate a story in the past, to recount an event in the past tense. K-Zetnik is unable to regard the Holocaust as past event but must relive it in the present, through the infinite traumatic repetition of a past that is not past, that has no closure and from which no distance can be taken.

Law, on the contrary, requires and provides distance from the Holocaust. Its inquiry and judgment are contingent on a separation between past and present. Law requires and brings closure and totalization of the evidence and of its meaning. This is why K-Zetnik's testimony, which defies at once legal reduction and legal closure, must remain unrealized, unfinished.

Part Two: Evidence in Law and Evidence in Art

— VI —

Between Law and Art

In 1964, a leading avant-garde literary critic in America, Susan Sontag, in a discussion of a German literary work about the role played by the pope during the Holocaust, surprisingly and quite provocatively argued that the Eichmann trial was "the most interesting and moving work of art of the past ten years."[44]

We live in a time [she wrote] in which tragedy is not an art form but a form of history. Dramatists no longer write tragedies. But we do have works of art (not always recognized as such) which attempt to resolve the great historical tragedies of our time . . . If then the supreme tragic event of modern times is the murder of six million Jews, the most interesting and moving work of art of the past ten years is the trial of Adolf Eichmann in Jerusalem in 1961.[45]

I do not believe, for my part, that the Eichmann trial—or any trial—can be reduced to, or subsumed in, the performance or the drama of a work of art. There is at least one crucial difference between an event of law and an event of art, no matter how dramatic they both are: a work of art cannot sentence to death. A trial, unlike art, is grounded in the sanctioned legal violence it has the power (and sometimes the duty) to enact.[46]

While it cannot be accepted at face value, Sontag's paradoxical remark about the Eichmann trial is nevertheless illuminating, not as a comment about trials but as an observation about art's relation to (juridical) reality. While the Eichmann trial can under no circumstances be regarded as a work of art, works of art have come today to imitate, to replicate or mimic, the legal structures of the Eichmann trial.

The strongest and most eloquent example of this trend (that reached its climax decades after Sontag's article) can be seen in the film *Shoah* by Claude Lanzmann, a work of art made of reality, whose legal, testimonial format is informed (and perhaps inspired) by the Eichmann trial[47] and of which it could indeed be said, in Sontag's words, that it is "the most interesting and moving work of art of the past years."[48]

I speak here of *Shoah* as emblematic of art after the Holocaust and as *paradigmatic* of the work of art of our times. I argue that the Eichmann trial is the complementary event (the legal correlative) of the contemporary process of art's invasion by the structures of the trial and of its transformation into testimony, a process by which writers like K-Zetnik (and like Elie Wiesel, Celan, Camus, and others) have precisely vowed to make of art itself a witness—to present, that is, historical and legal evidence by means of art. What, then, is the difference between law and art when both are underwritten by the legal process and when both vow to pursue reality? "Reality," says Arendt, "is different from, and more than, the totality of facts and events, which anyhow is unascertainable. Who says what is . . . always tells a story."[49] In Arendt's words, I argue that *law's story* focuses on ascertaining *the totality of facts* and events. *Art's story* focuses on *what is different from,* and *more than,* that totality. I argue that the breakdown of the witness in the Eichmann trial was (unwittingly) at once part of the totality of facts and part of what was different from, and more than, that totality. In that sense, it was *law's story* and *art's story* at the same time. "The truth" says Lanzmann, "kills the possibility of fiction."[50] In the same way that art is today transpierced, invaded by the language and the structures of the trial, the Eichmann trial—through K-Zetnik's court appearance—was transpierced, invaded by the artist's language, by the artist's testimony, and by the artist's astonishing collapse.

The artist's language cannot relegate traumatic suffering to the past. "The worst moral and artistic crime that can be committed in producing a work dedicated to the Holocaust," says Lanzmann, "is to consider the Holocaust as past. *Either the Holocaust is legend or it is present: in no case is it a memory.* A film devoted to the Holocaust . . . can only be an investigation into the present of the Holocaust or at least into a past whose scars are still so freshly and vividly inscribed in certain places and in the consciences of some people that it reveals itself in a *hallucinated timelessness.*"[51] In a similar way, K-Zetnik does not treat the Holocaust as past but lives it as a present that endlessly repeats itself in a hallucinated timelessness. The hallucinated timelessness—the time of traumatic repetition and the time of art—is the precise time of K-Zetnik's legal testimony. But legal temporality cannot admit, cannot include, cannot acknowledge timelessness except as a rupture of the legal frame. K-Zetnik's court appearance marks, thus, an invasion of the trial and of legal temporality by the endless, timeless temporality of art.

Law is a language of abbreviation, of limitation and totalization. Art is a language of infinity and of the irreducibility of fragments, a language of embodiment, of incarnation, and of embodied incantation or endless rhythmic *repetition*. Because it is by definition a discipline of limits, law distances the Holocaust; art brings it closer. The function of the judgment in the Eichmann trial was paradoxically to *totalize* and *distance* the event: the trial *made a past out of the Holocaust.*[52] And yet, within the courtroom, in the figure of K-Zetnik, the Holocaust returned as a ghost or as an incarnated, living present.

K-Zetnik's discourse in the trial has remained unfinished and, like art, interminable. In the courtroom, its lapse into interminability—into unconsciousness and silence—was paradoxically a physical reminder of the real, a physical reminder of a bodily reality that fractured the totality of facts sought by the law. But the testimonial power of this real, of this irreducible bodily presence of the witness, lay precisely in the pathos—in the crying power—of its legal muteness.

"But what can I do when I'm struck mute?" K-Zetnik will write almost thirty years after the Eichmann trial, in trying to explain at once the legal failure of his testimony and the very principle of interminability and inexhaustibility of his continued testimonial art:

> But what can I do when I'm struck mute? I have neither word nor name for it all. Genesis says: "And Adam gave names . . ." When God finished creating the earth and everything upon it, Adam was asked to give names to all that God had created. Till 1942 there was no Auschwitz in existence. For Auschwitz there is no name other than Auschwitz. My heart will be ripped to pieces if I say, "In Auschwitz they burned people alive!" Or "In Auschwitz people died of starvation." But that is not Auschwitz. People have died of starvation before, and people did burn alive before. But that is not Auschwitz. What, then, is Auschwitz? I have no words to express it; I don't have a name for it. Auschwitz is a primal phenomenon. I don't have the key to unlock it. But don't the tears of the mute speak his anguish? And don't his screams cry his distress? Don't his bulging eyes reveal the horror? I am that mute.[53]

Muteness in a courtroom is normally negative or void, devoid of legal meaning. Muteness in art, however, can be fraught with meaning. It is *out of its muteness* that K-Zetnik's writing in this passage *speaks*. It is out of its silence that his testimonial art derives its literary power. *Art is* what makes silence speak.

I would argue that it was precisely through K-Zetnik's *legal muteness* that the trial inadvertently *gave silence a transmitting power*, and—although not by intention—managed to transmit the legal meaning of collective trauma with the incremental power of a work of art. Once the trial gave transmissibility to silence, other silences became, within the trial, fraught with meaning.[54] At the limit of what could be legally grasped, something of the order of K-Zetnik's mute cry—something of the order of the speechlessness and of the interminability of art—was present in the courtroom as a silent shadow of the trial or as a negative of the proceedings. It was present in the interstices of the law as a ghost inside the house of justice. The poet Haim Gouri noted in his coverage of the trial:

> With an unmatched force, the court has managed to restrain the crushing power of the cry that burst out, now as if for the first time,

and to transmit it partially into a language of facts and numbers and dates, while letting the remainder of that cry float over the trial like a ghost.[55]

— VII —

The Judgment

Unlike K-Zetnik's testimony, the Eichmann trial did have closure. For his crimes against the Jewish people, his war crimes, and his crimes against humanity, the judges sentenced Eichmann to "the greatest penalty known to the law."[56] The judgment totalized a statement of the evidence. Like Arendt, the judges underscored the fact that their authority of doing justice (and of making justice seen) was contingent on the *force of limitation* of the law. "The Judgment in the Eichmann case," Arendt reports, for once approvingly, "could not have been clearer":

> All attempts to widen the range of the trial had to be resisted, because the court "could not allow itself to be enticed into provinces which are outside its sphere . . . The judicial process [wrote the judges] has ways of its own, which are laid down by law, and which do not change, whatever the subject of the trial may be." The court, moreover, could not overstep these limits without ending "in complete failure." Not only does it not have at its disposal "the tools required for the investigation of general questions, *it speaks with an authority whose very weight depends upon its limitation.*" (*EiJ*, 253–254; my emphasis)[57]

And yet, even the judges felt the need to point to the fact that there was something in the trial that went beyond their jurisdiction and beyond the jurisdiction of the law.

> If these be the sufferings of the individual [wrote the judges], then the sum total of the suffering of the millions—about a third of the Jewish people, tortured and slaughtered—is certainly beyond human understanding, and who are we to try to give it adequate expression? This is a task for the great writers and poets. *Perhaps it is symbolic that even the author who himself went through the hell named Auschwitz, could not stand the ordeal in the witness box and collapsed.*[58]

What the judges say is not simply that law and art are two modes of transmission of the Holocaust, two languages in which to translate the incomprehensible into some sort of sense, two modes of coping with collective trauma and of crossing the abyss of a mad and nightmarish history.

The judges recognize that even in the legal mode, within the language of the trial, the collapse of the writer and his breakdown as a witness was endowed with meaning. They further recognize that when the artist lapsed into unconsciousness, a dimension of infinitude and interminability registered itself within the trial *as what was uncontainable by its containment,* as what remained untotalizable precisely by and in the law's totalization, within the very legal text of the totalization that constitutes their judgment.

The judgment in the Eichmann trial takes note of the fact that, in the meeting point between law and art with which the courtroom was unwittingly confronted through K-Zetnik's testimony, *the law had a dialogue with its own limits* and touched upon a boundary of meaning in which sense and senselessness, meaning and madness seriously, historically commingled and could not be told apart. The court acknowledges, however, that this surprising legal moment that unsettled legal norms and threw the courtroom into disarray was a profoundly meaningful and not a senseless moment of the trial.

Part Three: Traumatic Narratives and Legal Frames

— VIII —

Story and Anti-Story: Between Justice and the Impossibility of Telling

I want now to return to Arendt's story, but to return to Arendt's story differently: to listen not just to her statement, but to her utterance; to seek to understand not only her juridical critique, but her own inadvertent testimony as a writer. I propose to show how Arendt's legal narrative in *Eichmann in Jerusalem* unwittingly encapsulates not only the reporter's critical account, but the thinker's own (erased) artistic testimony and the writer's own traumatic narrative.[59]

Like the judges, Arendt views K-Zetnik's fainting as a symbol.[60] But while for the judges, the writer's collapse encapsulates—within the trial and beyond it—the *collapse of language* in the face of uncontainable and unintelligible suffering, for Arendt, the writer's collapse encapsulates the *legal failure* of the trial. While for the judges, the collapse is a dramatization of *a failure of expression,* for Arendt, the collapse is a dramatization of *a failure of narration.*

"This," says Arendt, "to be sure, was an exception, but if it was an exception that proved the rule of normality, it did not prove the rule of simplicity or of ability to tell a story" (EiJ, 224). As an exception that confirms the rule of normality—that is, as a symbol of the legal abnormality of the trial as a whole—Arendt faults K-Zetnik for his *inability to tell a story* and thus to testify coherently. "Who says what is . . . always tells a story, and in this story the particular facts lose their contingency and acquire some humanly comprehensible meaning," Arendt will write in "Truth and Politics,"[61] doubtless remembering unconsciously the unforgettable essay called "The Storyteller" written by her dead friend Walter Benjamin, whose name she will in 1968—five years after the Eichmann book—redeem from anonymity and namelessness by publishing his work in the United States, but whose lost friendship she will silently mourn all her life as an intimate grievance, a wordless wound, a personal price that she herself has secretly paid to the Holocaust.[62] I hear a reference to "The Storyteller" in the conclusion of Arendt's account of K-Zetnik's testimony: "[I]t did not prove the rule of simplicity or of *ability to tell a story.*" There are several other references in *Eichmann in Jerusalem* to storytelling and to "The Storyteller."[63] While Benjamin's name is never mentioned and his text is never cited in the book, Benjaminian words and formulations unwittingly pervade its pages like stylistic echoes that form an impassioned philosophical *subtext* under and through the irony, the wryness and the dryness of the legalistic text. At stake in this subtext is a relation between death and writing, an intimately personal relation that the writing "I" cannot possess or formulate directly, but can relate to indirectly through Benjamin's reflection on the relation between death and storytelling. Benjamin's memory and presence—the presence of his death and of his text—unwittingly yet hauntingly, persistently inform Arendt's style and permeate her writing and her utterance. "Death," wrote Benjamin precisely in his essay, "is the sanction of everything that the storyteller has to tell. He has borrowed his authority from death" ("St.," 94).

Has Arendt in her turn borrowed her authority as storyteller of the trial from a legacy of death of which she does not speak and cannot speak? I would suggest indeed that, through its understated but repeated reference to the storyteller, *Eichmann in Jerusalem* is also Arendt's book of mourning.[64] It is, in other words, a book—an unarticulated statement—on the *relation between grief and justice*, as well as on the counterparts of grief and justice in narrative and storytelling. "It is perfectly true," Arendt will write in "Truth and Politics," "that 'all sorrows can be borne if you put them into a story or tell a story about them.'"[65] Both the Eichmann trial and Arendt's critical rehearsal of it are preoccupied—albeit in different styles—with the translation of grief into justice. Both are therefore mirror images of the translation of grief into grievance as what underlies precisely the capacity and the significance of saying "I accuse," of crying out "J'accuse" in the name of those who can no longer say it.[66]

Eichmann in Jerusalem, I would suggest, is inhabited by Arendt's mourned and unmourned ghosts. Benjamin is one of those. (Another ghost, I would suggest, is Heidegger, but I will not dwell here on his ghostly significance in *Eichmann in Jerusalem*.)[67]

In all language, Benjamin has argued, there is a lament that mutes it out.[68] "In all mourning there is an inclination to speechlessness, which is infinitely more than the disinclination or the inability to communicate."[69] Benjamin's unmentioned name and subterranean presence as an inadvertent and complex subtext of *Eichmann in Jerusalem* is linked, I argue, both to Arendt's testimony in this book and to her silence, a silence that in turn is linked not just to her discretion but to her speechlessness, that is, to her own *inability to tell a story*. There is, in other words, a crucial story Arendt does not tell and cannot tell that underlies the story of the trial she does tell.[70]

"Familiar though his name may be to us," wrote Benjamin, "the storyteller in his living immediacy is by no means a present force. He has already become something remote from us and something which is getting even more distant":

Less and less frequently do we encounter people with the ability to tell a tale properly . . . It is as if something that seemed inalienable to us . . . were taken from us: the ability to exchange experiences. ("St.," 83)

Benjamin intuitively knew that the inability to tell a story was related to the essence of traumatic experience.[71] Specifically, he linked this inability to tell to the collective, massive trauma of the war.

Was it not noticeable at the end of the war that men returned from the battlefield grown silent—not richer, but poorer in communicable experience? ("St.," 84)

Benjamin spoke of the First World War.[72] K-Zetnik's testimony at the Eichmann trial showed how people had returned even more tongue-tied—even poorer in communicable experience, grown even more silent—from the death camps and from the traumatic nightmare of the Second World War.

When I got out of Auschwitz [writes K-Zetnik] they went with me, they and the silent blocks, and the silent crematorium, and the silent horizons, and the mountain of ashes.[73]

* * *

I would argue differently from Arendt (and with hindsight she could not possess) that (unpredictably, unwittingly) it was the *inadvertent legal essence* and legal innovation and uniqueness of the Eichmann trial, and not its testimonial accident, to voice the muteness generated by the Holocaust and to *articulate the difficulty of articulation* of the catastrophic story, the difficulty of articulation and the tragic unnarratability of the ungraspable disaster and of its immeasurably devastating, unintelligible trauma. The impossibility of telling is not external to this story: it is the story's heart.[74] The trial shows how the inherent inability to tell the story is itself an integral part of the history and of the story of the Holocaust. The function of the trial thus becomes precisely to articulate the impossibility of telling through the legal process and to convert this *narrative impossibility* into *legal meaning*.[75]

* * *

My conception of the trial is, then, fundamentally different from that of Arendt. Logically speaking, it is, however, Arendt's text that has enabled me to read the trial differently from her. It is precisely Arendt's own surprised insistence on "how difficult it was to tell the story" (*EiJ*, 229) and her own *excessive* utterance—her own haunted allusions to Benjamin and to "The Storyteller"—that have contributed to shape my perspective. All along, I have been reading Arendt's text in an attempt to understand what was peculiar and unique about the trial. My own effort was to listen to the trial with the help of Arendt, to gain an insight into what in 1961 was happening in the courtroom through the magnifying lens of Arendt's sharp and critically insightful eyes. In this last chapter, I have suggested that besides the criticism there is also an unspoken element of grief in Arendt's text, that a relation between grief and justice indirectly and unconsciously informs Arendt's utterance, and that it is precisely this excessiveness of Arendt's utterance over her statement that gives her book authority and gives her text a literary depth, an existential density, and a political and legal-philosophical charisma that go beyond the conscious terms of her spoken argument.

I wish now to draw out this unspoken potential of Arendt's text and to pursue it further in my own way. In the remainder of my argument, I will go farther than Arendt does in drawing on the haunting relevance of Benjamin to *Eichmann in Jerusalem* and, more generally, in using Benjamin's reflection to highlight important aspects of the trial. Although I will, from this point on, use Benjamin to read the trial differently from Arendt (to argue with and argue *beyond* Arendt), my different understanding and my different proposition, to the extent that they rely in turn on Benjamin's authority and on his haunting presence, will also paradoxically be speaking *with* Arendt's text and *from her storyteller's silence:* from the unconscious pathos of her own excessive and yet silenced, *muted,* self-erased, and self-transcendent utterance.

— IX —

The Dramatic

In the wake of Benjamin, I argue therefore that the testimonial muteness underlying (and exceeding) Arendt's legal story reenacts, ironically enough, the literary muteness of K-Zetnik's story, and that K-Zetnik's *legal muteness*—his inability to tell a story in the trial—is part of the impossibility of telling that is at the trial's heart. Indeed, K-Zetnik's discourse prior to his fainting strives to *thematize* precisely the impossibility of telling, both in its use of the figure of "the other planet," testifying to the utter foreignness of Auschwitz and trying to convey the astronomic scale of distance separating its ungraspability and unnarratability from the narration in the courtroom in Jerusalem, and in its effort to narrate the scene of the extermination as a repeated scene of parting and of silence, a primal scene of silence whose sole meaning wordlessly resides in the exchange of looks between the living and the dying: between the not-yet-dead and the not-yet-surviving who remain behind for no other purpose than to tell and to retell the story that cannot be told.

But K-Zetnik's testimony does not simply tell *about* the impossibility of telling: it dramatizes it—*enacts it*—through its own lapse into coma and its own collapse into a silence. "It was the most *dramatic* moment of the trial," writes Tom Segev, "one of the most dramatic moments in the country's history."[76]

For Arendt as a critical legal observer and as a conscious representative of the traditional conception of the law, however,[77] *the dramatic* as such is by definition *immaterial* and extraneous to the trial. Arendt's view follows the classical axioms of jurisprudential thought. "The process," says Justice Oliver Wendell Holmes in one of the most authoritative statements of Anglo-Saxon jurisprudence in the twentieth century, "the process [of the law] is one, from a lawyer's statement of the case, eliminating as it does all the dramatic elements . . . , and retaining only the facts of legal import, up to the final analyses and abstract universals of theoretic jurisprudence."[78] This precisely is what Arendt tries to do, in discarding the dramatic and in theorizing in her legal proposition about the Eichmann trial the "abstract universal" of a new crime and of a new criminal without mens rea—without motive. "The banality of evil" is, in fact, strictly a "theoretical jurisprudential" concept: an *antiseptic* legal concept that is formed by the strict *reduction of the drama* that has given rise to its conceptual necessity. "If a man goes into law," says Holmes, "it pays to be a master of it, and to be a master of it means to look straight through all the dramatic incidents."[79]

Arendt therefore unambiguously discards the dramatic in the trial and denies it legal meaning. I would argue here, in contrast, that the dramatic *can be* legally significant. I submit that in the Eichmann trial (as the passing comment of the judges has in fact conceded) the dramatic *was* indeed endowed with *legal meaning*, meaning that the classical jurisprudential, legalistic view was programmed to miss and that Arendt consequently overlooked.

"As Hannah Arendt and others have pointed out," writes Susan

Sontag, "the juridical basis of the Eichmann trial, the relevance of all the evidence presented and the legitimacy of certain procedures are open to question on strictly legal grounds":

> But the truth is that the Eichmann trial did not, and could not, have conformed to legal standards only . . . The function of the trial was rather that of the tragic drama: above and beyond judgment and punishment, catharsis.
>
> . . . [T]he problem with the Eichmann trial was not its deficient legality, but *the contradiction between its juridical form and its dramatic function.*[80]

Arendt herself acknowledged in the epilogue of *Eichmann in Jerusalem* that, as the saying goes, "justice must not only be done but must be seen to be done" (*EiJ*, 277). The legal function of the court, in other words, is in its very *moral essence* a *dramatic* function: not only that of "doing justice" but that of *"making justice seen"* in a larger moral and historically unique sense.[81] It was through the perspective of this larger cultural and *historic visibility* the trial gave dramatically, historically, to justice that the Eichmann trial was (I would propose) *jurisprudentially dramatic.*

In a different context, Walter Benjamin in turn defines the dramatic:

> The mystery is, on the dramatic level, that moment in which it juts out of the domain of language proper to it into a higher one unattainable for it. *Therefore, this moment cannot be expressed in words but is expressible solely in representation:* it is the 'dramatic' in the strictest sense.[82]

Law in principle *rules out* what cannot be disclosed in words. In contrast, the dramatic, Benjamin says, is a beyond of words. It is a physical gesture by which language points to a meaning it cannot articulate.

Such is K-Zetnik's fall outside the witness stand. It makes a corpse out of the living witness who has sworn to remain anonymous and undifferentiated from the dead.

The witness's body has become within the trial what Pierre Nora would call *"a site of memory."*[83] In opposition to the trial's effort to create a conscious, totalizing memory and a totalizing historical consciousness, the site of memory is an unintegratable, residual, unconscious site that cannot be translated into legal consciousness and into legal idiom.

This site materializes in the courtroom memory of death both as a physical reality and as a limit of consciousness in history.

On this legal site, the witness testifies through his unconscious body. Suddenly, the testimony is invaded by the body. The speaking body has become a dying body. The dying body testifies dramatically and wordlessly beyond the cognitive and the discursive limits of the witness's speech.

The body's testimony thus creates a new dimension in the trial, a *physical legal dimension* that dramatically expands what can be grasped as legal meaning. This new dimension in its turn transforms and dramatically reshapes not just the legal process of the Eichmann trial, but the conception and the very frameworks of perception of the law as such.

The Caesura of the Trial: The Expressionless

How is it that the body can unconsciously transform the parameters of Law as such? The witness's fainting—the body's dramatic collapse in the midst of the witness's verbal testimony—could strikingly exemplify *within the structure of the trial* what Walter Benjamin calls "the expressionless":

The life undulating in it [Benjamin writes, and I would specify: the life undulating in the trial] must appear petrified and as if spellbound in a single moment . . . What . . . spellbinds the movement and interrupts the harmony is the expressionless . . . *Just as interruption by the commanding word is able to bring the truth out of the evasions . . . precisely at the point where it interrupts, the expressionless compels the trembling harmony to stop . . .* For it shatters whatever still survives of the legacy of chaos . . . the false, errant totality, the absolute totality. Only the expressionless completes the work [completes the trial], by shattering it into a thing of shards, into a fragment of the true world, into the torso of a symbol.[84]

To borrow Benjamin's inspired terms to describe the trial, I would argue that K-Zetnik's fainting and his petrified body stand for the "expressionless"—*das Ausdruckslose*—that suddenly erupts into the language of the law and *interrupts* the trial. In Benjamin's terms, K-Zetnik's collapse can be defined as "the caesura" of the trial:[85] a moment of petrification that interrupts and ruptures the articulations of the law, and yet that grounds them by shattering their false totality into "a fragment of the true world"; a sudden *"counter-rhythmic rupture"* in which (as Benjamin has put it) "every expression simultaneously comes to a standstill, in order to give free reign to an expressionless power."[86]

The fainting that cuts through the witness's speech and petrifies his body interrupts the legal process and creates a moment that is *legally traumatic* not just for the witness, but chiefly for the court and for the audience of the trial. I argue in effect that, in the rupture of the witness's lapse into a coma, it is the law itself that for a moment loses consciousness. But it is through this breakdown of the legal framework that history emerges in the courtroom and, in the legal body of the witness, exhibits its own inadvertently dramatic (nondiscursive) rules of evidence. It is precisely through this breach of consciousness of law that history unwittingly and mutely yet quite resonantly, memorably *speaks*.[87]

And it is for these moments in which history as injury dramatically, traumatically spoke—these moments that combined the legal, the dramatic, and the legally traumatic, yet whose eloquence and legal meaning could not be translated into legal idiom—that the Eichmann trial is remembered. It is precisely through these moments that the Eichmann trial has impressed itself on memory, as a remarkable legal event in which the law itself was shattered into a new level of perception and into a new historical and legal consciousness.

Part Four: Conclusion

This chapter has dealt with a legal moment that took the legal institution by surprise and stupefied at once the judges and the audience of the trial. In their written opinion, the judges marked the unique evidentiary position of this moment in the trial. They thought it was significant that it was here a literary writer who collapsed, and that it was an artist's testimony that the trial had exploded. Indeed, law has exploded here the literary framework. In turn, the conflation of the writer's literary testimony with the law has brought about a parallel explosion of the legal framework. Both the legal and the literary frameworks came apart as a result of their encounter in the trial. I argue that this breakdown—this caesura—was legally significant although (and because) it was legally traumatic.

This moment in which the human witness, flabbergasting both the audience and the judges, plunges into the abyss between the different planets and falls as though he were himself a corpse, is internal to the trial. I argue that it is a moment *inside law*, although its power comes from its interruption of the law, its interruption of discourse by what Walter Benjamin calls "the expressionless." The expressionless, I argue, grounds both the legal meaning of the trial and its inadvertent literary and dramatic power.

For the purpose of transmission of the Holocaust, literature and art do not suffice. And yet, a trial equally is insufficient. I believe that only the *encounter between law and art* can adequately testify to the abyssal meaning of the trauma.

It is remarkable that such an encounter between trauma, law, and art happens inside a trial. Inside the trial, in *the drama of the missed encounter* between K-Zetnik and the legal actors (judge and prosecutor), there is a unique confrontation between literature and law as two vocabularies of remembrance. The clash between these two dimensions and these two vocabularies brings about a breakdown of the legal framework through the physical collapse of the witness. Yet, through this inadvertent breakdown of the legal framework, history uncannily and powerfully speaks. "Everything," said Benjamin,

> Everything about history that, from the very beginning, has been untimely, sorrowful, unsuccessful, is expressed in a face,[88] or rather in a death's head.[89]

This death's head emerges in the trial as history is uncannily transmitted through K-Zetnik's fainting and through his endlessly reverberating courtroom silence.

*　*　*

In borrowing the words of Lanzmann, I therefore argue that what Arendt calls the *failures*[90] of the trial were *necessary failures*.[91] I argue that the Eichmann trial dramatically articulated legal meaning that no legal categories could apprehend, precisely through its failures. I further propose that it is in general a feature of pathbreaking trials to speak through the explosion of the legal framework, to legally say something (or show something) that is not containable precisely by the concepts and the logic of the legal. Moments of rupture of the legal framework can be—as they were in the Eichmann trial—moments of legal and conceptual breakthrough. Moments of institutional collapse and of "caesura" of the legal discourse—such as during K-Zetnik's fainting—

can be moments in which both art and history unwittingly speak in and through the legal tool.

I offer this as food for thought: Great trials are perhaps specifically those trials whose very failures have their own necessity and their own literary, cultural, and jurisprudential *speaking power.*

Abbreviations

Notes

Index

Abbreviations

The following abbreviations appear in citations in the text and the notes.

AJ Corr. Hannah Arendt and Karl Jaspers, *Correspondence: 1926–1969*, ed. Lotte Kohler and Hans Saner, trans. Robert and Rita Kimber (New York: Harcourt Brace, 1992)

BC Walter Benjamin, *A Berlin Chronicle*, in Walter Benjamin, *Reflections: Essays, Aphorisms, Autobiographical Writings*, trans. Edmund Jephcott, ed. with an introduction by Peter Demetz (New York: Schocken Books, 1986)

Brodersen Momme Brodersen, *Walter Benjamin: A Biography*, trans. Malcolm R. Green and Ingrida Ligers, ed. Martina Dervis (London: Verso, 1996)

"Critique" Walter Benjamin, "Critique of Violence," in Walter Benjamin, *Reflections: Essays, Aphorisms, Autobiographical Writings*, trans. Edmund Jephcott, ed. with an introduction by Peter Demetz (New York: Schocken Books, 1986)

EiJ Hannah Arendt, *Eichmann in Jerusalem: A Report on the Banality of Evil* (New York: Penguin Books, 1963)

EN Emmanuel Levinas, *Entre Nous: Thinking-of-the-Other*, trans. Michael B. Smith and Barbara Harshav (New York: Columbia University Press, 1998)

"GEA" Walter Benjamin, "Goethe's *Elective Affinities*," in Walter Benjamin, *Selected Writings, Volume I: 1913–1926*, ed. Marcus Bullock and Michael W. Jennings (Cambridge, Mass.: Harvard University Press, 1996)

Ill. Walter Benjamin, *Illuminations*, ed. with an introduction by Hannah Arendt (New York: Schocken Books, 1969)

"Kafka" Walter Benjamin, "Franz Kafka: On the Tenth Anniversary of His Death," in Walter Benjamin, *Illuminations*, ed. with an introduction by Hannah Arendt (New York: Schocken Books, 1969)

"MY" Walter Benjamin, "The Metaphysics of Youth," in Walter Benjamin, *Selected Writings, Volume I: 1913–1926*, ed. Marcus Bullock and Michael W. Jennings (Cambridge, Mass.: Harvard University Press, 1996)

Proceedings   *The Trial of Adolf Eichmann: Record of Proceedings in the District Court of Jerusalem,* Criminal Case 40/61 (Jerusalem), *Attorney General v. Eichmann* (1961), (English translation 1962, 1963)

R   Walter Benjamin, *Reflections: Essays, Aphorisms, Autobiographical Writings,* trans. Edmund Jephcott, ed. with an introduction by Peter Demetz (New York: Schocken Books, 1986)

RR   Paul de Man, *The Rhetoric of Romanticism* (New York: Columbia University Press, 1984)

Scholem   Gershom Scholem, *Walter Benjamin: The Story of a Friendship,* trans. Harry Zohn (New York: Schocken Books, 1988)

Segev   Tom Segev, *The Seventh Million: The Israelis and the Holocaust,* trans. Haim Watzman (New York: Farrar, Straus and Giroux, 1993)

Shivitti   Ka-Tzetnik 135633, *Shivitti: A Vision,* trans. Eliyah Nike De-Nur and Lisa Hermann (San Francisco: Harper and Row, 1986)

"SRK"   Walter Benjamin, "Some Reflections on Kafka," in Walter Benjamin, *Illuminations,* ed. with an introduction by Hannah Arendt (New York: Schocken Books, 1969)

"St."   Walter Benjamin, "The Storyteller," in Walter Benjamin, *Illuminations,* ed. with an introduction by Hannah Arendt (New York: Schocken Books, 1969)

SWI   Walter Benjamin, *Selected Writings, Volume I: 1913–1926,* ed. Marcus Bullock and Michael W. Jennings (Cambridge, Mass.: Harvard University Press, 1996)

TEM   *Trauma: Explorations in Memory,* ed. Cathy Caruth (Baltimore: Johns Hopkins University Press, 1995)

"Theses"   Walter Benjamin, "Theses on the Philosophy of History," in Walter Benjamin, *Illuminations,* ed. with an introduction by Hannah Arendt (New York: Schocken Books, 1969)

UAH   Friedrich Nietzsche, *The Use and Abuse of History for Life,* trans. Adrian Collins, introduction by Julius Kraft (New York: Liberal Arts Press, 1949, 1957)

UE   Cathy Caruth, *Unclaimed Experience: Trauma, Narrative, and History* (Baltimore: Johns Hopkins University Press, 1996)

Notes

Introduction

1. The word *trauma* means wound, especially one produced by sudden physical injury. The original use of the term derives from medicine; it has later been borrowed by psychoanalysis and by psychiatry to designate a blow to the self (and to the tissues of the mind), a shock that creates a psychological split or rupture, an emotional injury that leaves lasting damage in the psyche. Psychological trauma occurs as a result of an overwhelming, uncontrollable and terrifying experience, usually a violent event or events or the prolonged exposure to such events. The emotional damage often remains hidden, as though the person were unharmed. The full scope of the symptoms manifests itself only belatedly, sometimes years and years later. The trigger of the symptoms is often an event that unconsciously reminds the subject of the original traumatic scene, and is thus lived as a repetition of the trauma. Trauma thus results in lifelong psychological liabilities, and continues to have delayed aftereffects throughout one's existence. Classic examples of traumatic catalysts include wars, concentration camp experiences, prison experiences, terrorism incidents, auto and industrial accidents, and childhood traumas such as incest or sexual and physical abuse. Classic examples of traumatic symptoms include anxiety (for signs of danger) or, conversely, numbness and depression; addictions, compulsive repetition—in thought, speech, or fantasy—of the traumatic situation, or, conversely, amnesia; and repetitive nightmares in which the traumatic event is reproduced.

It is understood today that trauma can be collective as well as individual and that traumatized communities are something distinct from assemblies of traumatized persons; see Kai Erikson, "Notes on Trauma and Community," in *Trauma: Explorations in Memory,* ed. Cathy Caruth (Baltimore: Johns Hopkins University Press, 1995), pp. 183–199. Oppressed groups that have been persistently subject to abuse, injustice, or violence suffer collective trauma, much like soldiers who have been exposed to war atrocities. The twentieth century can be defined as a century of trauma.

2. In recent years, trauma has received a renewed attention both in the humanities and in the sciences—from psychiatrists, physicians, therapists, neurobiologists, brain researchers, sociologists, political thinkers, philosophers, historians and literary critics.

And yet, despite its topicality in modern thought, trauma theory has not yet penetrated jurisprudential studies. Since the consequence of every criminal offense (as well as of its legal remedy) is literally a trauma (death, loss of property, loss of freedom, fear, shock, physical and emotional destruction), I advance the claim that trauma—individual as well as social—is the basic underlying reality of the law. This book illustrates this claim and analyzes at the same time its particular relevance to contemporary history and its general implications (for law, for society, for history, for literature, for culture at large).

In the second half of the twentieth century, following in the footsteps of postwar Europe, post-Vietnam America has brought to the fore of contemporary research groundbreaking neurobiological, biochemical, and psychological studies of what is known as post-traumatic stress disorder," or PTSD. PTSD "reflects the imposition" and "engraving" on the mind and on memory of "the unavoidable reality of horrific events, the taking over of the mind, psychically and neurobiologically, by an event that it cannot control" and which it therefore suffers repeatedly beyond the shock of the first moment and beyond the terror of the original occurrence (57). But PTSD, Cathy Caruth writes, is not merely an effect of destruction; it is also "an enigma of survival" (57–58). Indeed, "trauma theory often divides itself into two basic trends: the focus on trauma as the 'shattering' of a previously whole self and the focus on the survival function of trauma as allowing one to get through an overwhelming experience" (131); And "it is only by recognizing traumatic experience as a paradoxical relation between destructiveness and survival that we can . . . recognize the legacy of . . . catastrophic experience" (58). References are to Cathy Caruth, *Unclaimed Experience: Trauma, Narrative, and History* (Baltimore: Johns Hopkins University Press, 1996); see also Caruth, "Introductions," in the interdisciplinary collection *Trauma: Explorations in Memory*, ed. Cathy Caruth (Baltimore: Johns Hopkins University Press, 1995), pp. 3–12, 151–157; for a discussion of the history of the notion of trauma and for recent attempts to define it, see *Trauma and Its Wake*, 2 vols., ed. Charles R. Figley (New York: Brunner-Mazel, 1985–1986).

For trauma theories generally and for discussions of trauma in specific settings, see also *Traumatic Stress: The Effects of Overwhelming Experience on Mind, Body, and Society*, ed. Bessel A. van der Kolk, Alexander C. McFarlane, and Lars Weisaeth (New York: Guilford Press, 1996); *International Responses to Traumatic Stress: Humanitarian, Human Rights, Justice, Peace and Development Contributions, Collaborative Actions and Future Initiatives*, ed. Yael Danieli, Nigel S. Rodley, and Lars Weisaeth with foreword by Boutros Boutros-Ghali (Amityville, N.Y.: Baywood Publishing, 1996); *Post-Traumatic Stress Disorder: Psychological and Biological Sequelae*, ed. Bessel A. van der Kolk (Washington, D.C.: American Psychiatric Press, 1984); *Psychological Trauma*, ed. Bessel A. van der Kolk (Washington, D.C.: American Psychiatric Press, 1987); *The Reconstruction of Trauma: Its Significance in Clinical Work*, ed. Arnold Rothstein (Madison, Conn.: International Universities Press, 1986); Robert Jay Lifton, *The Broken Connection: On Death and the Continuity of Life* (New York: Basic Books, 1979); *Massive Psychic Trauma*, ed. Henry Krystal (New York: International Universities Press, 1968); Dominick Lacapra, *Writing History, Writing Trauma* (Baltimore: Johns Hopkins University Press, 2000); Ruth Leys, *Trauma: A*

Genealogy (Chicago: University of Chicago Press, 2000); Giorgio Agamben, *Remnants of Auschwitz: The Witness and the Archive* (New York: Zone Books, 1999); H. W. Chalsma, *The Chambers of Memory: PTSD in the Life Stories of U.S. Vietnam Veterans* (Northvale, N.J.: Jason Aronson, 1998); *Children in Violent Society*, ed. Joy D. Osofsky (New York: Guilford Press, 1997); Alice Miller, *Thou Shalt Not Be Aware: Society's Betrayal of the Child*, trans. Hildegarde and Hunter Nannum (New York: New American Library, 1984); Judith Lewis Herman, *Trauma and Recovery: The Aftermath of Violence from Domestic Abuse to Political Terror* (New York: Basic Books, 1997); Inger Agger and Soren Buus Jensen, *Trauma and Healing under State Terrorism* (London: Zed Books, 1996); Inger Agger, *The Blue Room: Trauma and Testimony among Refugee Women: A Psycho-Social Exploration*, trans. Mary Bille (London: Zed Books, 1994); Dori Laub and Nanette Auerhahn, "Knowing and Not Knowing Massive Psychic Trauma: Forms of Traumatic Memory," *International Journal of Psychoanalysis* 74 (1993): 287–302; Nadine Fresco, "Remembering the Unknown," *International Review of Psychoanalysis* 11 (1984): 417–427; Robert Jay Lifton, *The Nazi Doctors: Medical Killing and the Psychology of Genocide* (New York: Basic Books, 1986); Robert Jay Lifton, *Thought Reform and the Psychology of Totalism: A Study of "Brainwashing" in China* (New York: W. W. Norton, 1969); Robert Jay Lifton, *Death in Life: Survivors of Hiroshima* (New York: Basic Books, 1967); D. W. Winnicott, "The Concept of Trauma in Relation to the Development of the Individual within the Family" (1965) and "Fear of Breakdown" (1963), in *Psychoanalytic Explorations*, ed. Clare Winnicott, Ray Sheperd, and Madeleine Davis (Cambridge, Mass.: Harvard University Press, 1989); Bruno Bettelheim, "Trauma and Reintegration," in *Surviving and Other Essays* (New York: Vintage Books, 1952).

3. Among the mass of clinical, scientific, and humanistic studies of traumatic experience (see note 2), this book is most indebted to the theorization of trauma offered by the works of Cathy Caruth (see Caruth, *Unclaimed Experience: Trauma, Narrative, and History*, hereinafter abbreviated *UE*, and *Trauma: Explorations in Memory*, ed. Caruth, hereinafter abbreviated *TEM*). The distinctive position of Caruth's contribution to this field of inquiry that she has helped to shape and to create derives from the fact that she is (uniquely among the researchers) a true *thinker of the field*, in fact its most authoritative, most original interdisciplinary theorist.

Caruth's pathbreaking work offers at once a new methodology of reading and an illuminating concept articulating trauma, psychoanalysis, and history into an integrated, comprehensive, innovative vision. This vision could be summarized by three main points that are also crucial to the readings in this book:

(1) Trauma is an essential dimension of historical experience, and its analysis provides a new understanding of historical causality;

(2) The aftermath of catastrophic experience is riddled by an enigma of survival; the legacy of traumatic experience imposes a reflection on, and provides a new type of insight into, the relation between destruction and survival;

(3) Because the experience of trauma addresses the Other and demands the listening of another, it implies a human and an ethical dimension in which the

Other receives priority over the self. This ethical dimension is tightly related to the question of justice.

In an exemplary analysis of Freud's as yet uncharted legacy of trauma in his last work, *Moses and Monotheism,* Caruth remarkably, paradigmatically, shows how the book itself—Freud's testament on *history as trauma*—is the site of an inscription of a historical trauma: that of Freud's dramatic departure from Vienna, then invaded and annexed by Hitler's Germany. Caruth's analysis reveals how Freud's own trauma in the face of persecutory Nazism is historically transformed into thought. It is indeed under the highly traumatic circumstances of his forced leaving of Vienna that Freud reflects on Moses' historical departure from Egypt and articulates his innovative and farsighted theory on history as trauma, exemplified by his analysis of the belated impact and the repetitive, traumatic history of the foundation of monotheism. In this way, Caruth exemplarily explores how the texts of psychoanalysis (as well as those of literature and theory) "both *speak about* and *speak through* the profound story of traumatic experience" (Caruth, *UE,* 4; emphasis mine).

Trauma, therefore, "does not simply serve as record of the past but precisely registers *the force of an experience*" that is "unclaimed," that is "not yet fully owned" (*TEM,* ed. Caruth, 151) and "cannot be placed within the schemes of prior knowledge" (*TEM,* 153). Caruth concretely analyzes, thus, the un-owned *human depth* of trauma (of the experience behind the theory), an experience through which trauma will *possess* the subject but will not become a simple narrative or a simple memory possessed or owned by him or her. "To be traumatized is precisely to be possessed by an image or event" (*TEM,* 4–5). Trauma is therefore the confrontation with "an event that is itself constituted . . . by its lack of integration into consciousness" (*TEM,* 152). Yet the event (as Freud observes in the life of individuals as well as of communities) registers a *belated* impact: it becomes precisely *haunting,* tends to historically return and to repeat itself in practice and in act, to the precise extent that it remains *un-owned* and unavailable to knowledge and to consciousness. Like the traumatic nightmares of returning soldiers that, years after the war, continue to repeat themselves and thus repeatedly relive the pain, the violence, the horror, and the unexpectedness of the original traumatizing scene, history is likewise subject, Freud suggests, to compulsive forms of (immemorial yet commemorative) traumatic repetitions. Freud thus shows how historical traumatic energy can be the motive-force of society, of culture, of tradition, and of history itself.

If PTSD (post-traumatic stress disorder, a concept officially acknowledged by the American Psychiatric Association in 1980) "must be understood as a . . . symptom," Caruth thus argues, "then *it is not so much a symptom of the unconscious, as it is a symptom of history.* The traumatized, we might say, carry an impossible history within them, or they become themselves the symptom of a history that they cannot entirely possess" (*TEM,* 5; emphasis mine).

Caruth's central insight, by which she translates and in which she locates Freud's central insight in *Moses and Monotheism,* is "that history, like trauma, is never simply one's own, that history is precisely the way we are implicated in each other's traumas" (*UE,* 24).

Caruth's theory of trauma is thus radically Other oriented. It is essentially a theory and practice of listening to the trauma of another, as "a means of passing out of the isolation imposed by the [traumatic] event" (*TEM*, 11). Caruth's compassionate, insightfully humane, and ethically committed readings underscore "the way in which one's own trauma is tied up with the trauma of another, the way in which trauma may lead, therefore, to the encounter with another" (*UE*, 8).

What Caruth propounds, in summary, in synthesizing philosophically, psychoanalytically, and literarily the interdisciplinary field of trauma studies, is *a new mode of reading and of listening* that "both the language of trauma, and the silence of its mute repetition of suffering, profoundly and imperatively demand" (*UE*, 9). The Other is necessary, Caruth insistently points out, for the history of trauma to be written, to be constituted at all. "The history of trauma, in its inherent belatedness, can only take place through the listening of another. The meaning of *trauma's address beyond itself* concerns, indeed, not only individual isolation but a wider historical isolation that, in our time, is communicated on the level of our cultures. Such an address can be located, for example, in Freud's insisting, from his exile in England, on having his final book on trauma—*Moses and Monotheism*—translated into English before he died; or in the survivors of Hiroshima first communicating their stories to the United States through the narrative written by John Hersey, or more generally in the survivors of the catastrophes of one culture addressing the survivors of another. This speaking and this listening—a speaking and a listening *from the site of trauma*—does not rely," Caruth suggests, "on what we simply know of each other, but on what we don't yet know of our own traumatic pasts." "In a catastrophic age . . . trauma itself may provide the very link between cultures" (*TEM*, 11; emphasis mine).

Caruth's theorization of trauma is largely recognized and widely cited as canonical, despite the recent academic controversies it has given rise to—polemics that in their turn acknowledge and confirm the centrality of this theorization that they are trying to dispute and undercut, but from whose creative momentum they are nourished and from which they draw the core of their own (secondary) insights.

These polemics are turning trauma studies into a field of academic struggles and of conflict of ideologies of knowledge and of scholarship, in which historians in particular—historians of ideas and historians of science—try to recuperate and annex the findings of the field. These territorial struggles and these claims to hegemony are, as a rule, not the concern of this book, because they are parasitic on the topic. But I will analyze here one such emblematic (symptomatic) book, in an attempt to demonstrate my general contention that it is the very claim to hegemony of these books that betrays at once their derivative position and, more importantly, their actual hidden agenda of denial of what they purport to investigate and what they so vocally discourse about.

A representative example of a book that feeds on controversy in such a way as to reduce the momentous stakes of trauma to the triviality of academic conflict is Ruth Leys's polemical work *Trauma: A Genealogy* (Chicago: Chicago University Press, 2000). The word *genealogy* is borrowed, after Nietzsche, from Foucault, but there is nothing Nietzschean (nothing truly philosophical) and nothing Foucaldian (nothing political or ethical) about the book. Its title is misleading. The book is far less interested in tracing history (in studying the past) than in witch hunting (in legislating the institutional future). A genealogy is by its very nature the opposite of a polemic. It would have been indeed extremely useful to have "a genealogy" of trauma that would have assembled all the various insights trauma theories have offered in the course of their historical development. But the agenda of this book is, on the contrary, to carry out primarily *a process of exclusion* of fellow contributors to the field. The dispute is based not just on argument but on pure verbal violence, as though one's own authority could be consolidated by arrogant and condescending epithets and by resentful personal disparagement of those researchers whose influence the book would like so badly to exclude. ("The reader who has come this far will not need to be told that my discussion of Caruth and van der Kolk has a critical edge that is absent from my discussion of earlier figures. In the first place, I am dismayed by the low quality of van der Kolk's scientific work . . . As for Caruth, I feel a similar impatience with the sloppiness of her theoretical arguments"; 305.)

As though by chance, the three main targets of the book happen to be three of the most creative and original contributors to the field: physician-clinician Judith Herman (who misguidedly believes in the veracity of traumatic memory), physician-clinician Bessel van der Kolk (who misguidedly believes in the literal engravement of trauma on the mind), and philosophical and literary theorist Cathy Caruth (who misguidedly accepts the "literality" of traumatic memory). However, Leys's book remains entirely derivative of the insights of those she attacks: her discussion of Pierre Janet feeds on van der Kolk's rediscovery and reevaluation of Janet; her discussion of the historical importance of World War I feeds on Judith Herman's pathbreaking analysis of the political importance of this war as a paradigm-shift and a gender-shift in trauma theory; her discussion of Freud feeds on the brilliant and pathbreaking readings of Freud's texts in Cathy Caruth's essential book, *Unclaimed Experience: Trauma, Narrative and History* (Baltimore: Johns Hopkins University Press, 1996).

When Leys repeats throughout the book that she will criticize Caruth, "whose ideas about trauma are today much in vogue in the humanities" (16) and whose approach "has received considerable approbation, not only from humanists in various fields but also from psychiatrists and physicians" (266), she acknowledges that what Caruth does is both "new" (304) and "surprising" (16) and that her work has naturally "a certain distinction and seeming authority" (16); but she keeps almost obsessively attributing both the substance of Caruth's theories and their authority to notions allegedly derived from Paul de Man (see, for instance, pp. 16, 17, 266, 275, 304, where Leys attributes to de Man Caruth's so-called "theory of the performative" and her theory of the "literality of the signifier"). What counts here is not Leys's glaring misrepresentation of de Man's alleged theories but, exemplarily, the way in which the "genealogy" is systematically taken for granted and misconstrued. Although Caruth had been, in fact, in her first book (*Empirical Truths and Critical Fictions* [Baltimore: Johns Hopkins University Press, 1991]), a distinguished philosophical and literary student of Paul de Man, her current work on trauma takes on a direction of its own that radically parts ways with her early teacher, who on principle shunned psychoanalysis as such. Indeed, the theory of "the literality of the signifier" here attributed to de Man in reality originates not in de Man but in Lacan, with whose pathbreaking perspective on trauma Leys is simply unacquainted. The (preconceived) connection to de Man is in the (haunted?) mind of the observer.

Trauma: A Genealogy sets out to offer, therefore, not a *genealogy of trauma* (unless it is de Man who is, genealogically, the real trauma behind this book) but, instead, a *genealogy of academic politics*. In its fixation on de Man, however, the book gets even this small-scale institutional history—this genealogy of academic politics—wrong.

The main trouble with the book, though, is not with its falsifying *institutionalization* of the stakes of trauma studies but with its far more substantive falsification of the work of Freud himself. The central proposition of the book is (admittedly, this time) derivative of Mikkel Borch-Jakobsen's proposal that "the mimetic paradigm serves as a key structuring principle in Freud's thought" (13). Accordingly, trauma is interpreted throughout the book in terms of so-called mimesis and antimimesis. "Mimesis" is based on the "notion of [the victim's] identification with the aggressor" and on the hysteric's tendency to imitate or "'mime' other disorders" (6). Because "it is well known that the rise of trauma theory was associated from the start with [hysteria and] hypnosis" (8), because "hypnosis was the means by which Charcot legitimated the concept of trauma by proposing that the hysterical crises that he suggestively induced in his patients were reproductions of traumatic scenes" (8), Leys claims by way of generalization that in Freud as well, and in his followers to come, "trauma was therefore understood as an experience of hypnotic imitation or identification—what I call *mimesis*" (8). In contrast, "the antimimetic tendency" would be "the tendency to regard trauma as if it were a purely external event" (10). Freud, according to Leys, is torn and remains undecided between these two poles, and so are all theories of trauma in his wake. This is the core premise of the book and also its repetitive conclusion: "My claim is that the concept of trauma has been structured historically in such a way as simultaneously to invite resolution in favor of one pole or the other of the mimetic/antimimetic dichotomy and to resist and ultimately defeat all such attempts at resolution" (299). "By now it should not need stating that as a historian or genealogist of trauma my project has been to reveal and investigate the tensions inherent in the mimetic-antimimetic structure" (306).

What is wrong with this artificial theory? To begin with, its barrenness of insight, its lack of human depth, and, by its own admission, its utter clinical irrelevance: "What, then, are the implications of my book?" asks Leys, and answers: "*The first* is that current debates over trauma are fated to end in *an impasse*, for the simple reason that they are the inescapable outcome of the mimetic-antimimetic oscillation" (305). "*A second implication* of my book is simply this: if it is true that the entire discourse on trauma in the West has been structured by an unresolvable tension and conflict between mimesis and antimimesis, then *it would be a mistake for therapists to think that treatment* for the victims of trauma *should follow theory*"(307; italics mine). Insensitive to textual, to clinical and to historical nuance alike, the eternal rediscovery of the same old ideology and of the same familiar academic categories (mimesis, non-mimesis) reduces the surprise and the unknown of trauma to the (purely academic) known. It *extrapolates* in fact from the complexity and from the foreignness of the unconscious an estheticizing and familiarizing terminology of consciousness. This terminology is also ahistorically essentializing. Irrespective of historical diversity and of concrete clinical and human singularity, "all these contradictions arise from *the same essential force,* the structural inability of the two paradigms to rigorously exclude the other" (301).

Far more severe than the essentializing thrust of this "genealogy" is its blatant falsification of the meaning of Freud's work. Because Freud is arrested here in the prehistory of psychoanalysis (hysteria and hypnosis), the book's understanding of Freud's notion of trauma is distortingly confined to sexual trauma. Freud's mature work and his late preoccupation with memory, with history, with violence, with culture, and with war, are here virtually ignored. It is both symptomatic and revelatory that this book discusses only a handful of cases of private trauma and seems totally oblivious to—has no real grasp of—the tragedies of genocide and the massive contemporary realities of collective trauma. The book misunderstands or fails to recognize the fact that the theory of trauma is far more consequential in the late Freud, where it is not always explicitly attached to the term *trauma* but has to be deciphered philosophically, textually, and literarily.

Although Freud is a cornerstone of Leys's book, Leys herself never provides any close reading or direct engagement with Freud's text, other than through the extensive citation of Caruth's interpretive work and the synoptical, "reader-digest" statements gleaned from secondary sources and "summarized" from a small number of secondary writers speaking about Freud (Laplanche, Borch-Jakobsen, Rose, the psychoanalytic dictionary of Laplanche and Pontalis). Thus, all actual readings of Freud's texts are in fact borrowed and their insights are quite literally *incorporated* from Caruth's criticized book, according to a process that in Leys's own terms has to be defined as "imitative," as exemplifying what Leys calls a "mimetic identification." In what could serve as a description of her own polemical and critical work, Leys writes: "according to Freud, violence is inherent in the imitative-identificatory process, which he describes as cannibalistic, devouring, incorporative identification that readily turns into a hostile desire to rid oneself of the other or enemy, with whom one has just merged" (30). "In short," writes Leys, "Freud places the hypnotic-suggestive tie or bond at the center of the traumatic paradigm . . . But what if—as Freud suggests—trauma is understood to consist in imitative or mimetic identification itself? So . . . the victim of a trauma identifies with the aggressor" (31–32).

The notion (central to Leys's book) that trauma is identical to a hypnotic or "mimetic identification"—the theory that identification is the defining feature of what trauma is about—is not only a complete misunderstanding and an incredible reduction, it is in fact an aberration. On this view, the disastrously traumatic events of September 11, 2001, in America (the collapse of the World Trade Center towers, the damage to the Pentagon, and the plane crash in Pennsylvania) would derive from, and would be defined by, the Americans' mimetic identification with the aggressors—with the terrorists.

The conceptual confusion that predominates in this "theory" derives from the book's (so-called genealogical) collapse of psychoanalysis on hypnosis: indeed, the "genealogy" proceeds as though the two historical experiences (psychoanalysis, hypnosis) were continuous and commensurate in all respects. "The conceptualization of trauma was inevitably connected with the rise of hypnosis . . . Hypnosis provided Freud with a model of unconscious identification" (36). Leys is oblivious to the fact that psychoanalysis was born (as Lacan points out) precisely from the *negative* procedure by which Freud chose to *forgo hypnosis.* The book misunderstands the way in which it is the rupture with hypnosis that is constitutive of the originality and radicality of psychoanalysis. The study thus derives from, and encapsulates, a miscomprehension of several different psychoanalytic concepts that are here collapsed upon each other with no critical awareness of their boundaries and of their crucial differences: unconscious, identification, imitation, trauma, narcissistic injury, hysterical disorders. The reduction of "Freud's conception of trauma" to "the archtrauma of identification" (32) amounts to the blatantly absurd assertion that there is no such thing as an *event* of trauma: "From this perspective, the traumatic 'event' is redefined as that which, precisely because it triggers the 'trauma' of emotional identification, strictly speaking cannot be defined as an event" (33). This perception misses everything about the reality of trauma. We may not understand what trauma is about or where it comes from. But if trauma is not an event (precisely a concrete and singular historical reality—a blow—we do not understand but have to take in), it is nothing. Trauma is, one might say, the event par excellence, the event as unintelligible, as the pure impact of sheer happening. But Leys's book reduces the event (as it reduces history) to what it calls "the *theme* of mimetic identification" (33, emphasis added). The thematic is, precisely (contrary to the event) what is already tamed and understood, what has already been reduced to meaning, to a vocabulary of consciousness. Trauma as a self-contained *thematic* meaning is reduced by Leys, essentially, to the disorders of a narcissistic injury. But to reduce trauma to a narcissistic injury is both to trivialize and to deny it, to recuperate its strangeness and its otherness. What is fatally lost sight of in this "theory" of trauma (a theory about the identifications of the self) is, indeed, the Other. *Trauma: A Genealogy,* a book that recognizes no events (and in which, consequently, nothing happens), is symptomatically a book in which narcissism is the only reality.

Hence Leys's attack on what she calls "the pathos of the literal" in Caruth's analysis. The disparagement and the exclusion of the literal (understood positivistically, reductively) quite naturally stems from the exclusion of the event. Where there is no event and no historic singularity (only an essence of "mimetic identification"), there obviously is no signifying (or symbolic) literality that can be grasped as such, that is to say, as *literally signifying,* literally symbolic, much like the Purloined Letter in Lacan's analysis. If Ruth Leys fails to see or grasp the nature of the letter and the nature of the signifier's literality in Caruth's text, it is because she looks for it positivistically and literal-mindedly, as the police precisely do in Poe's tale. Indeed, her persistent practice of critique of Caruth's text resides in a relentless spying on (the literality of) omitted words in Caruth's citations of Freud's text. The omissions are persistently detected and the elided words triumphantly restored, through an obsessively positivistic, self-congratulatory gesture of filling in the gaps. And yet, the letter (at once traumatizing and encapsulating the significance of trauma) is not found.

> Caruth's *omissions* here are not especially important—when she cites the same passage in her later book, *Unclaimed Experience,* she restores the second of the missing sentences. But they are symptomatic of her general rejection of Freud's Oedipal explanation of the neuroses. (278)

> Something else that Caruth disregards in Freud's text, an *omission* . . . That omission concerns Freud's adherence to Lamarck's theory. (284)

> Caruth also believes in the intergenerational transmission of trauma . . . If Caruth does not mention or need Freud's Lamarckian theories, this is because her de Manian version of that technology explains how texts themselves performatively achieve the same transformation of history into memory. (286)

> Caruth *omits nothing* significant in this passage . . . But her analysis depends on a ruse, because it involves *the omission* of the very words in the passage she cites that would appear to disprove her contention. I quote the passage again, this time with the elided words [in brackets] restored. (288)

"The police," writes Lacan in his famous analysis of "The Purloined Letter,"

> The police have looked *everywhere:* which we were to understand—vis-à-vis the area in which the police . . . assumed the letter might be found—in terms of a (no doubt theoretical) exhaustion of space . . . Have we not then the right to ask how it happened that the letter was not found *anywhere,* or rather observe that all we have been told of a more far-ranging conception of concealment does not explain, in all rigor, that the letter escaped detection, since the area combed did in act contain it, as Dupin's discovery eventually proves . . .
>
> Let us, in fact, look more closely at what happens to the police. We are spared nothing concerning the procedures used in searching the area submitted to their investigation: from the division of space into compartments from which the slightest bulk could not escape detection . . . to a microscope exposing the waste of any drilling at the surface of its hollow, indeed, the infinitesimal gaping of the slightest abyss . . .
>
> But the detectives have so immutable a notion of the real that they fail to notice that their search tends to transform it into an object.

(See Jacques Lacan, "Seminar on *The Purloined Letter,*" trans. Jeffrey Mehlman, in *Yale French Studies* 48 [1972], *French Freud,* ed. Mehlman, pp. 52–55.)

The detectives, says Lacan, fail to see the letter (and fail to grasp what literality means) because their search transforms it into an object—because they confuse the symbolic with the real; and so does Leys. Why, indeed, does Ruth

Leys need, like a detective at a crime scene, literally to spy on Caruth's and Freud's omitted words? Why this policing of the letter? Why this policing of the territory of knowledge? I venture to propose that it is precisely the vitality and force of Caruth's vision, and, more generally, the radicality of trauma itself—the way in which (precisely) the event of trauma destabilizes the security of knowledge and strikes at the foundation of the institutional prerogatives of what is known—that is experienced as a threat and needs thus to be tamed, contained and censored.

> Finally [writes Leys], in chapters 7 and 8 I examined the work of two post-Holocaust, post-Vietnam theorists of trauma, Bessel van der Kolk and Cathy Caruth . . . What is new in their work . . . is a fascination with . . . the currently modish idea that the domain of trauma is the unspeakable and unrepresentable . . . However, as I argued, there is no warrant in the mimetic theory for their insistence . . . that the traumatic experience stands outside or beyond representation as such . . . Both authors . . . emphasize the tendency of trauma to infect or contagiously influence others. In van der Kolk's work this takes the modest form of proposing that the therapist may be so affected by his patient's suffering that he or she comes to be traumatized in turn. In Caruth's work the topos of infection takes the more dramatic form of proposing that the trauma experienced by one generation can be contagiously . . . transmitted to ensuing generations, with the result that each of us can be imagined as receiving a trauma that we never directly experienced. (304–330)

In contrast, Ruth Leys denies the intergenerational transmission of trauma and the subversion of representation by the otherness of the event, which she experiences as nothing less than a scandal for (traditional) thought. She thus in principle denies the consequences by which trauma refuses to be pigeonholed and fundamentally subverts our frames of reference. Leys attempts to pass off this dread of consequences both as "science" and as "ethics," in proclaiming that Caruth's radical analysis of the unlocatability of trauma is seemingly "immoral" because it might induce us to confuse victims and perpetrators (78, 38–39, 292–297). But we are in no such danger, and if we were, no flat moralizing could protect us from it. No flat moralizing and no pseudo-scientific pigeonholing can erase the revolutionary consequences of traumatic experience. Pigeonholing is not ethics; still less is it science: it is dogma. "Conservatism," writes Charles Sanders Peirce, "in the sense of a dread of consequences, is altogether out of place in science—which has on the contrary always been forwarded by radicals and radicalism, in the sense of the eagerness to carry consequences to their extremes" (Charles Sanders Peirce, *Philosophical Writings*, ed. Justus Buchler [New York: Dover, 1955], p. 58). Unlike Caruth and van der Kolk, Ruth Leys does not have such an eagerness. Governed by what Peirce calls "the dread of consequences," which it sets out to suppress, police, *deny,* and *censor, Trauma: A Genealogy* construes itself as moralizing and as normalizing only at the cost of its uncritical and blind participation in the censorship of what it claims to talk about. "Denial, repression, and dissociation operate on a social as well as on an individual level," writes Judith Herman (*Trauma and Recovery,* [New York: Basic Books, 1997], p. 2). As this example demonstrates, there are (and thus *can* be) whole books on trauma whose actual subtextual and institutional agenda is (unconsciously or not) to participate in "the ordinary social processes of silencing and denial" (ibid., p. 9) of the bewildering phenomenon of trauma.

4. "Address by President George W. Bush to a Joint Session of Congress," delivered on September 20, 2001, text of the speech reproduced in the *Boston Globe,* September 21, 2001, 3rd ed., Section National/Foreign, p. A29 (transcript by eMediaMillWorks, Inc.).

5. Ibid.

6. "We're not deceived," said Bush, "by their pretenses to piety. We have seen their kind before. *They're the heirs of all the murderous ideologies of the twentieth century.* By sacrificing human life to serve their radical visions, by abandoning every value except the will to power, they follow in the path of fascism, Nazism, and totalitarianism" (ibid., italics mine).

7. These pages were written in the immediate aftermath of the events of September 11; the United States had just entered into a military war on terrorism whose ultimate historical developments and *judicial consequences* cannot be predicted or foreseen with total certainty or with a total clarity of moral vision. My point here is not political but analytical. Whatever the political and moral consequences, it is significant that the idea of justice by trial and by law was immediately envisioned and articulated as America's promised reply, and as Western civilization's most significant and most meaningful response precisely to the loss of meaning and the disempowerment occasioned by the trauma.

8. For references to the massive legal scholarship on the dichotomy between the private and the public, including the contemporary general rethinking of this dichotomy and the relevance of this rethinking to various cultural and political critiques and various critical legal movements, see Chapter 3, n. 48; see also Ruti Teitel, "The Universal and the Particular and International Criminal Justice: Symposium in Celebration of the Fiftieth Anniversary of the Universal Declaration of Human Rights," *Columbia Human Rights Law Review* 30 (1999): 285, and Gerry Simpson, "Conceptualizing Violence: Present and Future Developments in International Law and Policy on War Crimes and Crimes against Humanity: Didactic and Dissident Histories in War Crime Trials," in *Albany Law Review* 60 (1997): 801.

9. This juridical unconscious consists not only in the way in which the law repeats the trauma but also, more specifically, precisely in the way in which *what cannot be articulated in legal language* is, however, *played out on the legal stage* and is enacted and reenacted in the courtroom in two dramatic legal modes: (a) in compulsive structures of *legal* repetitions (Chapter 2), and (b) in moments of explosion and of interruption of the legal framework (Chapter 4).

10. Thus I show for instance (Chapter 4) how Benjamin is secretly present in Arendt's *Eichmann in Jerusalem* and how this secret presence sheds new light on Arendt's book not simply as a book on postwar trials but as a book of mourning: an unarticulated autobiographical mourning that wordlessly inscribes in Arendt's text her own loss and her own untold, silenced, traumatic story.

1. The Storyteller's Silence

1. Compare Franz Kafka, *The Trial*, trans. Willa and Edwin Muir; rev., with additional material trans. E. M. Butler (New York: Schocken Books, 1992), pp. 213–215.

2. Walter Benjamin, "Franz Kafka: On the Tenth Anniversary of his Death" (hereinafter abbreviated "Kafka"), in Walter Benjamin, *Illuminations*, ed. with an introduction by Hannah Arendt (New York: Schocken Books, 1969), p. 139. This collection will be referred to by the abbreviation *Ill.*

3. Walter Benjamin, "The Storyteller," in *Ill.*, 108. The essay "The Storyteller" will be indicated by the abbreviation "St."

4. At Nuremberg, history was asked in an unprecedented manner to account in court for historical injustices that were submitted for the first time to the legal definition of a crime. The prosecution and the judgment conceptualized as crimes atrocities and abuses of power that until then had not been justiciable: "crimes against humanity," crimes committed at the time of war against civilians, injustices that a totalitarian regime inflicts on its own subjects as well as on outsiders and opponents. On the pathbreaking concept of crimes against humanity and generally on the historical significance and vision of the Nuremberg trials, see "Introduction"; Chapter 3, Section V; and Chapter 4, Part One, subsection entitled "Two Visions of Historic Trial."

5. Compare Robert Cover, "Nuremberg and the Creation of a Modern Myth," in "The Folktales of Justice," in *Narrative, Violence, and the Law: The Essays of Robert Cover*, ed. Martha Minow, Michael Ryan, and Austin Sarat (Ann Arbor: University of Michigan Press, 1995), pp. 195–201; Jonathan Turley, "Symposium on Trials of the Century: Transformative Justice and the Ethos of Nuremberg," in *Loyola of Los Angeles Law Review* 33 (2000): 655; Gerry J. Simpson, "Conceptualizing Violence: Present and Future Developments in International Law and Policy on War Crimes and Crimes against Humanity: Didactic and Dissident Histories in War Crime Trials," in *Albany Law Review* 60 (1997): 801; Lawrence Douglas, "Film as Witness: Screening Nazi Concentration Camps before the Nuremberg Tribunal," *Yale Law Journal* 105 (1995): 449.

6. This change (which is related to the new tie between law and history) also entails and represents a basic reconfiguration of the relationship between "the private" and "the public" in criminal justice. Previously, criminal trials were "private" in the sense that they judged individual perpetrators (and their individual or private criminality) in the name of society and of its public interest. The new kind of trial puts on trial not only the private but also (through the private) the very realm of "the public." In the name of the public and of the collective interest, what is judged as criminal is henceforth both the private and the public.

7. Hannah Arendt precisely disputed the Eichmann trial's project to put history on trial in the name of the conservative jurisprudential necessity (requirement) to judge the private, to focus on the individual (the criminal), to target strictly the literal and not the representative responsibility of the accused. For a

discussion of Arendt's objections to a prosecution of history, see Chapter 3, Section III.

8. Walter Benjamin, "Theses on the Philosophy of History," in *Ill.*, 257. The essay will hereinafter be abbreviated "Theses." The "tradition of the oppressed" is the tradition of their silenced narratives and of their silenced trauma. For an analysis of this proposition through a close reading of Benjamin's "Theses," see here Part Two, the subsections entitled "A Philosophy of History" and "History and Speechlessness."

9. Compare Benjamin, "Goethe's *Elective Affinities*," trans. Corngold, in Walter Benjamin, *Selected Writings, Volume I: 1913–1926,* ed. Marcus Bullock and Michael W. Jennings (Cambridge, Mass.: Harvard University Press, 1996), pp. 340–341. The essay will hereinafter be abbreviated "GEA"; the volume will be abbreviated *SWI.*

10. In the expressionless, "every expression simultaneously comes to a standstill" ("GEA," 340).

11. Twentieth-century critiques of history include (but are not exhausted by) the postcolonial critiques of colonialism as well as more generally the antinationalist, antimilitarist, feminist, gay, antiracist critiques, including the economically oriented Marxist critiques, the critique of capitalism, and, more recently, the critique of globalization.

12. The expressionless, I argue, is a term that implicitly *conceptualizes trauma* and conceptualizes the inherent relation between trauma and literature. If trauma has in Benjamin a *literary* power of expression (the "shattering" power of its muteness), it is because, like literature, trauma in its turn is *an utterance that signifies although and because it has no possibility of statement.*

13. See the discussion of this concept later in this chapter (in Part Two, Section VII, the subsection entitled "Prosopopeia"), and the substantial discussion in Chapter 4, Part Three, Section IX, the subsection entitled "The Caesura of the Trial: The Expressionless."

14. Levinas in turn speaks of "the stripping away of expression as such." Emmanuel Levinas, "Philosophy, Justice, and Love," in Levinas, *Entre Nous: Thinking-of-the-Other,* trans. Michael B. Smith and Barbara Harshav, European Perspectives (New York: Columbia University Press, 1998), p. 145. (This collection of essays will be hereinafter abbreviated *EN.*) Although Levinas does not use the term *expressionless,* he situates in the expressionless face of the other (in the face stripped of expression) "the original locus of the meaningful" (*EN,* 145). For Benjamin, in turn, the expressionless is the original locus of the meaningful. Levinas's thought profoundly resonates with the thought of Benjamin, although it does not overlap with it on all points. The origin of meaning is for Levinas (as for Benjamin) "pure otherness." Pure otherness is signified in Levinas precisely by the image of the *expressionless* face of the other: the other's face is a naked, vulnerable, exposed human face, a face "before all particular expression . . . a nakedness and stripping away of expression as such; that is, extreme exposure, defenselessness, vulnerability itself" (*EN,* 145). This exposure, this vulnerability of the other is (for Benjamin as well as for Levinas) the original locus of the meaningful. I thus include in Benjamin's concept of the expression-

less the resonance of Levinas's concept of the face (and of the always present possibility of the erasure of the face by violence).

15. What follows is a definition of the synthetic, enlarged sense in which I use the Benjaminian concept, in applying it specifically to the context of the law and of the new relationship between law and history.

16. I borrow here the emphasis on the face from Levinas, for whom "the vision of the face" is a correlative of the emergence of ethics and of justice, and who rigorously defines violence (conceptualizes violence) as the effacement of the human face. This violent effacement of the living (human) face is also crucial, I propose, to Benjamin's concept of the expressionless. "What is there in a face?" asks Levinas. "The relation to the Face is both the relation to the absolutely weak—to what is absolutely exposed, what is bare and destitute . . . what is alone and can undergo the supreme isolation we call death and thus, in some way, an incitement to murder . . . and at the same time . . . the Face is also the 'Thou shall not kill' . . . ; it is the fact that I cannot let the other die alone, it is like a calling out to me" (EN, 146). Violence is what precisely effaces the face in obliterating both its vision and its mute call or its human appeal, the "Thou shall not kill." Struck by violence, a face that (through trauma or through its erasure by the other) loses the capacity to express life and to express itself becomes expressionless, expressing only the rigidity of death.

So far as Benjamin's linguistically precise use of the term *expressionless* is concerned (as distinguished from the added resonance of Levinas that I include in my enlarged use of the term), it should be noted, however: (1) that Benjamin deliberately never said that some person is expressionless (which in German would be the traditional use of the term as implying a lack of expression in a face or in a person), but only that specific acts (including speech acts), both moral and artistic, are expressionless in his sense; (2) that the expressionless paradoxically is the only form in which specific acts and phenomena can possibly find expression (rather than being excluded from it and first having to find a way to express themselves). For a detailed philological analysis of the concept of the expressionless in Benjamin, see Winfried Menninghaus: "Walter Benjamin's Variations of Imagelessness," in *Jewish Writers, German Literature: The Uneasy Examples of Nelly Sachs and Walter Benjamin*, ed. Timothy Bahti and Marilyn Sibley Fries (Ann Arbor: University of Michigan Press, 1995), pp. 155–173.

17. "There is no document of civilization," Benjamin writes, "that is not at the same time a document of barbarism." The "cultural treasures," therefore, have an origin that a historical materialist "cannot contemplate without horror" ("Theses," 256).

18. "Not man or men, but the struggling, oppressed class itself is the depository of historical knowledge" ("Theses," 260).

19. The political unconscious consists in the structure of oppressions and repressions specific to a given historical moment. Compare Fredric Jameson, *The Political Unconscious: Narrative as a Socially Symbolic Act* (Ithaca: Cornell University Press, 1982).

20. In this apparently Messianic theme, Benjamin again predicts the new relationship between trials and the dead, a relationship that will predominate some

of the later "trials of the century" and that this book will in its turn study and attempt to think through and concretely meditate about. See Chapters 3 and 4.

21. Mariana Varverde, "Derrida's Justice and Foucault's Freedom: Ethics, History, and Social Movements," *Law and Social Inquiry* 24 (1999): 657. Compare Jacques Derrida, *Specters of Marx: The State of Debt, the Work of Mourning, and the New International,* trans. Peggy Kamuf (New York: Routledge, 1994).

22. Benjamin, "Critique of Violence" (hereinafter abbreviated "Critique"), in Walter Benjamin, *Reflections: Essays, Aphorisms, Autobiographical Writings,* trans. Edmund Jephcott, ed. with an introduction by Peter Demetz (New York: Schocken Books, 1986), p. 277. This collection is hereinafter abbreviated *R (Reflections).*

23. It was to some extent this critique of legal violence, this awareness of the problematic nature of the law and of the limits and flaws of prosecutorial trials that (among other reasons) was at the origin of the contemporary institution (in South Africa and elsewhere) of an alternative mode of dealing with the crimes of history: the Truth and Reconciliation Commissions.

24. For a synthetic summary of this well-known critique of the Nuremberg trials as "victor's justice," compare for instance Gerry Simpson, "Conceptualizing Violence: Present and Future Developments in International Law and Policy on War Crimes and Crimes against Humanity: Didactic and Dissident Histories in War Crime Trials," *Albany Law Review* 60 (1997): 805–806: "In the absence of a uniform and global approach, the trials of war criminals generally occurred only where defeat and criminality coincide. This was undoubtedly the case at Nuremberg and Tokyo. The phrase 'victor's justice' is by now a truism. The victorious allied powers tried their German and Japanese adversaries without considering the possibility of applying these same laws to their own war-time behavior." See also Cover, "Nuremberg and the Creation of a Modern Myth," in "The Folktales of Justice," in *Narrative, Violence and the Law,* pp. 195–201; Lawrence Douglas, "Film as Witness: Screening Nazi Concentration Camps before the Nuremberg Tribunal," *Yale Law Journal* 105 (1995): 449; Ruti Teitel, "The Universal and the Particular and International Criminal Justice: Symposium in Celebration of the Fiftieth Anniversary of the Universal Declaration of Human Rights," *Columbia Human Rights Law Review* 30 (1999): 285.

25. Compare Robert Cover, "Bringing the Messiah" and "Nuremberg and the Creation of a Modern Myth," in "The Folktales of Justice," in *Narrative, Violence and the Law,* pp. 185–187 and p. 201: "Integrity [in judges] . . . is the act of maintaining the vision that it is only that which redeems that is law."

26. The dead can have an afterlife, but they cannot come back to life, and if they do, they do so *as precisely dead.* Benjamin is well aware of this reality, and of the fact that the historical *resuscitation* of the dead *does not entail their resurrection.* "The angel [of history] would like to stay, awaken the dead and make whole what has been smashed," but he cannot make whole what has been broken: his wings are impotently caught in the wind (the storm) of "progress" ("Theses," 257–258).

27. Emmanuel Levinas, "Uniqueness," in *EN,* 196.

28. Hannah Arendt, "Introduction," *Ill.,* 5–18.

29. Compare Franz Kafka, *The Trial,* pp. 213–215.

30. Benjamin, "Kafka," 131. Indeed, as Benjamin notes after Brecht, "Kafka perceived what was to come without perceiving what exists in the present" ("Some Reflections on Kafka" [*Ill.,* 143], hereinafter abbreviated "SRK"). And Benjamin adds: "He perceived it essentially as an *individual* affected by it" (ibid.). Like Kafka's, Benjamin's perception of the future proceeds, I argue, from his position as affected individual, from his insight, that is, into his historical position as a persecuted subject.

31. Kafka, *The Trial,* pp. 227–229, italics mine.

32. Hannah Arendt, *Eichmann in Jerusalem: A Report on the Banality of Evil* (New York: Penguin Books, 1963), pp. 125–126; hereinafter abbreviated *EiJ.* Arendt is commenting on the collaboration of the *Judenrat:* "Wherever Jews lived, there were recognized Jewish leaders, and this leadership, almost without exception, cooperated in one way or another, for one reason or another, with the Nazis" (*EiJ,* 125). But this cooperation between victim and executioner (the essence of the moral calamity triggered by the Nazis) was not specific to Jews, Arendt insists. "David Rousset, a former inmate of Buchenwald, described what we know happened in all concentration camps: 'The triumph of the S.S. demands that the tortured victim allow himself to be led to the noose without protesting, that he renounce and abandon himself to the point of ceasing to affirm his identity. And it is not for nothing. It is not gratuitously, out of sheer sadism, that the S.S. men desire his defeat. They know that the system which succeeds in destroying its victim before he mounts the scaffold . . . is incomparably the best for keeping a whole people in slavery. In submission. Nothing is more terrible than these processions of human beings going like dummies to their deaths' (*Les Jours de notre mort,* 1947)" (Arendt, *EiJ,* 11–12).

33. See Kafka, *The Trial,* p. 227–228 (emphasis mine): "The two of them laid K. down on the ground, propped him against the boulder, and settled his head upon it. But *in spite of the pains they took and all the willingness K. showed, his posture remained contorted* and unnatural-looking." Compare Benjamin, "Kafka," 135 (emphasis mine): "This story takes us right into the milieu of Kafka's world. No one says that *the distortions which it will be the Messiah's mission to set right someday* affect only our space; surely they are *distortions of our time* as well. Kafka must have had this in mind."

34. *EN,* 187.

35. Walter Benjamin, "The Metaphysics of Youth" (hereinafter abbreviated "MY"), in Benjamin, *SWI,* p. 6.

36. "The Task of the Translator," *SWI,* 261.

37. Ibid., 259.

38. Ibid., 257.

39. Hannah Arendt, *On Revolution* (London: Penguin, 1990), p. 11.

40. Ibid., pp. 11–18.

41. Ibid., p. 11.

42. This textual juxtaposition of the theory and the autobiography will be illuminated, in its turn, by Benjamin's work as a literary critic, especially in the early literary essays on Hölderlin, on Dostoevsky, and on Goethe's *Elective Af-*

finities. I will thus borrow metaphors from Benjamin's own literary criticism and will in turn use them as interpretive tools and as evocative stylistic echoes. My methodology will be attentive, therefore, to three distinct levels of the text that the analysis will bring together: the conceptual level of the theory, the narrative level of the autobiography, and the figurative level of the literary criticism.

43. *SWI*, 18–36.

44. Ibid., p. 33.

45. "St.," 83.

46. "Karl Kraus," *R*, 242. Compare "St.," *Ill.*, 88–91. Information and narration are not simply two competing modes of discourse (two functions of language). They are in fact two strategies of living and communicating, two levels of existence within culture. Narration seeks a listener; information, a consumer. Narration is addressed to a community, information is directed toward a market. Insofar as listening is an integral part of narration, while marketing is always part of information, narration is attentive and imaginatively productive (in its concern for the singularity, the unintelligibility of the event), while information is mechanical and reproductive (in its concern for the event's exchangeability, explainability, and reproducibility).

Benjamin was concerned not only with communication but (implicitly, essentially) with education. Educationally, these two modes conflict not only as two separate roles or institutions. They wage a battle *within* every institution and *within* every discipline of knowledge. They are in conflict, in effect, *within* every pedagogy. They struggle (to this day) within every university.

47. "Today people live in rooms that have never been touched by death and . . . when their end approaches they are stowed away in sanatoria or hospitals by their heirs" ("St.," 94).

48. "Death is the sanction of everything the storyteller has to tell. He has borrowed his authority from death" ("St.," 94).

49. Since the storyteller (in Leskov and his tradition) is "a righteous man," a "teacher," and a "sage" ("St.," 108), what now falls to muteness is the very possibility of righteousness. Similarly, literature as teacher of humanity (in the manner of Leskov) has lost its voice. In the collapse of narrative as a generic, literary mode of discourse, literature as ethics—"counsel," education—is thus inherently, historically, and philosophically reduced to silence.

50. Among the theories of history that Benjamin critiques and "deconstructs" are pure theology (religion), pure historicism (positivism), pure liberalism (idealism), and pure Marxism (uncritical historical materialism).

51. Compare Hitler's harangue to his top civilians and military officials in 1939, on the occasion of the invasion of Poland: "Destruction of Poland is in the background. The aim is elimination of living forces, not the arrival at a certain line . . . I shall give a propagandistic cause for starting the war—never mind whether it be plausible or not. The victor shall not be asked later on whether he told the truth or not. In starting and making a war, not the right is what matters but victory." Quoted by Robert Jackson in his introduction to Whitney Harris, *Tyranny on Trial: The Evidence at Nuremberg* (New York: Barnes and Noble, 1954, 1995), p. xxxi.

52. In this conception, Benjamin is the intepreter—the synthesizer—of the diverse legacies of Nietzsche, Marx, and Freud.

53. Walter Benjamin, "Paralipomènes et variantes des *Thèses 'Sur le concept de l'histoire,'*" *Écrits français,* ed. Jean-Maurice Monnoyer (Paris, 1991), p. 352; my translation.

54. The reality of history is grasped (articulated) when the historian *recognizes* a historical *state of emergency* that is, precisely, *not* the one the ruler has declared or that (in Hobbes's tradition, in Carl Schmitt's words) is "decided by the sovereign." Compare Carl Schmitt, *Politische Theologie* (Munich and Leipzig, 1922), a work cited and discussed by Benjamin in *The Origin of German Tragic Drama* (1928; London: NLB, 1977), pp. 65, 74, 239, nn. 14–17.

55. *A Berlin Chronicle* (hereinafter abbreviated *BC*), in *R*, 56–57.

56. "GEA," 355. Redemption seems, therefore, to be linked to the moment of illumination that suddenly and unexpectedly gives us the capacity to *hear the silence*—to *tune into* the unarticulated and to *hear* what is in history deprived of words. Redemption starts by redeeming history from deafness.

57. For a historiography free of complicity, we must disassociate ourselves from our accustomed thinking: "Thinking involves not only the flow of thoughts, but their arrest as well. Where thinking suddenly stops in a configuration pregnant with tensions, it gives that configuration a shock, by which it crystallizes into a monad. A historical materialist approaches a historical subject only where he encounters it as a monad. In this structure he recognizes a sign for a Messianic cessation of happening, or, put differently, *a revolutionary chance* in the fight for the oppressed past" (XVII, *Ill.,* 262, emphasis mine).

58. The original and current German title of the essay is, precisely, "On the Concept of History."

59. Letters, p. 76. Quoted in *SWI,* 499.

60. "The Role of Language in *Trauerspiel* and Tragedy," in *SWI,* p. 60.

61. Compare Momme Brodersen, *Walter Benjamin: A Biography,* trans. Malcolm R. Green and Ingrida Ligers, ed. Martina Dervis (London: Verso, 1996), p. 118. This biography is hereinafter referred to by the abbreviation Brodersen.

62. "Two Poems by Friedrich Hölderlin: 'The Poet's Courage' and 'Timidity,'" in *SWI,* pp. 18–36.

63. Brodersen, 118.

64. Paul de Man, "Autobiography as De-Facement," in *The Rhetoric of Romanticism* (New York: Columbia University Press, 1984), p. 81. This book will hereinafter be referred to by the abbreviation *RR*.

65. "On Language as Such and On the Language of Man," in *SWI,* p. 73. "Even where there is only a rustling of plants, there is always a lament. Because she is mute, nature mourns. Yet the inversion of this proposition leads even further into the essence of nature; the sadness of nature makes her mute" (ibid.).

66. Benjamin, *The Origin of the German Tragic Drama,* p. 106.

67. The incomprehension of the audience then could ironically today stand for the incomprehension of Benjamin's contemporary critics with respect to the

significance of the event (and of its subsequent inscription as a silence) in Benjamin's life and in his work.

68. "The child's inability to express itself continues to have a crippling effect on the speech of Dostoyevsky's characters" (*SWI*, 81). Damaged youth is marked, thus, at once by a condensation of "immortal" life and by a damaged (silent) language.

69. "Experience" (1913).

70. "The greater the share of the shock value in particular impressions . . . , the less do these impressions enter experience [*Erfahrung*]," Benjamin will later write in his essay "On Some Motifs in Baudelaire" (*Ill.*, 163). As Freud explained in *Beyond the Pleasure Principle*, memory fragments "are often the most enduring when the incident which left them behind was one that never entered consciousness" (ibid., 160). "Put in Proustian terms this means that only *what has not been experienced explicitly and consciously*, what has not happened to the subject as an experience, can become the object of the *mémoire involontaire*" (ibid., 160–161). "Perhaps the special achievement of shock defense may be seen in its function of assigning to an incident *a precise point in time at the cost of the integrity of its content*" (ibid., 163; my emphasis). The *integrity of content* of the war experience—the integrity of its narration—is thus lost to consciousness and lost to language.

71. There may have been additional reasons for the impossibility of giving the suicidal couple a proper burial: religious reasons (Heinle's girlfriend was Jewish; Jewish communities had their separate communal graveyards); sociological reasons (middle-class families owned large familial burial sites potentially sufficient for the accommodation of their entire family, but the couple obviously did not qualify to be buried as family members by either family). The Selikson family (the wealthier of the two) would have probably accused Heinle of having dragged their daughter to suicide.

72. To overcome, that is, ironically and lengthily, "the precaution of the subject represented by the 'I,' which is entitled not to be sold cheap" (*BC*, 16).

73. Hannah Arendt, *On Revolution*, p. 20.

74. *BC*, 18; my emphasis.

75. "For childhood, having no preconceived opinions, has none about life. It is as dearly attached . . . to the realm of the dead, where it juts into that of the living, as to life itself" (*BC*, 28).

76. In addressing his impossible narration to a child, Benjamin returns to his original (early) concern with pedagogy and with education, a concern that in turn has been struck by silence but that he has never in effect abandoned. "But who would trust a cane wielder who proclaimed the mastery of children by adults to be the purpose of education? *Is not education, above all, the indispensable ordering of the relationship between generations* and therefore mastery . . . of that relationship and not of children?" (*One-Way Street*, *SWI*, 487; emphasis mine).

77. "Experience and Poverty," in *Gesammelte Schriften*, ed. Hermann Schweppenhauser and Rolf Tiedemann (Frankfurt am Main: Suhrkamp, 1977), vol. 2, p. 219.

78. Compare Benjamin, "Theses," IX: "A Klee painting named *Angelus Novus* shows an angel looking as though he is about to move away from something he is fixedly contemplating. His eyes are staring, his mouth is open, his wings are spread. This is how one pictures the angel of history. His face is turned toward the past. Where we perceive a chain of events he sees one single catastrophe which keeps piling wreckage upon wreckage and hurls it in front of his feet. The angel would like to stay, awaken the dead and make whole what has been smashed. But a storm is blowing from Paradise; it has got caught in his wings with such violence that the angel can no longer close them. This storm irresistibly propels him into the future to which his back is turned, while the pile of debris before him grows skyward. This storm is what we call progress" (257–258).

79. Or the unfinished text on Baudelaire and the Arcades.

80. "On the Topic of Individual Disciplines and Philosophy," in *SWI*, p. 404.

81. Peter Demetz, "Introduction," in Walter Benjamin, *Reflections*, p. xv.

82. The monument (sponsored by the German government) was planned and built by the Arbeitskreis selbstandiger Kulturinstitute (ASKI).

83. Hannah Arendt, "Introduction," in Walter Benjamin, *Illuminations:* "There is another . . . element . . . which is involved in the life of those 'who have won victory in death.' It is *the element of bad luck,* and this factor, very prominent in Benjamin's life, cannot be ignored here because he himself . . . was so extraordinarily aware of it. In his writing and also in conversation he used to speak about 'the little hunchback,' . . . a German fairy-tale figure . . . out of . . . German folk poetry. The hunchback was an early acquaintance of Benjamin . . . His mother . . . used to say, 'Mr Bungle sends his regards' whenever one of the countless little catastrophes of childhood had taken place. The mother referred to 'the little hunchback,' who caused the objects to play their mischievous tricks upon children . . . *(With a precision suggesting a sleepwalker [Benjamin's] clumsiness invariably guided him to the very center of misfortune . . .)* . . . Wherever one looks in Benjamin's life, one will find the little hunchback . . .

"On September 26, 1940, Walter Benjamin, who was about to emigrate to America, took his life at the Franco-Spanish border . . . *But the immediate occasion for Benjamin's suicide was an uncommon stroke of bad luck*" (pp. 5–18; emphasis mine).

84. Benjamin, *The Origin of German Tragic Drama,* p. 108.

85. Benjamin in this way reenacts, beyond the moral speechlessness of Heinle's story, a more effective transformation of the corpse into a message. If "storytelling is always the art of repeating stories" ("St.," 91), it goes without saying that *not every repetition is an art.* In "the age of mechanical reproduction," not every reiteration is endowed with what "The Storyteller" calls "the gift of retelling" (ibid.), a gift that is specifically, says Benjamin, *a listener's gift*—an insight born out of the capacity for silent listening. Benjamin's "gift of retelling" is both autobiographical and theoretical: it is at once a literary gift and a historical force of perception; it is compellingly subjective (it pays the ultimate subjective price) and compellingly objective (it speaks with the intentionless authority of history). There are various ways of "repeating stories"—with or without historical surprises, with or without new meaning, with or without historical

authority. Benjamin's historical retelling of the story of the suicide is authoritative, because it makes *transmissible* what it repeats, because it rescues the past suicide from its meaninglessness and from its original forgettability, in endowing it with a transmissible historical intelligibility.

86. Gershom Scholem, *Walter Benjamin: The Story of a Friendship*, trans. Harry Zohn (New York: Schocken Books, 1988), p. 188; hereinafter referred to by the abbreviation Scholem.

2. Forms of Judicial Blindness

1. For recent overviews and general discussions of the field of law and literature, see (in chronological order): Brook Thomas, "Reflections on the Law and Literature Revival," *Critical Inquiry* 17 (1991): 510–537; C. R. B. Dunlop, "Literature Studies in Law Schools," *Cardozo Studies in Law and Literature* 3 (1991): 63–110; Richard H. Weisberg, *Poethics: And Other Strategies of Law and Literature* (New York: Columbia University Press, 1992); John Fischer, "Reading Literature / Reading Law: Is There a Literary Jurisprudence?" *Texas Law Review* 72 (1993): 135–160; Richard H. Weisberg, "Three Lessons from Law and Literature," *Loyola of Los Angeles Law Review* 27 (1993): 285–303; Gary Minda, *Postmodern Legal Movements: Law and Jurisprudence at Century's End* (New York: New York University Press, 1995), pp. 149–166; Ian Ward, *Law and Literature: Possibilities and Perspectives* (New York: Cambridge University Press, 1995); *Law and Literature: Perspectives*, ed. Bruce Rockwood (New York: Peter Lang, 1996); Theodore Ziolkowski, *The Mirror of Justice: Literary Reflections of Legal Crises* (Princeton: Princeton University Press, 1997).

For problematizations of the field, see: Richard Posner, *Law and Literature: A Misunderstood Relation* (Cambridge, Mass.: Harvard University Press, 1988); Richard Rorty, *Contingency, Irony, and Solidarity* (New York: Cambridge University Press, 1989); Stanley Fish, *Doing What Comes Naturally: Change, Rhetoric, and the Practice of Theory in Literary and Legal Studies* (Durham: Duke University Press, 1989).

For thematic studies and for rhetorical and philosophical interpretations of representations of the law in works of art, see, among others: Robert M. Cover, *Justice Accused: Antislavery and the Judicial Process* (New Haven: Yale University Press, 1975), pp. 1–7; Barbara E. Johnson, "Melville's Fist: The Execution of *Billy Budd*," in *The Critical Difference: Essays in the Contemporary Rhetoric of Reading* (Baltimore: Johns Hopkins University Press, 1980); Richard H. Weisberg, *The Failure of the Word: The Lawyer as Protagonist in Modern Fiction* (New Haven: Yale University Press, 1984); Shoshana Felman, "Crisis of Witnessing: Albert Camus's Postwar Writings," *Cardozo Studies of Law and Literature* 3 (1991): 197–242, reprinted in Shoshana Felman and Dori Laub, *Testimony: Crises of Witnessing in Literature, Psychoanalysis and History* (New York: Routledge, 1992).

For legal "hermeneutics" and for rhetorical interpretations of legal opinions, statutes, and legal texts, see, among others: James Boyd White, *The Legal Imagination: Studies in the Nature of Legal Thought and Expression* (Boston: Little,

Brown, 1973); Sanford Levinson, "Law as Literature," *Texas Law Review* 60 (1982): 373–403; Owen M. Fiss, "Objectivity and Interpretation," *Stanford Law Review* 34 (1982): 739–763; James Boyd White, *Heracles' Bow: Essays on the Rhetoric and Poetics of the Law* (Madison: Wisconsin University Press, 1985); Ronald Dworkin, "How Is Law Like Literature?" in *A Matter of Principle* (Cambridge, Mass.: Harvard University Press, 1985); Jack M. Balkin, "Deconstructive Practices and Legal Theory," *Yale Law Journal* 96 (1987): 743–86; John Leubsdorf, "Deconstructing the Constitution," *Stanford Law Review* 40 (1987): 181–201; *Interpreting Law and Literature: A Hermeneutic Reader*, ed. Sanford Levinson and Steven Mailloux (Evanston: Northwestern University Press, 1988); Robert A. Ferguson, "The Judicial Opinion as Literary Genre," *Yale Journal of Law and Humanities* 2 (1990): 201–219; James Boyd White, *Justice as Translation: An Essay in Cultural and Legal Criticism* (Chicago: University of Chicago Press, 1990); *Deconstruction and the Possibility of Justice*, *Cardozo Law Review* 11 (1990); Richard H. Weisberg, "Legal Rhetoric under Stress: The Example of Vichy," *Cardozo Law Review* 12 (1991): 1371–1415; Barbara E. Johnson, "Double Mourning and the Public Sphere," in *The Wake of Deconstruction* (Oxford: Blackwell, 1994); Judith Butler, *Excitable Speech: A Politics of the Performative* (New York: Routledge, 1997); Barbara E. Johnson, "Anthropomorphism in Lyric and Law," *Yale Journal of Law and the Humanities* 10 (1998): 549–574.

For narratological interpretations of legal storytelling and for general discussions of the relation between law and narrative, see, among others: James R. Elkins, "On the Emergence of Narrative Jurisprudence: the Humanistic Perspective Finds a New Path," *Legal Studies Forum* 9 (1985): 123–156; Derrick Bell, *And We Are Not Saved: The Elusive Quest for Racial Justice* (New York: Basic Books, 1987); Mari Matsuda, "Looking to the Bottom: Critical Legal Studies and Reparations," *Harvard Civil Rights–Civil Liberties Law Review* 22 (1987): 323–399; James R. Elkins, "The Quest for Meaning: Narrative Accounts of Legal Education," *Journal of Legal Education* 38 (1988): 577–598; Richard Delgado, "Storytelling for Oppositionists and Others: A Plea for Narrative," *Michigan Law Review* 87 (1989): 2411–2441; Kathryn Abrams, "Hearing the Call of Stories," *California Law Review* 79 (1991): 971–1052; *Narrative and the Legal Discourse: A Reader in Storytelling and the Law*, ed. David Ray Papke (Liverpool: Deborah Charles, 1991); Patricia Williams, *The Alchemy of Race and Rights: Diary of a Law Professor* (Cambridge, Mass.: Harvard University Press, 1991); Robin West, *Narrative, Authority, and Law* (Ann Arbor: University of Michigan Press, 1993); Daniel A. Farber and Suzanna Sherry, "Telling Stories Out of School: An Essay on Legal Narratives," *Stanford Law Review* 45 (1993): 807–855; Richard Sherwin, "Law Frames: Historical Truth and Narrative Necessity in a Criminal Case," *Stanford Law Review* 47 (1994): 39–83; *Narrative, Violence, and the Law: The Essays of Robert Cover*, ed. Martha Minow, Michael Ryan, and Austin Sarat (Ann Arbor: University of Michigan Press, 1995); *Critical Race Theory: The Cutting Edge*, ed. Richard Delgado (Philadelphia: Temple University Press, 1995); *Critical Race Theory: The Key Writings That Formed the Movement*, ed. Kimberlé Crenshaw et al. (New York: New Press, 1995); *Law's*

Stories: Narrative and Rhetoric in the Law, ed. Peter Brooks and Paul Gewirtz (New Haven: Yale University Press, 1996); Austin Sarat, "Narrative Strategy and Death Penalty Advocacy," *Harvard Civil Rights–Civil Liberties Law Review* 31 (1996): 353–381.

For the relation between law and poetry, see: Barbara E. Johnson, "Apostrophe, Animation and Abortion," in *A World of Difference* (Baltimore: Johns Hopkins University Press, 1987); Thomas C. Grey, *The Wallace Stevens Case: Law and the Practice of Poetry* (Cambridge, Mass.: Harvard University Press, 1991); and Barbara Johnson, "Anthropomorphism in Lyric and Law," in *Yale Journal of Law and the Humanities* 10 (1998): 549–574.

2. I will use "law in literature" to analyze not only law as literature but also literature as jurisprudence. The analysis that follows does not merely "cross the boundaries" between the disciplines; it shifts those boundaries, it challenges both disciplines' epistemological and legal definition. I do not assume that authority (truth, knowledge, facts, reality) is a prerogative of law. I do not assume that literature, however disempowered, does not act in the real world and does not have power.

3. Indicted by the State of California for the June 12, 1994, stabbing and slashing murders of his ex-wife, Nicole Brown-Simpson, and her companion Ronald Goldman, O. J. Simpson was unanimously acquitted on October 1995. The sensational, fully televised criminal case was dubbed "trial of the century" because it held television viewers (in America and across the Atlantic) spellbound on a daily basis for over a year as Simpson's "dream team" of high-priced lawyers picked apart what prosecutors thought was "a mountain of evidence." The families of the two victims, thinking that Simpson had "gotten away with murder," brought a wrongful death civil suit against him that ended in January 1997 with a jury finding the former football star and actor responsible for the deaths and liable for $33.5 million in damages to the victims' families. In May 1997, lawyers for Simpson formally filed a notice of appeal for a new trial, hoping to overturn the civil jury's verdict. (This was after Simpson's lawyers had lost the first legal round when the judge in the civil trial refused to set aside the jury decision and reduce the $33.5 million damage award.) In January 2001 a California appeals court upheld the civil jury's finding that Simpson was liable for the two deaths. The three-judge panel on California's Second Court of Appeals said, "In effect, the jury found that Simpson committed two deliberate, vicious murders. This is the most reprehensible conduct that society condemns and is ordinarily punished under California criminal law by a sentence of death or life imprisonment without the possibility of parole." In their unanimous sixty-seven-page opinion, the appeals court judges said, "The harm suffered by the victims was the maximum possible; they were intentionally killed." They rejected Simpson's argument that the damages were excessive. Simpson, who had won against the Brown family the legal battle over custody of his two children with Nicole, had moved from California to Florida, where he lives with his two children.

4. The unanimous verdict of the criminal trial ("not guilty," October 1995) did not close the case, because it gave rise to the civil trial. But the following conclusion of the civil trial by a unanimous verdict of liability (January 1997) did

not, in its turn, bring an ending to the case: the defense immediately filed notice of appeal for a new trial. More profoundly, the civil verdict did not close the case because it could not cancel out its contradiction by the criminal acquittal, whose historical impact cannot be undone and whose outcome is, thus, irreversible, not merely legally but epistemologically. Society now knows it cannot produce, on Simpson's guilt, an *undivided* justice (a legal truth not subject to a systematic— and systemic—legal crisis).

5. Such an analytical tool is not limited to murder cases or to criminal law. More broadly, it constructs a psychoanalytical (and a psychoanalytically informed literary/philosophical) approach to jurisprudence.

6. The O. J. Simpson trial is not the only trial that has been called the trial of the century. "A number of high-profile 20th-century courtroom events . . . have each in turn been dubbed the trial of the century," writes Marjorie B. Garber (who analyzes the Scopes trial and the Rosenberg trial) in *Symptoms of Culture* (New York: Routledge, 1998), p. 107. Gerald F. Uelman caustically notes that his research "has uncovered at least thirty-two trials since 1900 that have been called 'the trial of the century'" (*Lessons from the Trial: The People v. O. J. Simpson* [Kansas City: Andrews and McMeel, 1996], p. 204. I would suggest, nonetheless, that the redundancy of the title does not undermine the accuracy of its expressive historical significance. In referring to a trial as the trial of the century, the media names a visceral public perception that the trial is a mirror of something larger than itself, and that the courtroom drama marks the ways in which a larger cultural crisis has come to a head. This perception is fundamentally correct. The O. J. Simpson criminal trial is nevertheless unique in that, as Erwin Chemerinsky has noted, "it received more media attention than any other legal proceeding in American or world history" (Erwin Chemerinsky, "Lawyers Have Free Speech Rights, Too: Why Gag Orders on Trial Participants Are Almost Always Unconstitutional," *Loyola of Los Angeles Entertainment Law Journal* 17 [1997]: 311–331.) Other trials that have been called "the trial of the century" include the 1921 trial of Italian-born anarchists Nicola Sacco and Bartolomeo Vanzetti; the 1925 Scopes ("Monkey") trial; the 1945–1946 Nuremberg War Crimes Tribunal; and the 1951 treason (espionage) trial of Julius and Ethel Rosenberg. It is interesting to note that, in addition to major political and international crimes, several of these notorious trials of the (twentieth) century deal with private atrocities and, in particular, with the murder and abuse of women and children: the 1924 trial of Nathan Leopold and Richard Loeb for the murder of a fourteen-year-old boy; the 1932 trial of Bruno Richard Hauptmann for the kidnapping and killing of Charles Lindbergh's baby; and the 1954 trial of Sam Sheppard, a prominent physician, for the beating to death of his wife, Marilyn (thirty-one years old and four months pregnant). The O. J. Simpson criminal case is the last "trial of the century." In 1906, the first trial of the century evokes a similar triangular criminal scene, in which Harry K. Thaw, the madly jealous (millionaire) husband of Evelyn Nesbit, a chorus girl, is prosecuted for the murder of his wife's lover, the famous architect Stanford White (killed while dining atop Madison Square Garden, which White designed).

It is interesting to note that, even in a symposium on international law and its legal "conceptualization" of contemporary ("crimes against humanity") violence, Michael Scharf (in a discussion of the Tadic case) associates quite naturally (in passing) to the O. J. Simpson case, which he mentions in the same category with "other renowned trials" (to differentiate them from the Tadic trial): "the treason trial of Ethel and Julius Rosenberg, the Chicago Seven trial, the Watergate trials, the Rodney King case and the O. J. Simpson trial." (Michael P. Scharf, "The Prosecutor v. Dusko Tadic: An Appraisal of the First International War Crimes Trial since Nuremberg (Symposium: Conceptualizing Violence: Present and Future Developments in International Law: Panel II: Adjudicating Violence: Problems Confronting International Law and Policy on War Crimes and Crimes against Humanity)," *Albany Law Review* 60 (1997): 861–882, at 863.)

7. Lance Morrow, "A Trial for Our Times," *Time,* October 9, 1995, p. 28.

8. David Shribman, "Sad, But True: Titillating Case Defines Our Times," *Boston Globe,* October 8, 1995, p. A32.

9. Not to speak of a presiding judge who is neither black nor white. See also: Cynthia Kwei Yung Lee, "Beyond Black and White: Racializing Asian Americans in a Society Obsessed with O. J.," *Hastings Women's Law Journal* 6 (1995): 167–207.

10. Stanley Crouch, "The Agonizing Whine Down," *Los Angeles Times,* October 8, 1995, p. M1.

11. Trauma theory, I argue, can become a powerful tool for the analysis of law, in much the same way that it has become a powerful tool for the analysis of literature. See Introduction, notes 1, 2, and 3. For examples of the application of trauma theory to literary analysis, see the remarkable philosophical and literary studies in Cathy Caruth, *Unclaimed Experience: Trauma, Narrative, and History* (Baltimore: Johns Hopkins University Press, 1996). See also: Geoffrey H. Hartman, "On Traumatic Knowledge and Literary Studies," *New Literary History,* Summer 26 (1995): 537; Maurice Blanchot, *The Writing of the Disaster,* trans. Ann Smock (Lincoln: University of Nebraska Press, 1986); essays by Bataille, Bloom, Felman, Lanzmann, Newmark, in *Trauma: Explorations in Memory,* ed. Cathy Caruth (Baltimore: Johns Hopkins University Press, 1995); Jacques Derrida, "Passages: From Traumatisms to Promise," interview with Elisabeth Weber, in Elisabeth Weber, *Points . . . Interviews, 1974–1994* (Stanford: Stanford University Press, 1995); Jean-François Lyotard, "Critical Reflections," in *Artforum* 29 (1991): 92; Jean-François Lyotard, "Ticket to a New Decor (Millenium)," *Harper's Magazine* 276 (1988): 26; Michael Holquist, "A New Tower of Babel: Recent Trends Linking Comparative Literature Departments, Foreign Language Departments, and Area Studies Programs," in *ADFL* 27 (1995): 6–12; Thomas Keenan, *Fables of Responsibility: Aberrations and Predicaments in Ethics and Politics* (Stanford: Stanford University Press, 1997); Thomas Pepper, *Singularities: Extremes of Theory in the Twentieth Century* (Cambridge: Cambridge University Press, 1997); *Holocaust Remembrance: The Shapes of Memory,* ed. Geoffrey H. Hartman (Oxford: Blackwell, 1994); Elaine Scarry, *The Body in Pain: The Making and Unmaking of the World* (New York: Oxford University Press, 1985); Jacqueline Rose, *States of Fantasy* (Oxford: Clarendon

Press, 1995); Laura E. Tanner, *Intimate Violence: Reading Rape and Torture in Twentieth-Century Literature* (Bloomington: Indiana University Press, 1994); Jacqueline Rose, *Why War? Psychoanalysis, Politics, and the Return to Melanie Klein* (Oxford: Blackwell, 1993); Shoshana Felman and Dori Laub, *Testimony: Crises of Witnessing in Literature, Psychoanalysis and History* (New York: Routledge, 1992); Ernest van Alphen, *Caught by History: Holocaust Effects in Contemporary Art, Literature and Theory* (Stanford: Stanford University Press, 1997); Dori Laub and Daniel Podel, "Art and Trauma," *International Journal of Psychoanalysis* 67 (1995): 991–1005.

Related works implicating trauma in philosophy and in the conjunction of philosophy, psychoanalysis, and literary theory include (among others): Emmanuel Levinas, *Ethique et infini* (Paris: Fayard, 1982); Emmanuel Levinas, *Le Temps et l'autre* (Paris: Quadrige/PUF, 1994); Emmanuel Levinas, "As If Consenting to Horror," *Critical Inquiry* 15 (1989): 485; Emmanuel Levinas, "The Face of a Stranger," *UNESCO Courier* (July–August 1992): 66; Michel de Certeau, *Heterologies,* trans. Brian Massumi (Minneapolis: University of Minnesota Press, 1986); Michel de Certeau, *The Writing of History,* trans. Tom Conley (New York: Columbia University Press, 1988); Emmanuel Levinas, "Reflections on the Philosophy of Hitlerism," *Critical Inquiry* 17 (1990): 62; Emmanuel Levinas, *Totality and Infinity: An Essay on Exteriority,* trans. Alphonso Lingis (Pittsburgh: Duquesne University Press, 1969); Jacques Derrida, *Adieu: À Emmanuel Levinas* (Paris: Galilée, 1997); Jacques Derrida, *Résistances: De la psychanalyse* (Paris: Galilée, 1996); Jacques Derrida, *Passions* (Paris: Galilée, 1993); Jacques Derrida, *Limited Inc.,* trans. Samuel Weber (Evanston: Northwestern University Press, 1988); Jacques Derrida, *Mémoires: For Paul de Man* (New York: Columbia University Press, 1986); Jacques Derrida, *Writing and Difference,* trans. Alan Bass (Chicago: University of Chicago Press, 1978); Vladimir Jankélévitch, *L'Imprescriptible* (Paris: Seuil, 1986); Jean-François Lyotard, "A Postmodern Fable," *Yale Journal of Criticism* 6 (1993): 237; Jean-François Lyotard, *The Differend: Phrases in Dispute,* trans. Georges Van Den Abbeele (Minneapolis: University of Minnesota Press, 1988); Jean-François Lyotard, *Heidegger and "the Jews,"* trans. Andreas Michel and Mark Roberts (Minneapolis: University of Minnesota Press, 1990); Jean-François Lyotard, *La Condition postmoderne* (Paris: Minuit, 1979); Jean-François Lyotard, *Political Writings,* trans. Bill Readings and Kevin Paul Geiman (Minneapolis: University of Minnesota Press, 1993); Pierre Vidal-Naquet, *Les Assassins de la mémoire* (Paris: La Découverte, 1987); Gillian Rose, *Mourning Becomes the Law* (Cambridge: Cambridge University Press, 1996); Barbara Johnson, *A World of Difference* (Baltimore: Johns Hopkins University Press, 1987); Barbara Johnson, *The Critical Difference* (Baltimore: Johns Hopkins University Press, 1980); Barbara Johnson, *Défigurations: Du langage poétique* (Paris: Flammarion, 1979); Michael Levine, *Writing through Repression: Literature, Censorship, Psychoanalysis* (Baltimore: Johns Hopkins University Press, 1994); Paul de Man, *Allegories of Reading* (New Haven: Yale University Press, 1979); Paul de Man, *The Rhetoric of Romanticism* (New York: Columbia University Press, 1984); Paul de Man, *Blindness and Insight* (Minneapolis: University of Minnesota Press, 1983); Paul de

Man, *The Resistance to Theory* (Minneapolis: University of Minnesota Press, 1986); *Critical Encounters: Reference and Responsibility in Deconstructive Writing*, ed. Cathy Caruth and Deborah Esch (New Brunswick: Rutgers University Press, 1995); Slavoj i ec, *For They Know Not What They Do* (New York: Verso, 1991); Ned Lukacher, *Primal Scenes: Literature, Philosophy, Psychoanalysis* (Ithaca: Cornell University Press, 1986); Cathy Caruth, *Empirical Truths and Critical Fictions* (Baltimore: Johns Hopkins University Press, 1991); Christopher Miller, *Blank Darkness* (Chicago: Chicago University Press, 1985); James Baldwin, *The Evidence of Things Not Seen* (New York: Holt, Rinehart and Winston, 1985); Anna Deavere Smith, *Fires in the Mirror: Crown Hights, Brooklyn, and Other Identities* (New York: Anchor Books, 1993); Anna Deavere Smith, *Twilight: Los Angeles, 1992* (New York: Anchor Books, 1994).

12. For writers who struggle against this fragmentation of our legal fields of vision and who work to counteract the shadows of invisibility and judicial blindness cast by the race trauma and the gender trauma on each other, see, among others: Angela P. Harris, "Race and Essentialism in Feminist Legal Theory," *Stanford Law Review* 42 (1990): 581–616; Kimberlé Crenshaw, "Mapping the Margins: Intersectionality, Identity Politics and Violence against Women of Color," *Stanford Law Review* 93 (1991): 1241–1299. See also: Cheryl I. Harris, "Myths of Race and Gender in the Trials of O. J. Simpson and Susan Smith: Spectacles of Our Times," *Washburn Law Journal* 35 (1996): 225–253. (Harris examines how the O. J. Simpson and the Susan Smith trials reinscribed prevailing ideologies of race and gender.)

13. Sigmund Freud, *Moses and Monotheism*, trans. Katherine Jones (New York: Vintage Books, 1967; orig. pub. 1939).

14. Compare, for instance, the way in which the criminal trial of Emile Zola in France (in 1898, following the publication of his pamphlet *J'accuse*—criminal proceedings instituted as the French government's response to this pamphlet's printed trial of the army and the state) reopened the closed case of the Dreyfus affair (reopened, that is, the first trial and conviction of Dreyfus, 1894, and the second trial and acquittal of Esterhazy, 1898, for an additional hearing, and for a redeliberation and a reexamination of the evidence), and eventually enabled a rejudgment and a rehabilitation of Dreyfus (1906). In a similar way, I would view the Eichmann trial in Israel (1961) not just as a simple repetition or continuation of the international Nuremberg trials (1945–1946) but more specifically as a traumatic reenactment of the (legal trauma of) the Kastner trial in Israel (1956). (For an intellectual history of the Dreyfus affair, see Jean-Denis Bredin, *The Affair: The Case of Alfred Dreyfus*, trans. Jeffrey Mehlman [New York: G. Braziller, 1986]. For an intellectual history of the Eichmann and Kastner cases, see Pnina Lahav, *Judgment in Jerusalem: Chief Justice Simon Agranat and the Zionist Century* [Berkeley: University of California Press, 1997], 121–162).

In these series of historic repetitions (or of historical dualities), my point is to underscore and to explore something that is legally specific, or that is specific to the legal structure. Because the social function of the legal institutions is to close disputes and not to open them, the legal system cannot, in principle, accept the reopening of a case (as distinguished from the reconsideration of a precedent) except as a scandal and a shock. A case therefore requires another trial to repeat itself in order either to reverse its verdict or to change the understanding or the reading of its evidence. Judicial re-vision must take place through another trial. I believe that such an analytical perspective on historical dualities and on traumatic legal repetition can be illuminating for an understanding of some critical, strategic moments in the history of trials.

15. The relationship between law and politics has been discussed in a variety of contexts. Throughout the early decades of this century, for example, legal realists radically challenged the very distinction between politics and law. The legal realists' attack on the autonomy (and pseudo-neutrality) of law consequently lay the foundations for many contemporary movements, including the law and society movement, law and economics, critical legal studies, legal feminism, and critical race theory. Jaspers's counterchallenge, his European skepticism and his philosophical question is, however, not about the political (nonautonomous) nature of the law but about the capacity of the law (of legal concepts) to accurately articulate (exhaust, truly define) the political.

16. Karl Jaspers, letter to Hannah Arendt, December 16, 1960, in Hannah Arendt and Karl Jaspers, *Correspondence, 1926–1969,* ed. Lotte Kohler and Hans Saner, trans. Robert and Rita Kimber (New York: Harcourt Brace Jovanovich, 1992), p. 413; this volume is hereinafter abbreviated *AJ Corr.*

17. Arendt to Jaspers, December 23, 1960, *AJ Corr.,* 417.

18. Would this coincidence of cases mean, then, that Tolstoy is *our contemporary* (implicitly *ahead of his own time*)? Or could it rather mean that we ourselves, in some major respects, are still quite retrograde, that we *have not yet truly come out of the nineteenth century?*

19. Quoted in Henri Troyat, *Tolstoy,* trans. Nancy Amphoux (New York: Penguin Literary Biographies, 1987; orig. pub. Paris, 1965), p. 660.

20. Quoted in David Magarshack, "Afterword," in Leo Tolstoy, *The Death of Ivan Ilych and Other Stories* (New York: New American Library, 1960), p. 301.

21. Troyat, *Tolstoy,* p. 664.

22. Quoted in David Mcduff, "Translator's Introduction," in Leo Tolstoy, *The Kreutzer Sonata and Other Stories* (New York: Penguin Classics, 1985), p. 16.

23. For interpretations of Tolstoy's text see, among others: Robert Jackson, "In the Darkness of the Night: Tolstoy's *Kreutzer Sonata* and Dostoevsky's *Notes from the Underground,*" in *Dialogues with Dostoevsky: The Overwhelming Questions* (Stanford, Calif.: Stanford University Press, 1993), pp. 208–227; Dorothy Green, "*The Kreutzer Sonata:* Tolstoy and Beethoven," in *Tolstoy's Short Fiction,* ed. Michael R. Katz (New York: W. W. Norton, 1991); Stephen Baehr, "Art and *The Kreutzer Sonata:* A Tolstoyan Approach," ibid., pp. 448–455; all these readings are mainstream, "orthodox" readings of Tolstoy. For a heretic's reading, see the provocatively insightful chapter on Tolstoy in Andrea Dworkin, *Intercourse* (New York: Free Press, 1987), pp. 3–20.

24. It is the universalizing, threateningly generalizing nature of this proposition, I would argue (and not the public's simple prurience into Tolstoy's pri-

vate life and into what might be, presumably, his own unique confession) that accounts for the scandal, for the heat and for the controversy caused by *The Kreutzer Sonata* (by the daring literary treatment of the legal case). It is, in other words, not the singularity or the exceptional nature of the case of the murder of the wife but, on the contrary, its general and unexceptional validity that Tolstoy precisely emphasizes in *his* trial of the century: the general and unexceptional (though generally invisible) relation between marriage and abuse (marriage and violence) that the case merely reveals in bringing it to its concretely visible extremes.

This unsettling emphasis is central to my reading and is in any case constitutive of my own understanding of the story; it accounts for the scandalous boldness of the text and in particular for its provocative and paradoxical "didacticism," i.e., its *collective* lesson.

25. Leo Tolstoy, *The Kreutzer Sonata,* in *The Kreutzer Sonata and Other Stories,* trans. with an introduction by David Mcduff (New York: Penguin Classics, 1985). Unless otherwise indicated, page numbers in parenthesis refer to this edition. In all cited texts, emphasis is mine unless otherwise indicated.

26. On sexual addiction as a clinical symptom of trauma defined by "a life of self-destruction," see Patrick Carnes, *Don't Call It Love: Recovery from Sexual Addiction* (New York: Bentham Books, 1991).

27. Compare Simpson's statement to an interviewer: "Let's say I committed this crime . . . ; even if I did do this, it would have to have been because I loved her very much." Celia Farber, "Whistling in the Dark" (interview with O. J. Simpson), *Esquire* (February 1998): 120.

28. This last paragraph is rendered not in Penguin's English version, but in Henri Troyat's translation; see Troyat, *Tolstoy,* p. 667.

29. John Gregory Dunne, "The Simpsons," *New York Review of Books,* September 22, 1994, p. 36.

30. "If jealousy hadn't been the pretext, some other one would have been found" (81).

31. Justice, as is well known, is customarily represented as a blindfolded goddess (see Raphael's fresco *Justice*). In this concrete image, the blindness stands of course for impartiality. The metaphor of the blindness of justice has been underscored by the vocabulary of legal liberalism: an impartial constitution is often presumed to be color-blind as well as gender-blind.

32. Seeing as a metaphor of judgment has a rather concrete history in the jury box. For years, federal and state courts upheld juror qualification statutes that precluded "individuals with immutable characteristics such as blindness, deafness, and paralysis" from jury service. In 1993 the Supreme Court of the District of Columbia declared categorical exclusions a violation of the Rehabilitation Act, the Americans with Disabilities Act, and the Civil Rights Act of 1871 (*Galloway v. Superior Court of the District of Columbia,* 816 F. Supp. 12 [D.D.C. 1993]). See Andrew Weis, "Peremptory Challenges: The Last Barrier to Jury Service for People with Disabilities," *Willamette Law Review* 33 (1997): 1–66, at 18. The court allowed, however, for exclusion in particular cases, i.e., cases "*with a great deal of visual and physical evidence* or if the right to a fair trial is

threatened" (emphasis mine). See, similarly, Robert J. Brookes, "Symposium: Municipal Liability: Recent ADA and Rehabilitation Act Cases," *Syracuse Law Review* 44 (1993): 861–873, at 871. Still, nothing protects an abused victim from the possibility of *cultural* blindness (or from the unwritten prescription not to see).

33. Compare Charles Nesson's argument that evidentiary rules and the rules governing the conduct of judges and juries help the legal system to project substantive legal rules and behavioral messages by facilitating public acceptance of the verdicts as statements about events (rather than about evidence presented at trial): Charles Nesson, "The Evidence or the Event? On Judicial Proof and the Acceptability of Verdicts," *Harvard Law Review* 98 (1985): 1357–1392.

34. Compare Martha Minow, "Speaking and Writing against Hate," in *Deconstruction and the Possibility of Justice, Cardozo Law Review* 11 (1990): 1393; and Judith Butler, "Implicit Censorship and Discursive Agency," in *Excitable Speech,* pp. 127–163.

35. I take it as a pure coincidence that Louis Althusser, the famous, brilliant French philosopher who combined Marxism with Lacanian psychoanalysis and became an authority on ideology, ethics, and political philosophy, also ended up murdering his wife, in one of the most notorious French crimes of the century (1980). Declared "unfit to plead," Althusser was spared a trial. However, he later felt that "the absence of a trial" deprived him of the possibility of a public debate he would have desired. This is why he later wrote a confession, an "autobiography" that was published after his death under the title *The Future Lasts Forever.* "The fact is I strangled my wife, who meant everything to me, during an intense and unforseeable state of mental confusion, in November 1980," wrote Althusser when he was released from his first period of confinement following the murder. "In the case of someone held responsible, a straightforward procedure is set in motion . . . The person is brought before a court and there is a debate in public. On the other hand, if someone is held not to be responsible in *juridico-legal terms,* he is denied the whole procedure of a public, confrontational court appearance . . . If the murderer is acquitted after a public trial, he can return home with his head held high (in principle at least, since the public may be indignant at his acquittal and make its feelings known . . .) . . . I want to free myself from the murder and above all from the dubious effects of having been declared unfit to plead, which I could not challenge in law . . . But I can also help others to reflect upon a concrete case. No one before me has made such a critical confession . . . I lived through an experience of the most acute and horrifying nature which I cannot fully comprehend, since it raises a number of legal, penal, medical, analytical, institutional, and intimately ideological and social questions . . . When I speak of that trying experience, I refer not just to the period of confinement but to my life since then and what I clearly see I shall be condemned to for the rest of my days, if I do not intervene *personally* and *publicly* to offer my own testimony." Louis Althusser, *The Future Lasts Forever: A Memoir,* ed. Olivier Corpet and Yann Moulier Bountang, trans. Richard Veasey (New York: New Press, 1992), pp. 3, 18–29; Althusser's italics.

36. Louis Althusser, *Lire le Capital* (Paris: F. Maspero, 1968), vol. 1, pp. 26–

28 (author's italics; my translation). Compare Judith Butler's analysis of the way in which the Simi Valley jurors failed to see the beating of Rodney King: "This is not a simple seeing, an act of direct perception, but the racial production of the visible, the workings of racial constraints on what it means to 'see.'" Judith Butler, "Endangered/Endangering: Schematic Racism and White Paranoia," in *Reading Rodney King / Reading Urban Uprising,* ed. Robert Gooding-Williams (New York: Routledge, 1993), pp. 15–22.

37. See *Trauma: Explorations in Memory,* ed. Caruth. See also Caruth, *Unclaimed Experience.*

38. Andrea Dworkin, writing in the *Los Angeles Times,* cites another stupefying case concerning the recalcitrant invisibility of beating (a case, however, whose political invisibility seems to relate to gender rather than to race): "On the same day the police who beat Rodney King were acquitted in Simi Valley, a white husband who had raped, beaten and tortured his wife, also white, was acquitted of marital rape in South Carolina. He had kept her tied to a bed for hours, her mouth gagged with adhesive tape. He videotaped a half-hour of her ordeal, during which he cut her breasts with a knife. The jury, which saw the videotape, had eight women on it. Asked why they acquitted, they said, he needed help. *They looked right through the victim.*" (Andrea Dworkin, "Trying to Flee," *Los Angeles Times,* October 8, 1995, p. M6; italics mine.)

39. "The English law of legalized wife beating was transplanted to America through Blackstone's reference to the doctrine of moderate chastisement. 'For, as [the husband] is to answer for her misbehaviour, the law thought it reasonable to intrust him with this power of restraining her, by domestic chastisement, in the same moderation that a man is allowed to correct his apprentices or children'" (1 William Blackstone, *Commentaries on the Laws of England* 444 [University of Chicago Press, 1979; orig. pub. 1850], quoted in Marina Angel, "Susan Glaspell's Trifles and a Jury of Her Peers: Woman Abuse in a Literary and Legal Context," *Buffalo Law Review* 45 (1997): 779–844, at 792).

"During the nineteenth century, an era of feminist agitation for reform of marriage law," writes Reva Siegel, "authorities in England and the United States declared that a husband no longer had the right to chastise his wife. Yet, for a century after courts repudiated the right of chastisement, the American legal system continued to treat wife beating differently from other cases of assault and battery. While authorities denied that a husband had the right to beat his wife, they intervened only intermittently in cases of marital violence: men who assaulted their wives were often granted formal and informal immunities from prosecution, in order to protect the privacy of the family and to promote 'domestic harmony.'" (Reva B. Siegel, "'The Rule of Love': Wife Beating as Prerogative and Privacy," *Yale Law Journal* 105 (1996): 2117–2207). It was the feminist movement of the 1970s that began the process of fighting against such social malpractices by promoting both conceptual and legal changes of perception (see, for example, Catharine A. MacKinnon, *Toward a Feminist Theory of the State* [Cambridge, Mass.: Harvard University Press, 1989]). But as Senator Joseph Biden, author of the Violence against Women Act, acknowledges in an address to the Senate, "this common law principle has left *a legacy of legal blind-*

ness toward violence against women" (Joseph R. Biden, "Domestic Violence a Crime, Not a Quarrel," *Trial*, June 1993, p. 56; emphasis mine).

See also Linda Gordon, *Heroes of Their Own Lives: The Politics and History of Family Violence, Boston 1880–1960* (New York: Viking, 1988); Bernadette Dunn Sewell, "History of Abuse: Societal, Judicial, and Legislative Responses to the Problem of Wife Beating," *Suffolk University Law Review* 23 (1989): 983–1017; *The Public Nature of Private Violence: The Discovery of Domestic Abuse,* ed. Martha Albertson Fineman and Roxanne Mykitiuk (New York: Routledge, 1994).

40. Estimates are that "in the United States, a woman falls victim to domestic abuse at the hands of her husband or boyfriend once every nine seconds"; it has also been estimated that "more than half of the women murdered in America are killed by their male partners" (see Jill Lebowitz, "Pursuit of Tort Claims for Domestic Violence in New Jersey and the Creation of a New Tort Cause of Action for 'Battered Woman's Syndrome': Case Comment—*Giovine v. Giovine,*" *Women's Rights Law Reporter* 17 [1996]: 259). Estimates are also that domestic violence is the most underreported crime in America, with only one in ten victims making a report (*Chattanooga Free Press,* September 30, 1997, p. C2). Catharine MacKinnon notes that "sexual violation is a sexual practice." She adds that "because the inequality of the sexes is socially defined as the enjoyment of sexuality itself, gender inequality appears consensual." "Women are systematically beaten in our homes by men with whom we are close. It is estimated that between one quarter and one third of married women experience serious violence in their homes—some studies find as many as 70 percent. Four out of five murdered women are killed by men; between one third and one half are married to their murderers. When you add the boyfriends and former spouses, the figures rise" (Catharine A. MacKinnon, *Feminism Unmodified: Discourses on Life and Law* [Cambridge, Mass.: Harvard University Press, 1987], pp. 6–7, 24).

41. Law takes up, thus, indirectly and unwittingly (implicitly), the traditional tasks of historiography. Historiography, however, is inherently a cognitive or constative endeavor, whereas law is, and remains, inherently performative: it inadvertently competes with historiography (or duplicates its organizing or interpretive functions) only through the radical difference of its performative endeavor, in its essence as performativity.

42. Law relates to trauma through the social function of the trial as a structural (procedural and institutional) remedy to trauma. In a different, larger philosophical sense, Walter Benjamin (see Chapter 1) has inaugurated (in the wake of Marx, but with a different kind of insight and emphasis) an innovative tradition of historiography whose goal is to articulate the past historically (always against the version of official or established "history"), not from the perspective of "the victors" but from the perspective of "the tradition of the oppressed," in which Benjamin underscores precisely the centrality of the experience of trauma. "To articulate the past historically," writes Benjamin, "does not mean to recognize [the past] 'the way it really was' . . . It means to seize hold of a memory as it flashes up at a moment of danger . . . The tradition of the oppressed teaches us that the 'state of emergency' in which we live is not the exception but the rule. We must attain to a conception of history which is in keeping with this insight.

Then we shall clearly realize that it is our task to bring about a real state of emergency . . . Where we perceive a chain of events, [the angel of history] sees one single catastrophe which keeps piling wreckage upon wreckage" ("Theses," 255–257).

43. "The forgotten recalls itself in acts," says Jacques Lacan ("L'oublié se rappelle dans les actes"). Jacques Lacan, "Fonction et Champ de la parole et du langage," in *Écrits* (Paris: Seuil, 1966), p. 262 (my translation).

44. Cf. Pierre Nora, "Entre mémoire et histoire," introductory essay to *Les Lieux de mémoire*, ed. Pierre Nora, vol. 1: *La République* (Paris: Gallimard, 1984). An English version of excerpts of this introduction ("Between Memory and History: Les Lieux de mémoire," trans. Mark Roudebush) was published in *Representations* 26, special issue, *Memory and Counter-Memory* (Spring 1989).

45. See Freud, *Moses and Monotheism*, p. 64 and chap. 7 of part II, throughout.

46. What acquitted Simpson is, thus, history: a repetitive historical pattern of abuse of African Americans by agents of the law. Those who voted or who would have voted for acquittal (and they are not limited to blacks) wanted to exonerate black trauma, to vindicate, to exculpate, and to empower the historical defenselessness of African Americans before the law. It is an entire history of trauma that weighed on the decision. What acquitted Simpson is the way in which his confrontation with the law allowed him (irrespective of his guilt or innocence) to play an inadvertent role he did not seek and did not in effect desire: that of a physical custodian—a keeper in his very body—of black collective memory. This legal and symbolic, mythic role begins unwittingly when Simpson chooses to attempt to earn freedom by a physical escape or by a run in the face of the law. The dramatic televised pursuit—the mute scenario of the slow-speed chase and Simpson's ultimate surrender and return as state property—enacts or reenacts in the collective memory at once the recent drama of the high-speed chase of Rodney King (ironically pursued for speeding), and a more ancient primal scene of running slaves pursued so as to be returned to their proper, *legal* owners. Not only in the case of gender, therefore, but in the case of race as well, the traumatic legal story of the twentieth century has not entirely emerged from a traumatic story of the nineteenth century (Dred Scott, 1857).

In his embodied posture as a captured runaway and in the need to be or to become now *a survivor of the law* (or of the legal system), Simpson symbolically recovers a collective cultural past he had been trying to forget and to deny, and a shared history he had been trying, his life long, to run away from. In running from the law, he runs back toward the past. In Simpson's very body (and in his bodily presence in the court), blackness historically returns as erased (forgotten) memory; it *returns* therefore *as unconscious or repressed:* repressed, erased by Simpson's own assimilation. This (in part at least) accounts for the emotional explosion at the verdict. The intensity of the triumphant identification of the black community with Simpson's *survival of the law* derived precisely from the force of this *historical return of the repressed,* all the more forceful for symbolically returning an *erased* collective and traumatic memory.

From this perspective, the legal drama of the century became a legal narrative of black survival, and of the survival and resuscitation of black memory. (Ironically, this narrative of recall doomed to forgetfulness the story of the murder.)

47. Cf. *The Kreutzer Sonata*, p. 80: "Yes, he was a musician, a violinist . . . He had moist eyes, like almonds, smiling red lips, and a little moustache . . . He was slight of physique . . . and he had a particularly well-developed posterior, as women have . . . He and his music were the real cause of it all. At my trial the whole thing was made to look as though it had been caused by jealousy. Nothing could have been further from the truth."

48. Like the crime scene in the O. J. Simpson case, the scene of *The Kreutzer Sonata* (the confession) takes place in a literal obscurity outlined only by shadows and by shades. (See Jackson, "In the Darkness of the Night: Tolstoy's *Kreutzer Sonata* and Dostoevsky's *Notes from the Underground*," pp. 208–227.) It is nighttime, dark both outside and inside the train; the story is surrounded (governed) by a darkness, in which (metaphorically and literally) nothing is entirely or simply readable: "It was too dark to read, so I closed my eyes and pretended I wanted to go to sleep," says the narrator (36). Pozdnyshev confesses in this total darkness, which protects him; his voice is heard, but his face, symbolically and literally, is never clearly seen. Like O. J. Simpson, he remains "a shadowy figure." The story never entirely emerges from the darkness in which it is plunged: "It was *so dark* that I *could not see his face*, only hear his forceful, pleasant voice" (38). "His face kept altering strangely in the *semi-darkness* where he sat" (42). "'The light is getting in my eyes—do you mind if we pull the shade over it?' he said, pointing to the lamp" (53). "I started to get a sinister feeling, lying there in the dark, and I struck a match . . . He continued his story . . . and all that could be heard in the *semi-darkness* was the rattling of the windows . . . In the half-light of the dawn, *I could no longer make out Pozdnyshev's features*. All I could hear was his voice" (101–102).

49. "And so we continued to live, in a perpetual fog, without ever being aware of the situation we were in. If what finally happened hadn't happened . . . I would never have come to perceive the abyss of unhappiness, the loathsome falsehood in which I was wallowing" (75).

50. On the way in which trauma resists awareness, see Alice Miller, *Thou Shalt Not Be Aware: Society's Betrayal of the Child*, trans. Hildegarde and Hunter Nannum (New York: New American Library, 1984).

51. Cf. Lisa Kennedy: "The karmic payback of this verdict [O. J. Simpson] for that injustice [Rodney King] has an *empty* quality (*Village Voice*, October 17, 1995, p. 25), and Henry Louis Gates: "It is a discourse . . . in which everyone speaks of payback and nobody is paid . . . And so an *empty* vessel like O. J. Simpson becomes filled with meaning, and more meaning—more meaning than any of us can bear" (Henry Louis Gates, Jr., "Thirteen Ways of Looking at a Black Man," *New Yorker*, October 23, 1995, p. 65; reprinted in Gates, *Thirteen Ways of Looking at a Black Man* [New York: Random House, 1997], pp. 121–122).

52. Robert A. Jordan, "No Victory, No Defeat, Only an Angry Divide," *Boston Globe*, October 8, 1995 ("Focus").

53. Francis X. Clines, "And Now, the Audience Rests," *New York Times*, October 8, 1995, p. 4.

54. Isabel Wilkerson, "Whose Side to Take: Women, Outrage and the Verdict on O. J. Simpson," *New York Times*, 8 October 1995, p. 4.

55. In his famous essay "Violence and the Word," Robert Cover underscores the systematic way in which the violent, traumatizing side of the law is always underplayed, denied, or altogether ignored. As a result, we emphasize law as (legal) meaning. But "pain and death" are limits on the possibility of totalizing this meaning. Pain and death (which the law inflicts) are by definition what cannot be understood, what cannot be transformed into meaning by those who suffer them. Legal meaning, therefore, is not shared by those whom the law overwhelms. See "Violence and the Word," in *Narrative, Violence, and the Law*, pp. 203–238; and Cover, *Justice Accused*. See also: Walter Benjamin, "Critique of Violence," in *Reflections*, 277–300; Jacques Derrida, "Force of Law: The 'Mystical Foundation of Authority,'" in *Deconstruction and the Possibility of Justice, Cardozo Law Review* 11 (1990): 921–1045.

56. While the injuries of race and sex abuse are comparable—and have indeed been compared throughout history—the legal remedy of one has been sometimes achieved (as in this case) at the expense of the other. During Reconstruction, for example (when marital "chastisement" was no longer recognized as a husband's right), southern judges responded to the abolition of slavery by closing the law's eye to domestic abuse. (See Laura F. Edwards, "'The Marriage Covenant Is at the Foundation of All Our Rights': The Politics of Slave Marriages in North Carolina after Emancipation," *Law and History Review* 14 [1996]: 81–124, at 81–89.) To the extent that this (willed) form of judicial blindness was triggered by the reawakened need to protect the integrity of the domestic sphere, it may be viewed as a post-traumatic legal and jurisprudential response to the political subversion/loss of "the domestic institution" (as slavery was called). One "domestic institution" (beaten wives) substituted for another (slavery). One trauma compensated for another, through the legal medium of a symptomatic (and symptomatically prescribed) judicial blindness. "If no permanent injury has been inflicted," argued a 1874 legal opinion, "nor malice, cruelty nor dangerous violence shown by the husband, it is better to *draw the curtain, shut out the public gaze*, and leave the parties to forget and forgive" (North Carolina; quoted in Siegel, "'The Rule of Love': Wife Beating as Prerogative and Privacy," p. 2158; emphasis mine). Even in the North, it seems, the destabilization of the boundaries of "domesticity" may have had post-traumatic legal compensations concerning women: in several cases northern juries acquitted husbands who had murdered their wife's lover. (For a discussion of such cases in a different framework, see Hendrik Hartog, "Lawyering, Husbands' Rights and 'the Unwritten law' in Nineteenth-Century America," *Journal of American History* 84 [1997]: 67–96.)

Conversely, race was made to compensate for the trauma of gender. Lynching, masquerading as justice (and sometimes complicitly applied through the judicial institution), was meant to be a pseudo-legal remedy for the underlying *gender trauma* of the failed white male attempt to control the (white) woman's sexuality. Lynching was thus also (among other things) meant to remedy the uncontrollability (the uncontainability) of female sexuality as such. Race subordination and gender subordination acted in concert. Even the black activist Ida B. Wells, who crusaded against lynching during the late nineteenth century and spoke on behalf of its black (male *and* female) victims, wrote that "white men used their ownership of the body of white females as a terrain on which to lynch the black male" (quoted in Dorothy E. Roberts, "Rape, Violence, and Women's Autonomy," *Chicago-Kent Law Review* 69 [1993]: 359, 366). Almost a century later Catharine MacKinnon notes that the definition of rape as a crime committed by black men against white women has obscured and legitimated the more common incidents of sexual abuse by acquaintances. (MacKinnon, *Feminism Unmodified,* pp. 81–82; see, in this conjunction, Nancy S. Ehrenreich, "Perceptions and Decision Making: Gender Perspectives, O. J. Simpson and the Myth of Gender/Race Conflict," *University of Colorado Law Review* 67 [1996]: 931, 939–940; see, similarly, Jacquelyn Dowd Hall, "'The Mind That Burns in Each Body': Women, Rape and Racial Violence," in *Powers of Desire: The Politics of Sexuality,* ed. Ann Snitow, Christine Stansell, and Sharon Thompson [New York: Monthly Review Press, 1983]; and Dorothy E. Roberts, "Rape, Violence, and Women's Autonomy," ibid.)

Unlike these authors (with whom I am in basic agreement), my own emphasis is not on the mutual reinforcement of the ideological *stereotypes* of race and gender but on the mutual reinforcement of the two *traumas* (histories of suffering subject to a specific psychoanalytic logic), and on the traumatizing impact of the trial (meant to be a remedy) as a result. The black women jurors in the O. J. Simpson trial identified so deeply with the suffering of the defendant (with the terror of his flight and with the desperation of his struggle with the law) that they were blinded to the gender trauma. They relived, through the spectacular dramatization of the trial, (what they took to be) an all-too-familiar *reenactment* of *a primal lynching scene.* In this view, O. J. Simpson was implicitly accused of having had sex with a white woman; the prosecution's argument (and visual evidence) concerning Simpson's regular behavior of sexual abuse was lived (and screened) precisely as a dejà vu, an *already seen* (an all-too-seen) charge of an interracial sexual crime, for which O. J. Simpson was now going to be lynched, according to the archetypal script of history. It was for this primal scene and for its wounding repetition that the black women jurors sought a *legal remedy.* They *acquitted trauma* (and vindicated black males' innocence). Marcia Clark, on the other hand, identified so deeply with the trauma of the battered woman (which she in turn relived) that she was blinded (not ideologically, I submit, but traumatically) to the race trauma. Ideologically, on the contrary, she was "colorblind." Despite the advice of her jury consultant, she could not believe that women jurors would not listen to her, and would not *see* the evidence—and the battered face. She did not know that she was talking to them across an abyss of trauma. She did not believe in judicial blindness. For her and for all those who, like her, felt the suffering of Nicole (and did not or could not believe in blindness), the verdict was an added injury inflicted on the battered face. (On violent misuses of "the lynching metaphor," see Kendall Thomas, "Strange Fruit," in

Race-ing Justice, En-gendering Power, ed. Toni Morrison [New York: Pantheon Books, 1992], pp. 364–389.)

57. Wilkerson, "Whose Side to Take," pp. 1, 4.

58. "Two Nations, Divisible: The Intolerable Lesson of the O. J. Simpson Trial," *Economist,* October 7, 1995. The depth of the amazement at the depth of the race cleavage was itself, however, yet another symptom of how history is inherently deprived of memory: forgetful of the still not so remote legal enforcement of "two countries"—two Americas—through racist segregation laws.

59. Compare Robert Cover's definition of law as bridge: "Law is neither to be wholly identified with the understanding of the present state of affairs nor with the imagined alternatives. *It is the bridge*—the committed social behaviour which constitutes the way a group of people will attempt to get from here to there." Each community, Cover emphasizes, builds its bridges in its own way. "Thus, visions of the future are more or less strongly determinative of *the bridge which is 'law'* depending upon the commitment and social organization of the people who hold them." (Robert M. Cover, "The Folktales of Justice: Tales of Jurisdiction," in *Narrative, Violence, and the Law,* pp. 173–202, at 176–177, 201). On law as bridge, see also Sarat, "Narrative Strategy and Death Penalty Advocacy," p. 366.

60. The legal thinker who comes closest to this view is Robert Cover. Cover has proposed, indeed, a uniquely sophisticated reflection on the connection and on the difference between law and literature. To know law, Cover insists, one must understand a literature and a tradition. To understand law one must also recognize its connection (and commitment) to reality. Judges often exercise caution, as they should do, but in so doing they "risk losing law to the overpowering force of what is and what is dominant. Integrity . . . is the act of maintaining the vision that it is only that which redeems which is law." Literature and tradition, according to Cover, teach commitments that we then use to build *"bridges to the future."* In stories one may find an insight into a legal ideal that real judges are cautious not to provoke (Cover, "The Folktales of Justice: Tales of Jurisdiction," pp. 176–177, 201). However, Cover adds, there is a crucial element that radically differentiates between literature and law: the very real violence of the judicial institution, its performative injurious power. This is all too often forgotten in the treatment of "law as literature." "I fully agree [says Cover] that the dominant form of legal thought ought to be interpretive. However, the emergence of interpretation as a central motif does not, by itself, reflect upon the way in which the interpretive acts of judges are simultaneously performative utterances in an institutional setting for violent behavior" (Cover, "Violence and the Word," p. 216, n. 24). "We begin, then, not with what the judges say but with what they do. The judges deal pain and death . . . In this they are different from poets, from artists. It will not do to insist on the violence of strong poetry, of strong poets. Even the violence of weak judges is utterly real . . . Whether or not the violence of judges is justified is not now the point—only that it exists in fact and differs from the violence that exists in literature or in the metaphoric characterizations of literary critics and philosophers" (ibid., 213–214).

To add to this remarkable analysis, my study insists on the way in which the law as such is inhabited not simply by a (very real) violence, but also more precisely (as I show) by *an abyss*. The abyss exists *inside the law* as well as inside literature. Unlike Cover, I insist on the fact that the difference between law and literature resides not simply in the difference between *literal violence* (the judge's, the criminal's) and *metaphorical violence* (Tolstoy's), but in the fact that *literature opens the trial that the law closes*. The law exhibits (and gives to see) the violence of the criminal, but hides its own. Literature lays open and exposes the violence that is hidden in culture (including the violence of law).

61. Paul Celan, "The Meridian" (speech given in 1960, on the occasion of Celan's receipt the Georg Büchner Prize from the German Academy for Language and Literature), trans. Jerry Glenn, *Chicago Review* 29 (1978): 34.

62. See Shoshana Felman and Dori Laub, *Testimony: Crises of Witnessing in Literature, Psychoanalysis, and History* (New York and London: Routledge, 1992).

63. Compare, for instance, the way in which, during the Second World War, messengers (such as the Polish underground courier Ian Karski) and escapees from Nazi concentration camps failed to inform the world about the Nazis' final aims. Information was forthcoming, but it could not reach its destination; knowledge existed, but it could not be effectively *transmitted* either to the Allied governments or to the endangered victims. Most Jews in Europe had at least heard rumors about horrible events in Western Europe. But the rumors either were not believed or it was assumed that "it cannot happen here." The bearers of the rumors were stigmatized as unreliable or mad. (See Felman and Laub, ibid., chaps. 3, 4, 6, 7, esp. pp. 103–105 and 231–239.)

64. See Felman and Laub, ibid., pp. xx and 12–40, 52.

65. Quoted in Magarshack, "Afterword," in Tolstoy, *The Death of Ivan Ilych and Other Stories*, p. 301.

66. Cf. Joanna Coles, "My Dinner with OJ," *The Guardian*, May 16, 1996, pp. 1–3.

67. Ibid., p. 2.

68. Simpson quoted (from a British television interview) by Stuart Jeffries, in "OJ Survives 10-Minute Trial by Television," *International Guardian*, May 14, 1996, p. 2.

69. Quoted in Coles, "My Dinner with OJ," p. 3.

70. Quoted in Dunne, "The Simpsons."

71. Albert Camus, "L'Espoir et l'absurde dans l'oeuvre de Franz Kafka," Appendix to *Le Mythe de Sisyphe* (Paris: Collection Folio, Gallimard, 1942), p. 187; my translation.

72. Troyat, *Tolstoy*, p. 664.

73. Medria Williams, quoted in Wilkerson, "Taking Sides: Women, Rage and O. J. Simpson," p. 4.

74. The main difference, in effect, between the criminal trial and its legal repetition in the civil trial derived from the fact that in the civil trial, Simpson was compelled to testify. But his testimony, in its absolute denial of reality against all evidence ("I never owned such shoes—absolutely not"; "I never hit my wife—absolutely not"), still essentially continued to maintain his choice of legal silence

(even in his courtroom speech) through his absolute *refusal to become a witness;* a witness not just to the crime, but *to the trial;* a witness to himself—and to the evidence.

75. Albert Camus, *La Chute* (Paris: Collection Folio, Gallimard, 1956), p. 148; my translation.

76. Clines, "And Now, the Audience Rests," p. 4.

77. Wilkerson, "Taking Sides: Women, Rage and O. J. Simpson," p. 4.

78. Franz Kafka, letter to Max Brod (July 5, 1922), in *The Basic Kafka,* ed. Michael Kowal (New York: Pocket Books, 1979), p. 295.

3. Theaters of Justice

1. Hannah Arendt, *Eichmann in Jerusalem: A Report on the Banality of Evil* (New York: Penguin Books, 1994; first published in the United States by Viking Press, 1963). The abbreviation *EiJ* refers to the Penguin edition.

Arendt traveled to Jerusalem, along with many other foreign correspondents, to report for the *New Yorker* on the trial whose dramatic announcement in Israel had provoked international excitement and captured the world's attention. See Criminal Case 40/61 (Jerusalem), *Attorney General v. Eichmann* (1961, English translation of the Proceedings 1962) and Criminal Appeal 336/61, *Eichmann v. Attorney General* (1962). Pnina Lahav summarizes the facts of the case: "Adolf Eichmann was head of Department IV B 4 in the RSHS (the Reich security services) and in charge of Jewish Affairs and Evacuation. He proved his excellent managerial skills first by performing the modest task of expelling Vienna's Jews from Austria, then by engineering the systematic murder of the majority of European Jewry. In 1944, weeks before the red army marched on Budapest, he reactivated the Auschwitz crematoria to add 400,000 Hungarian Jews to his 5.5 million victims. [*Eichmann v. Attorney General* (1962), English translation (1963) Part III, at 11–12, 17–35.] After the war, Eichmann escaped to Argentina and assumed a false identity. On May 11, 1960, as Israel was celebrating its [twelfth anniversary,] Israeli security agents abducted Eichmann and brought him to face charges in Jerusalem . . . To ensure Eichmann's security, he was seated [in the courtroom] in a specially constructed bulletproof glass booth . . . Cameras were allowed into the . . . courtroom, a rarity in the common law world and unprecedented in Israeli judicial procedure. A battery of simultaneous translators [interpreted the trial—conducted in Hebrew—into the earphones of the foreign correspondents and of the accused and his defense attorney. However, the judges cross-examined the accused in German, without earphones and without the mediation of translators.] . . . After the conviction, Eichmann was hung in the summer of 1962. He was the first, and so far the only, person executed by the State of Israel." (Pnina Lahav, "The Eichmann Trial, the Jewish Question, and the American-Jewish Intelligentsia," *Boston University Law Review* 72 (1992): 555, 558–559.)

2. On Arendt's definition of evil, see, among others: Marie-Claire Caloz Tschopp, *Hannah Arendt: La Banalité du mal comme mal politique* (Paris: L'Harmattan, 1998); Berel Lang, "Hannah Arendt and the Politics of Evil," in

Hannah Arendt, Critical Essays, ed. Lewis P. Hinchman and Sandra K. Hinchman (Albany: State University of New York Press, 1994), pp. 41–56; Joseph Beatty, "Thinking and Moral Considerations: Socrates and Arendt's Eichmann," ibid., pp. 57–74; Dana Villa, "Beyond Good and Evil: Arendt, Nietzsche, and the Aesthetization of Politics," *Political Theory* 20 (1992): 274–308; George Kateb, *Hannah Arendt: Politics, Conscience, Evil* (Totowa, N.J.: Rowman and Allanheld, 1984); Shiraz Dossa, "Hannah Arendt on Eichmann: The Public, the Private and Evil," *Review of Politics* 46 (1984): 163–182, reprinted in Shiraz Dossa, *Public Realm and Public Self: The Political Theory of Hannah Arendt* (Waterloo, Iowa: Wilfrid Laurier University Press, 1989); Nathan Rottenstreich, "Can Evil Be Banal?" *Philosophical Forum* 16 (1984): 50–62; Barry Clarke, "Beyond the Banality of Evil," *British Journal of Political Science* 10 (1980): 417–439; J. Robinson, *And the Crooked Shall Be Made Straight: The Eichmann Trial, the Jewish Catastrophe, and Hannah Arendt's Narrative* (Philadelphia: Jewish Publication Society, 1965); "'Eichmann in Jerusalem': An Exchange of Letters between Gershom Scholem and Hannah Arendt," *Encounter* 22 (1964); L. Abel, "The Aesthetics of Evil: Hannah Arendt on Eichmann and the Jews," *Partisan Review* 30 (1963).

On Arendt generally, see, among others: Julia Kristeva, *Le Génie féminin,* vol. 1: *Hannah Arendt* (Paris: Fayard, 1999); Julia Kristeva, *Hannah Arendt,* trans. Ross Guberman (New York: Columbia University Press, 2001); Julia Kristeva, *Hannah Arendt: Life Is a Narrative,* trans. Frank Collins (Toronto: University of Toronto Press, 2001); Etienne Tassin, *Trésor perdu: Hannah Arendt, L'Intelligence de l'action politique* (Paris: Payot, 1999); *Hannah Arendt, Revue internationale de philosophie* 208 (1999); Yvette Theraulaz and Marie-Claire Caloz Tschopp, *Hannah Arendt: Les Sans-états et le droit d'avoir des droits* (Paris: L'Harmattan, 1998); Eslin, *Hannah Arendt: L'Obligée* (Paris: Michalon, 1996); Martha Minow, "Stories in the Law," in *Law's Stories: Narrative and Rhetoric in the Law,* ed. Peter Brooks and Paul Gewirtz (New Haven: Yale University Press, 1996), pp. 24–36; Seyla Benhabib, *The Reluctant Modernism of Hannah Arendt* (London: Sage Publications, 1994); Maurizio Passerin D'Entrève, *The Political Philosophy of Hannah Arendt* (New York: Routledge, 1994); *Hannah Arendt: Critical Essays,* ed. Lewis Hinchman and Sanra Hinchman (Albany: State University of New York Press, 1994); P. Hansen, *Hannah Arendt* (Cambridge: Polity Press, 1993); M. Canovan, *Hannah Arendt: A Reinterpretation of Her Political Thought* (Cambridge: Cambridge University Press, 1992); D. Watson, *Arendt* (London: Fontana Press, 1992); G. Tolle, *Human Nature under Fire: The Political Philosophy of Hannah Arendt* (Lanham, Md.: University Press of America, 1992); D. Barnouw, *Visible Spaces: Hannah Arendt and the German-Jewish Experience* (Baltimore: Johns Hopkins University Press, 1990); L. Bradshaw, *Acting and Thinking: The Political Thought of Hannah Arendt* (Toronto: University of Toronto Press, 1989); *Hannah Arendt: Thinking, Judging, Freedom,* ed. G. T. Kaplan and C. S. Kessler (Sydney: Allen and Unwin, 1989); *Amor Mundi: Explorations in the Faith and Thought of Hannah Arendt,* ed. J. W. Bernauer (Dordrecht: Martinus Nijhoff, 1987); *La Pluralità irrapresentabile: Il pensiero politico di Hannah Arendt,* ed. R. Esposito (Urbino: Edizioni Quattro

Venti, 1987); James Bernauer, "On Reading and Misreading Hannah Arendt," *Philosophy and Social Criticism* 11 (1985): 20; D. May, *Hannah Arendt* (Harmondsworth: Penguin Books, 1986); A. Enegren, *La Pensée politique de Hannah Arendt* (Paris: PUF, 1984); Elisabeth Young-Bruehl, *Hannah Arendt: For Love of the World* (New Haven: Yale University Press, 1982); J. B. Parekh, *Hannah Arendt and the Search for a New Political Philosophy* (London: Macmillan, 1981); S. Whitefield, *Into the Dark: Hannah Arendt and Totalitarianism* (Philadelphia: Temple University Press, 1980); *Hannah Arendt: The Recovery of the Public World,* ed. Melvin A. Hill (New York: Saint Martin's Press, 1979).

3. "When I speak of the banality of evil," Arendt explains in the "Postscript" in *Eichmann in Jerusalem,* "I do so only on the strictly factual level, pointing to a phenomenon that stared one in the face at the trial. Eichmann was not Iago and not Macbeth . . . Except for an extraordinary diligence in looking out for his personal advancement, *he had no motives at all* . . . He merely, to put the matter colloquially, *never realized what he was doing*" (*EiJ,* 287; emphasis mine).

4. Arendt insisted, Pnina Lahav writes, "that 'civilized jurisprudence prided itself . . . [most] on . . . taking into account . . . the subjective factor' of mens rea. But *the Nazis formed a new category of criminals, men and women who did not possess mens rea*. This new category, Arendt insisted, had to be recognized as a matter of law" (*EiJ,* 276–277; Lahav, "The Eichmann Trial, the Jewish Question, and the American-Jewish Intelligentsia," pp. 555, 570; italics mine).

My emphasis is slightly different. I see the crux of Arendt's concept of "banality of evil" not only in the new conception of "a criminal without mens rea," but also in the added legal and linguistic factor of the superimposition of a *borrowed (Nazi) language*—of recognizable and structuring *clichés*—on this absence of subjective motive. Eichmann's quasi-parodic German, a German limited to an anachronistic use of Nazi bureaucratic jargon (noticeable during the trial by every native German speaker as the farcical survival of a sort of robot-language), *takes the place of mens rea*. This unintentional *linguistic parody that substitutes for mens rea* is what makes Arendt call Eichmann "a clown" (*EiJ,* 54) and view in general the German-language version of the trial as "sheer comedy" (a comedy compounded by a farcical, inadequate simultaneous translation into German) (*EiJ,* 3, 48). "The German text of the taped police examination . . . corrected and approved by Eichmann, constitutes a veritable gold mine," writes Arendt, in showing how "the horrible can be not only ludicrous but outright funny. Some of the comedy cannot be conveyed in English, because it lies in Eichmann's heroic fight with the German language, which invariably defeats him . . . Dimly aware of a defect that . . . [during the trial] amounted to a slight case of aphasia—he apologized, saying, 'Officialese [*Amtssprache*] is my only language.' But the point here is that *officialese became his language because he was genuinely incapable of uttering a single sentence that was not a cliché* . . . what he said was always the same, expressed in the same words. The longer one listened to him, the more obvious it became that his inability to speak was closely connected with an inability to *think*, namely to think from the standpoint of somebody else. *No communication was possible with him, not because he lied but because he was surrounded by the most reliable safeguards against the words and the presence of others, and hence against reality as such"* (*EiJ*, 48–49; italics mine). As a parrotlike "clown," Eichmann does not *speak* the borrowed (Nazi) language: he is rather *spoken by it, spoken for* by its clichés, whose criminality he does not come to realize. This total loss of a sense of reality regarding Nazi crimes is what encapsulates, for Arendt, the utmost moral scandal (the *ventriloquized mens rea,* the criminal linguistic "banality") typified by Eichmann. Eichmann's continued impersonation during the trial (his autistic ventriloquism) of technocratic Nazi language is what incriminates him above all in Arendt's eyes. (In this sense, it is perhaps symbolic that, as the prosecutor notes, "Eichmann almost never looked into the courtroom." Gideon Hausner, *Justice in Jerusalem* [New York: Harper and Row, 1996], p. 332.)

5. For a similar emphasis on the jurisprudential essence of "the banality of evil," but from a different interpretive perspective, see Laurence Douglas, "The Memory of Judgment: The Law, the Holocaust and Denial," *History and Memory* 7 (1996): 100, 108. "The banality of evil thus can be understood to describe a bureaucratic and a legal phenomenon. Organizationally removed from the mass killing they sanctioned, functionaries such as Eichmann could claim to have participated in the Final Solution *out of a feeling of legal obligation. So conceived, the Holocaust could be viewed as the perfection, rather than as the perversion, of legal positivism*—the idea that the legitimacy of a legal command derives from its status as law, and not from any underlying normative content" (italics mine).

6. This, in my eyes, is the quintessence of Arendt's paradox and of her unexpected legal reading of the crime. This reading stands, of course, in sharp contrast to the prosecution's version and to the court's juridical interpretation, both of which attributed to Eichmann undoubtable mens rea, or a hyperbolic ("monstrous," monstrously self-conscious and self-willed) criminal intention: "Eichmann," wrote Israeli supreme court justice Simon Agranat, "performed the extermination order at all times and in all seasons *con amore . . .* with genuine zeal and devotion to that objective." Cr. App. 336/61, *Eichmann v. Attorney General,* P.D. 16, 2033, 2099 (Hebrew, 1962); *Eichmann* Supreme Court Opinion, I-70 (English). Quoted in Pnina Lahav, *Judgment in Jerusalem: Chief Justice Simon Agranat and the Zionist Century* (Berkeley: University of California Press, 1997), p. 157. For an elaborate account of the court's views in this and other legal matters, see Lahav, ibid., pp. 145–162.

7. Arendt to Jaspers, *AJ Corr.,* letter 50, p. 69.

8. *AJ Corr.,* letter 274, pp. 215–217.

9. See, for instance, Gershom Scholem's characteristic interpretation in his public letter to Arendt of June 23, 1963: "[Y]our description of Eichmann as a 'convert to Zionism' could only come from somebody who had a profound dislike of everything to do with Zionism. These passages in your book . . . amount to a mockery of Zionism; and I am forced to the conclusion that this was, indeed, your intention." "'Eichmann in Jerusalem': An Exchange of Letters between Gershom Scholem and Hannah Arendt," *Encounter* 22 (1964): 53.

10. Against an international hue and cry disputing Israeli jurisdiction in the wake of Israel's abduction of Eichmann from his hiding place in Argentina, Arendt defends Israel's right both to try Eichmann and to execute him. Al-

though she criticizes the philosophy behind the district court opinion, she supports wholeheartedly the verdict and condones the punishment, which she deems just (*EiJ*, 234–265, 277–279). She goes as far as to condone the kidnapping, which she acknowledges as the sole realistic (if illegal) means to bring Eichmann to justice. ("This, unhappily, was the only almost unprecedented feature in the whole Eichmann trial, and certainly it was the least entitled ever to become a valid precedent . . . *Its justification was the unprecedentedness of the crime and the coming into existence of a Jewish State.* There were, however, important mitigating circumstances in that there hardly existed an alternative if one indeed wished to bring Eichmann to justice . . . In short, *the realm of legality offered no alternative to kidnapping.* Those who are convinced that justice, and nothing else, is the end of law will be inclined to condone the kidnapping act, though not because of precedents" [*EiJ*, 264–265; emphasis mine].) A founding legal act, Arendt implies, is always grounded in an act of violence. (On the general relation between the foundation of the law and violence, compare Jacques Derrida, "Force of Law," in *Deconstruction and the Possibility of Justice, Cardozo Law Review* 11 [1990]: 920, 941–942; Walter Benjamin, "Critique of Violence," in *SWI*, 237–252; and Robert Cover, "Violence and the Word," in *Narrative, Violence, and the Law: The Essays of Robert Cover*, ed. Martha Minow, Michael Ryan, and Austin Sarat [Ann Arbor: University of Michigan Press, 1995], pp. 203–238.)

All these points, in summary, establish Arendt's stance (contrary to common opinion) as *pro*-Zionist, though critical of the Israeli government and of its handling of the trial. "How you could believe that my book was 'a mockery of Zionism,'" Arendt writes to Scholem, "would be a complete mystery to me, if I did not know that many people in Zionist circles have become incapable of listening to opinions or arguments which are off the beaten track and not consonant with their ideology. There are exceptions, and a Zionist friend of mine remarked in all innocence that the book, the last chapter in particular (recognition of the competence of the court, justification of the kidnapping), was very pro-Israel, as indeed it is. What confuses you is that my argument and my approach are different from what you are used to; in other words, the trouble is that I am independent." Letter of reply of Arendt of July 24, 1963, in "'Eichmann in Jerusalem': An Exchange of Letters," p. 55.

11. Arendt criticizes the jurisdiction in Israel of religious law over family law: pragmatically, this subordination of family law to religious law does not enable intermarriage with non-Jews; Arendt provocatively compares this exclusionary jurisdiction of Israeli religious law with the racist exclusions of the 1935 Nuremberg laws of the Third Reich (*EiJ*, 7).

12. Arendt summarizes these spectacular (spectacularized) political and didactic ends: "Thus, the trial never became a play, but the 'show' Ben Gurion had had in mind to begin with did take place, or, rather, the 'lessons' he thought should be taught to Jews and Gentiles, to Israelis and Arabs . . . These lessons . . . Ben Gurion had outlined them before the trial started, in a number of articles designed to explain why Israel had kidnapped the accused. There was the lesson to the non-Jewish world: 'We want to establish before the nations of the world

how millions of people, because they happened to be Jews, and one million babies, because they happened to be Jewish babies, were murdered by the Nazis.'
. . . 'We want the nations of the world to know . . . and they should be ashamed.'
The Jews in the Diaspora were to remember how Judaism, four thousand years
old . . . , had always faced 'a hostile world,' how the Jews had degenerated until
they went to their death like sheep, and how only the establishment of the Jewish
state had enabled the Jews to hit back, as Israelis had done in the War of Independence . . . And if the Jews outside Israel had to be shown the difference between Israeli heroism and Jewish submissive meekness, there was a lesson for
those inside Israel too: 'the generation of Israelis who had grown up since the
holocaust' were in danger of losing their ties with the Jewish people and, by implication, with their own history. 'It is necessary that our youth remember what
happened to the Jewish people. We want them to know the most tragic facts in
our history.' Finally, one of the motives in bringing Eichmann to trial was to fer-
ret out other Nazis—for example, the connection between the Nazis and some
Arab rulers" (*EiJ*, 9–10). These well-known and much discussed political, ideological, and educational objectives of the state in the Eichmann trial are not my
concern here. My own focus in what follows is, instead, on the achievements of
the trial as an unprecedented legal event *exceeding its own ideology*. Arendt's debate is with the policies of the state around the trial. These policies, and the official ideological purposes of the trial, have been thoroughly described and analyzed in Hausner, *Justice in Jerusalem;* Tom Segev, *The Seventh Million: The
Israelis and the Holocaust,* trans. Haim Watzman (New York: Farrar, Straus and
Giroux, 1993), pp. 323–366, hereinafter abbreviated Segev; Lahav, *Judgment
in Jerusalem,* pp. 145–164; Lahav, "The Eichmann Trial, the Jewish Question,
and the American-Jewish Intelligentsia," p. 555; Annette Wieviorka, *Le Procès
Eichmann* (Paris: Editions Complexe, 1989); Annette Wieviorka, *L'Ère du
témoin* (Paris: Plon, 1998).

    13. Arendt claims Ben Gurion distorts justice by making the trial serve the
state's political aims (see previous note), and by using the sharp polarization between good and evil that the trial dramatizes (equating the accused with absolute
evil) as a strategy to equate the prosecuting state with absolute good, and thus to
legitimate the state and to legitimate uncritically (beyond criticism) any policies
or measures the state deems necessary to ensure its continued existence. Thus
(Arendt paraphrases Ben Gurion's "lessons" in the trial), Israeli youth was in
particular supposed to learn how the Jews in the Diaspora, persecuted and surrounded by a hostile world, "had degenerated until they went to their death like
sheep, and how only the establishment of the Jewish state had enabled the Jews
to hit back, as Israelis had done in the War of Independence, in the Suez adven-
ture, and in the almost daily incidents on Israel's unhappy borders" (*EiJ*, 10).
Arendt does not mention explicitly the Palestinians, but it is hard today (in
2002) not to think in this connection of the Palestinian tragedy (ensuing from
the Israeli right to justice) and not to recognize the Palestinians' equal right to
justice tragically asserted in the violence and in the daily conflicts on Israel's (today's) still more "unhappy borders." (Here again, as in the Simpson trial, two
conflicting traumas—the Jewish trauma and the Palestinian trauma—strive to *si-*

lence each other and to suppress and mute each other's cry for justice.) "For a period in the history of the Israeli state [with the arrival of the Likkud government, sixteen years after the Eichmann trial], Eichmann would come to symbolize not just European Nazism but Palestinian terrorism and Arab anti-Zionism as well," writes Gerry Simpson ("Conceptualizing Violence," *Albany Law Review* 69 [1997]: 828). Although this claim is totally anachronistic with respect to the Eichmann trial itself, the subsequent use of legal means to justify state violence would retrospectively prove Arendt's foresight. (Compare Idith Zertal, "From the People's Hall to the Wailing Wall: A Study in Memory, Fear and War," *Representations* 69 [2000]: 39–59.) This then dissident, then iconoclastic Arendtian vision, which subversively contrasts and radically *polarizes Justice and the State,* is nowadays accepted and upheld in Israel by the "post-Zionist" historians and by a large part of the Israeli left, which has adopted many of Arendt's views. The Israeli left, denouncing the violent injustices (blockades, extrajudicial killings) the state legitimates as self-defense against Palestinian terrorism, and vehemently struggling against the policies of occupation of their own government, identifies in principle today with Arendt's statement (on a different issue) in her letter to Gershom Scholem: "wrong done by my own people naturally grieves me more than wrong done by other people" (quoted in Young-Bruehl, *Hannah Arendt: For Love of the World,* p. 344).

14. Compare prosecutor Hausner's own memoirs of the trial: "But the court generally considered the evidence on Jewish resistance to be extraneous to the charge, and we were soon engaged in heated arguments over different portions of this testimony. After parts of it were heard, the presiding judge remarked . . . that 'the testimony digressed quite far from the object of the trial,' and that we should have asked the witness to abstain from speaking on 'external elements which do not pertain to the trial.' I replied that these matters were certainly relevant, as would become even clearer when I delivered my final address to the court . . . The presiding judge replied that . . . the court had its own view about the trial according to the indictment, and that the prosecution should restrict itself to the court's rulings. 'You have got a hostile tribunal,' one of the foreign correspondents jested as he passed me during the lunch recess that followed" (Hausner, *Justice in Jerusalem,* p. 333).

15. "The latter's rule," Arendt proceeds, "as Mr. Hausner is not slow in demonstrating, is *permissive;* it *permits* the prosecutor to give press-conferences and interviews for television during the trial . . . it *permits* frequent side glances into the audience, and the theatrics characteristic of a more than ordinary vanity, which finally achieves its triumph in the White House with a compliment on 'a job well done' by the President of the United States. *Justice does not permit anything of the sort;* it demands seclusion, it permits sorrow rather than anger, and it prescribes the most careful abstention from all the nice pleasures of putting oneself in the limelight" (*EiJ,* 5–6; italics mine).

16. Of course, Arendt was not part of the critical legal studies movement. It is worth noting, however, the ways in which Arendt's approach prefigures that of the later legal movement. Both methodologies are deconstructive; both set out to analyze and to *unmask* the strategies of power that disguise themselves in the

proceedings of the law; both critically lay bare the political nature of legal institutions and of trials. But whereas the later legal movement challenges in principle the presumed line of demarcation between law and politics, Arendt's critique is driven, on the contrary, by a demand for purer justice—or by a claim for a strict separation between the legal and the political in the Eichmann trial.

On critical legal studies and legal scholars' challenges to the law-politics boundary, see *Critical Legal Studies,* ed. James Boyle (New York: New York University Press, 1992); *The Politics of Law: A Progressive Critique,* ed. David Kairys, rev. ed. (New York: Basic Books, 1998); Mark Kelman, *A Guide to Critical Legal Studies* (Cambridge, Mass.: Harvard University Press, 1987).

17. I define "event" by the capacity of happenings to shock and to surprise—in excess of their own deliberateness. An event is always what surpasses its own planning, what exceeds its own deliberateness, what happens in a form of surprise to—and in excess of—the ideological intentions that have given rise to it. Arendt criticizes the deliberateness of the Eichmann event: with such orchestrated deliberateness on the part of the state, the trial, in her eyes, cannot but involve an element of fraud. In the same vein, Mark Osiel writes, "If collective memory can be created deliberately, perhaps it can be done only dishonestly, that is, by concealing this very deliberateness from the intended audience." (Mark J. Osiel, "Ever Again: Legal Remembrance of Administrative Massacre," *University of Pennsylvania Law Review* 144 [1995]: 463, 467.) My argument, however, is that Arendt's very presence at the trial, and her impact on the historiography and on the memory of the event, precisely prove that the event has gone beyond the known parameters that were set as its limits, and has reached over to some new parameters that were unknown and unexpected. Certainly the state did not plan, and no one could have expected, Arendt's charismatic contribution to the meaning and the impact of the Eichmann trial. This is one concrete example in which the event surpassed its own deliberateness. I argue that the deepest significance of the event (the legal event as well as the historical event) lies precisely in its self-transcendence. An event is that of which the consequences are incalculable, irrespective of its conscious architecture and of its ideological intentionality.

18. Pierre Nora, "Le Retour de l'événement," in *Faire de l'histoire: Nouveaux problèmes,* vol. 1, ed. Jacques Le Goff and Pierre Nora (Paris: Gallimard, 1974), pp. 220, 223; my translation.

Nora speaks of the event as a historian and as a philosopher of history. Compare, from the complementary vantage point of political theory, Arendt's own reflection on the event: "Events, past and present—not social forces and historical trends, not questionnaires and motivation research . . . —are the true, the only reliable teachers of political scientists, as they are the most trustworthy source of information for those engaged in politics." (*The Origins of Totalitarianism,* rev. ed. [New York: Meridian, 1968], p. 482.)

19. Friedrich Nietzsche, *The Use and Abuse of History for Life,* trans. Adrian Collins, introduction by Julius Kraft (New York: Liberal Arts Press, 1949, 1957), pp. 12–17. Hereinafter abbreviated *UAH.*

20. Scholem, in "'Eichmann in Jerusalem': An Exchange of Letters," p. 51.

21. The monumental legal vision, as I see it, is not identical with the ideological and educational objectives of the state concerning the trial. For a discussion of the state's deliberate objectives, see references in note 12, above. My interest, as I have stated earlier, is in the way in which the monumental legal event dramatizes a legal vision that exceeds its own ideological, self-conscious, and conscious deliberateness (see above, note 17.)

22. "In justification of the Eichmann trial," Arendt writes, "it has frequently been maintained that although the greatest crime committed during the last war had been against the Jews, the Jews had been only bystanders at Nuremberg, and the judgement of the Jerusalem court made the point that now, for the first time, the Jewish catastrophe 'occupied the central place in the court proceedings, and [that] it was this fact which distinguished this trial from those which preceded it,' at Nuremberg and elsewhere" (*EiJ*, 258).

23. Ben Gurion responds to the international debate and legal controversy triggered by the announcement of the trial, a world polemics in which some Western legal scholars put in question Israeli jurisdiction by calling for the constitution of a more neutral international tribunal to try Eichmann.

24. David Ben Gurion, *Israel: A Personal History,* trans. Nechemia Meyers and Uzy Nystar (New York: Funk and Wagnalls, 1971), p. 575. Compare Michael Keren, "Ben Gurion's Theory of Sovereignty: The Trial of Adolf Eichmann," in *David Ben Gurion: Politics and Leadership in Israel,* ed. Ronald W. Zweig (New York: Frank Cass, 1992), p. 38.

25. *Attorney General v. Eichmann* (Proceedings of the District Court of Jerusalem, 1962). Quoted in Hausner, *Justice in Jerusalem,* p. 325.

26. "I kept asking myself," Hausner recalls, "what the victims themselves would have wished me to say on their behalf, had they had the power to brief me as their spokesman, now that the roles were reversed and that the persecuted had become the prosecutors. I knew that the demand for retribution had resounded in many of the last messages bequeathed by the dead: 'Avenge our blood!' . . .

"There was no way to implement this in the literal sense. The historic 'vengeance' was Jewish survival itself . . . After much heart-searching I felt that I should interpet the last will and testament of the departed as a demand to set a course for scrupulous fairness. For they had been put to death though innocent of any crime. That their chief murderer should now receive a meticulously just trial was the only way they could be truly avenged. This, I thought, would be the real vindication of their memory." (Hausner, *Justice in Jerusalem,* p. 322.)

27. *Attorney General v. Eichmann* (Proceedings of the District Court of Jerusalem, 1962). Quoted in Hausner, *Justice in Jerusalem,* pp. 323–324; Arendt, *EiJ,* 260.

28. It is not surprising that, in thus establishing for the first time the victims' story and their monumental history, the prosecution tends to censor what Arendt famously will analyze and underscore as the victims' own collaboration with their executioners (*EiJ,* 121–125, 132–134: "Wherever Jews lived," Arendt insists, "there were recognized Jewish leaders, and this leadership, almost without exception . . . cooperated with the Nazis . . . I have dealt with this chapter of the story, which the Jerusalem trial failed to put before the eyes of the world in

its true dimensions, because it offers the most striking insight into the totality of the moral collapse the Nazis caused . . . not only among the persecutors but also among the victims.") "Hausner," writes Tom Segev, "would almost completely ignore the Judenrats," avoiding an exposure of the coerced collaboration of the Jewish Councils in the deportations. In contrast to the state's discretion on, and to the trial's marginalization of, this chapter of collaboration of the Jewish leadership in the death of their own people, the state would try to underscore the victims' heroic activism: Hausner and Ben Gurion organized the trial so that it "would emphasize both the inability of the Jews to resist and their attempts to rebel" (Segev, 348). By highlighting the rare cases of Jewish resistance to the Holocaust, prosecutor Hausner aimed to help young Israelis overcome their "repugnance for the nation's past," a repugnance based on their impression that their grandparents had "allowed themselves to be led like lambs to the slaughter" (Hausner, *Justice in Jerusalem*). "The younger generation were to learn that Jews were not lambs to be led to the slaughter but, rather, a nation able to defend itself, as in the War of Independence, Ben Gurion told the *New York Times*" (Segev, 328). Prosecutor Hausner "sought to design a national saga that would echo through the generations," in concert with Ben Gurion's underlying grand vision that "something was required to unite Israeli society—some collective experience, one that would be gripping, purifying, . . . a national catharsis" (Segev, 336, 328).

I submit that these pragmatic goals, while carried out, were also overwhelmed and exceeded by the subterranean force and the volcanic impact of the trial's reference to the dead, which took on a legal momentum of its own, later picked up by the victims' own testimonial discourse.

29. I analyzed in Chapter 2 what I call "the cross-legal nature" of historic trials: their typical articulation through a reference to a different trial, of which they reenact the legal memory and the traumatic legal content. I have thus shown how what Freud calls "historical dualities"—the tendency of great historical events to happen twice, to give rise to a twin historical event emerging as a post-traumatic duplicate or a belated double—applies to legal history as well, and structures in particular key trials touching on great collective traumas, that equally quite often manifest a tendency to duplication or to what I termed (in conjunction with the O. J. Simpson case) "a compulsion to a legal repetition" in structurally picking up (unconsciously or by deliberate design) on the traumatic legal meaning of a previous trial. A psychoanalytic logic of traumatic repetition often governs inadvertently what seems to be the purely legal logic of proceedings dealing with major historical phenomena of trauma. (See Sigmund Freud, *Moses and Monotheism*, trans. Katherine Jones [New York: 1967; orig. pub. 1939], p. 64 and part 2, chap. 7, throughout; and Chapter 2 here.) The Eichmann trial is yet another illustration of this phenomenon. Not only does the trial try to heal the legal trauma of the Kastner trial that took place in Israel five years earlier (see Lahav, "The Eichmann Trial, the Jewish Question, and the American-Jewish Intelligentsia," pp. 555, 573). It also formulates precisely the unprecedented nature of its case in reference to a different case articulated in a different language, in a different century, and through a different legal culture

(the Dreyfus case, France 1984–1906). The Eichmann trial thereby chooses to articulate, quite paradoxically, its very claim to legal originality in reference to (the legal trauma of) a previous trial.

30. "Yes, each dead person leaves a little goods, his memory, and asks that it be taken care of," writes the French historian Jules Michelet. "For the sake of him who has no friends, the magistrate, the judge, must substitute for friends. For the law, justice is more reliable than all our forgetful tendernesses, our tears so quickly dried.

"This magistrate's jurisdiction is History. And the dead are, to borrow an expression from Roman law, these *miserabilis personae* with whom the judge has to preoccupy himself.

"Never in my whole career have I lost sight of this historical duty. I have given to many forgotten dead the assistance of which I myself will have need when the time comes.

"I have exhumed them for a second life . . .

"History welcomes and renews these disinherited glories . . . Its justice [creates] a common city between the living and the dead." (Jules Michelet, *Oeuvres complètes*, vol. 21 *Histoire de France* [Paris: Flammarion, 1971], p. 268; my translation.)

31. Thus Socrates, as a condemned philosopher and as role model, gives the example of refusing to escape from Athens to avoid the death sentence the polis has unjustifiably inflicted on him. His only recourse, the philosopher tells his disciple Crito, is persuasion of the court within the legal framework of the trial. Socrates thereby accepts and legally assumes and consummates his role as victim of injustice so as to safeguard (and teach) the supreme principle of the rule of law. See Plato, *Crito*, in *The Dialogues of Plato*, trans. R. E. Allen, vol. 1 (New Haven: Yale University Press, 1984), pp. 123–129.

32. Compare note 29, above, and Chapter 2, section II, subsection "2. The cross-legal nature of the trial."

33. Quoted in Jean-Denis Bredin, *The Affair: The Case of Alfred Dreyfus*, trans. Jeffrey Mehlman (New York: George Brasiller, 1986), p. 456; translation modified.

34. Emile Zola, *J'accuse*, in *J'accuse . . . ! La Vérité en marche* (Paris: Editions Complexe, 1988), pp. 111–113. Emile Zola, *The Dreyfus Affair: J'accuse and Other Writings*, ed. Alain Pagès, trans. Eleanor Levieux (New Haven: Yale University Press: 1996), pp. 52–53; English translation occasionally modified by me according to the French original (modification signaled with "tm" ["translation modified"]). Unless otherwise indicated, page references in parentheses following Zola's quotations will be to the English edition.

35. Zola, "Letter to France," January 7, 1898, in *The Dreyfus Affair*, p. 42.

36. Zola, "Déclaration au jury," in *J'accuse . . . ! La Vérité en marche*, p. 127; my translation.

37. "Ma protestation enflammée n'est que le cri de mon âme" ("My ardent protest is but a cry from my very soul"), Zola said. The challenge Zola met was that of a *translation* of "the cry" to a creative legal action. It is a similar challenge that confronts the prosecutor at the Eichmann trial: the central legal ques-

tion in the trial is how to articulate creatively—yet in a legal idiom that all recognize—the cry (the victim's cry, the soul cry, the cry of the dead, the cry of history that no one has as yet heard within the space and in the language of a trial).

38. Hannah Arendt, *The Origins of Totalitarianism* (New York: Harcourt Brace, 1958, 1973), p. 91

39. Ibid., p. 92. Arendt extends her own suspicion of the state machine (normally concentrated on *totalitarian abuses* of the state machine) to her analysis—and her critique (her "critical history")—of the State of Israel's handling of the Eichmann trial. In this sense, *Arendt formulates her own "J'accuse"* against the state and its judicial system (the nonseparation between church and state that she sarcastically equates with reverse racism: Israeli law indicted right at the outset; *EiJ*, 6–7). Arendt speaks truth to power, unwittingly adopting in her turn Zola's antireligious, antiracist, *antinationalistic, antistatist stance*. Arendt challenges, indeed, Hausner's prerogative to quote Zola in pointing out that Hausner is "a government-appointed agent," not a defiant individual who undertakes to challenge the very justice of the state and the legitimacy of the state's implementation of its judicial system. With her usual sarcasm focused on the chief prosecutor, Arendt writes: "The 'J'accuse,' so indispensable from the viewpoint of the victim, sounds, of course, much more convincing in the mouth of a man who has been forced to take the law into his own hands than in the mouth of a government-appointed official who risks nothing" (*EiJ*, 266). Ironically and without meaning to do so, Arendt will also, like Zola, open herself to trial by the defenders of the state. The Dreyfus affair is thus, in more than one sense, archetypal of positions in the Eichmann trial. The Eichmann trial takes place in the shadow of the distant lessons and of the structural cross-legal memory of the Dreyfus case. See above, note 29.

40. Compare Arendt's report in *EiJ:* "The aim of the conference was to coordinate all efforts toward the implementation of the Final Solution . . . It was a very important occasion for Eichmann, who had never before mingled socially with so many 'high personnages' . . . He had sent out the invitations and had prepared some statistical material . . . for Heydrich's introductory speech—eleven million Jews had to be killed, an undertaking of some magnitude—and *later he had to prepare the minutes*. In short, he *acted as secretary of the meeting*.

"There was another reason that made the day of that conference unforgettable for Eichmann. Although he had been doing his best right along to help in the Final Solution, he had still harbored some doubts about 'such a bloody solution through violence,' and these doubts had now been dispelled. *'Here now, during this conference, the most prominent people had spoken, the Popes of the Third Reich.'* Now he could see with his own eyes and hear with his own ears that not only Hitler . . . but the elite of the good old Civil Service were vying and fighting with each other for the honor of taking the lead in these 'bloody' matters. *'At that moment, I sensed a kind of Pontius Pilate feeling, for I felt free of all guilt'"* (*EiJ*, 113–114; emphasis added).

41. David Ben Gurion, *Israel: A Personal History*, p. 599. Compare Michael

Keren, "Ben Gurion's Theory of Sovereignty: The Trial of Adolf Eichmann," in *David Ben-Gurion: Politics and Leadership in Israel*, ed. Ronald W. Zweig (New York: Frank Cass, 1992).

42. Arendt thus offers what Henry Louis Gates calls a "counternarrative" to the official story of the Eichmann trial. "People," writes Gates, "arrive at an understanding of themselves and the world through narratives—narratives purveyed by schoolteachers, newscasters, 'authorities,' and all the other authors of our common sense. Counternarratives are, in turn, the means by which a group contests that dominant reality and the framework of assumptions that supports it. Sometimes delusion lies that way, sometimes not. There's a sense in which much of black history is simply counternarrative that has been documented and legitimized, by slow, hard-won scholarship." Henry Louis Gates, *Thirteen Ways of Looking at a Black Man* (New York: Random House, 1997), pp. 106–107. Arendt's critical history is the decanonizing and iconoclastic *counternarrative* of a resistant reader, whose faith is in diversity and separation (rather than in unity and in communal solidarity) and who speaks truth to power, from a "position . . . close to the classical anarchist—with anarchy understood to mean the absence of rulers, not the absence of law." (I am borrowing this definition of the anarchist position from Robert Cover, "The Folktales of Justice: Tales of Jurisdiction," in *Narrative, Violence, and the Law*, p. 175.)

43. In Arendt's eyes, the focus on the victims trivializes both the nature of the accusation (the indictment) and the nature of the crime (of the offense). "For just as a murderer is prosecuted because he has violated the law of the community, and not because he has deprived the Smith family of its husband, father and breadwinner, so these modern, state-employed murderers must be prosecuted because they violated the order of mankind, not because they killed millions of people" (*EiJ*, 273).

44. Compare Hausner, *Justice in Jerusalem*, p. 331: "It was often excruciating merely to listen to one of these tales. Sometimes we felt as if our reactions were paralyzed, and we were *benumbed*. It was a story with an unending climax" (emphasis added).

45. Richard Rorty, "Feminism and Pragmatism," *Michigan Quarterly Review* 30 (1991): 231–232.

46. The difficulty of listening was underscored even by the prosecutor. "The narratives," he later writes, "were so overwhelming, so shocking, that we almost stopped observing the witnesses and their individual mannerisms. What impressed itself on the mind was an anonymous cry; it could have been voiced by any one of the millions who had passed through that Gehenna. The survivors who appeared before us were almost closer to the dead than to the living, for each had only the merest chance to thank for his survival . . .

"It was often excruciating merely to listen to one of these tales. Sometimes we felt as if our reactions were paralyzed, and we were benumbed. It was a story with an unending climax. Often I heard loud sobbing behind me in the courtroom. Sometimes there was a commotion, when the ushers removed a listener who had fainted. Newspaper reporters would rush out after an hour or two, explaining that they could not take it without a pause . . .

"The prosecution team was thankful for the 'documentation sessions.'" (Hausner, *Justice in Jerusalem*, pp. 227, 331.)

47. "I was there, and I don't know. How can you possibly know when you were elsewhere?" Elie Wiesel asked Hannah Arendt. "Her reply: 'You're a novelist; you can cling to questions. I deal with human and political sciences. I have no right not to find answers.'" Elie Wiesel, *All Rivers Run to the Sea: Memoirs*, vol. 1 (1928–1969) (New York: Harper Collins, 1995), p. 348.

48. In consciously unsettling the dichotomy (the segregation and the opposition) between the private and the public, the Eichmann trial was, in 1961, ahead of other legal movements (such as feminism, black studies, gay studies) that would equally seek to unsettle this dichotomy in their political struggles during the seventies, the eighties, and the nineties.

For feminist critiques of the public/private divide, see, for example, Catharine A. MacKinnon, "Feminism, Marxism, Method and the State: Toward Feminist Jurisprudence," *Signs: Journal of Women in Culture and Society* 8 (1983): 635; Frances Olsen, "The Family and the Market: A Study of Ideology and Legal Reform," *Harvard Law Review* 96 (1983): 1497; Carole Pateman, "Feminist Critiques of the Public/Private Dichotomy," in *The Disorder of Women: Democracy, Feminism and Political Theory* (Cambridge: Polity, 1989), p. 118; Elizabeth M. Schneider, "The Violence of Privacy," *Connecticut Law Review* 23 (1992): 973; Nicola Lacey, "Theory into Practice? Pornography and the Private/Public Dichotomy," *Journal of Law and Society* 20 (1993): 93. For critiques of the dichotomy of private/public by critical race theorists, see, for instance, Kimberlé Crenshaw, "Demarginalizing the Intersection of Race and Sex: A Black Feminist Critique of Antidiscrimination Doctrine, Feminist Theory and Antiracist Politics," *University of Chicago Legal Forum* (1989): 139; Mari Matsuda, "Public Response to Racist Speech: Considering the Victim's Story," *Michigan Law Review* 87 (1989): 2320; Charles R. Lawrence, "If He Hollers Let Him Go: Regulating Racist Speech on Campus," *Duke Law Journal* (1990): 431; Patricia Williams, *The Alchemy of Race and Rights, Diary of a Law Professor* (Cambridge, Mass.: Harvard University Press, 1991). For critiques of the public/private distinction from a gay-rights perspective, see, for instance, "The Constitutional Status of Sexual Orientation: Homosexuality as a Suspect Classification," *Harvard Law Review* 98 (1985): 1285; Mary Anne Case, "Couples and Coupling in the Private Sphere: A Comment on the Legal History of Litigating for Lesbian and Gay Rights," *Virginia Law Review* 79 (1993): 1643. On the history of the public/private distinction generally, see Morton J. Horwitz, "The History of the Public/Private Dichotomy," *Pennsylvania Law Review* 130 (1982): 1423; Duncan Kennedy, "The Stages of the Decline of the Public/Private Distinction," *Pennsylvania Law Review* 130 (1982): 1349.

In her perspicacious analysis of the Eichmann trial, Pnina Lahav analyzed the trial's deconstruction of the public/private dichotomy with respect not to the victim experience but to the fact of Jewishness and its relevance. See Lahav, "The Eichmann Trial, the Jewish Question, and the American-Jewish Intelligentsia," p. 555. See also Lahav, *Judgment in Jerusalem*, pp. 145–164, and Annette Wieviorka, "L'Avènement du témoin," in *L'Ère du témoin*, pp. 81–126.

For analyses of the ways in which Arendt's political theory contested traditional understandings of private and public (based on Arendt's own analytical distinction between "the Private" and "the Public" and between "the Social" and "the Political" in *The Human Condition* and in *On Revolution*) see, among others, Benhabib, *The Reluctant Modernism of Hannah Arendt*, pp. 173–215; Hanna Fenischel Pitkin, "Justice: On Relating Private and Public," in *Hannah Arendt: Critical Essays*, pp. 261–288; see also Shiraz Dossa, "Hannah Arendt on Eichmann: The Public, the Private and Evil," reprinted in Dossa, *Public Realm and Public Self*.

49. Ka-Tzetnik 135633, *Shivitti: A Vision*, trans. Eliyah Nike De-Nur and Lisa Herman (San Francisco: Harper and Row, 1987), p. x; Hebrew original: K-Zetnik, *Tsofan: Edma* (Tel Aviv: Hakibbutz Hameuhad, 1987), p. 8. I am using Arendt's orthography to transcribe the writer's name (K-Zetnik).

50. *Shivitti*, pp. 1–2, translation modified; Hebrew ed., p. 18.

51. Ibid., pp. 31–32, translation modified.

52. *Shoah: The Complete Text of the Film by Claude Lanzmann* (New York: Pantheon Books, 1985), pp. 12–13.

53. This definition is inspired by the analysis of the political psychiatrist Thomas Szasz, in his book *Ideology and Insanity: Esssays on the Psychiatric Dehumanization of Man* (New York: Doubleday/Anchor Books, 1970), p. 5: "Rulers have always conspired against their subjects and sought to keep them in bondage; and, to achieve their aims, they have always relied on force and fraud. Indeed, when the justificatory rhetoric with which the oppressor conceals and misrepresents his true aims and methods is most effective—. . . the oppressor succeeds not only in subduing his victim but also in robbing him of a vocabulary for articulating his victimization, thus making him a captive deprived of all means of escape." Compare the philosophical analysis of Jean-François Lyotard in *The Differend: Phrases in Dispute*, trans. Georges Van Den Abbeele (Minneapolis: University of Minnesota Press, 1988), pp. 3, 5: "You are informed that human beings endowed with language were placed in a situation such that none of them is now able to tell about it. Most of them disappeared then, and the survivors rarely speak about it. When they do speak about it, their testimony bears only upon a minute part of this situation. How can you know that the situation itself existed? . . . In all of these cases, to the privation constituted by the damage is added the impossibility of bringing it to the knowledge of others, and in particular to the knowledge of a tribunal." For other theories of victimhood, see, among others, Martha Minow, *Between Vengeance and Forgiveness: Facing History after Genocide and Mass Violence* (Boston: Beacon Press, 1998); Martha Minow, "Surviving Victim Talk," *UCLA Law Review* 40 (1993): 1411; Joseph Amato: *Victims and Values: A History and Theory of Suffering* (New York: Greenwood Publishing Group, 1990); Orlando Patterson, *Slavery and Social Death* (Cambridge, Mass.; Harvard University Press, 1982); and William Ryan, *Blaming the Victim* (New York: Vintage Books, 1976).

54. Compare Rorty, "Feminism and Pragmatism," p. 133: "For until then only the language of the oppressor is available, and most oppressors have had the wit to teach the oppressed a language in which the oppressed will sound crazy—

even to themselves—if they describe themselves as oppressed." Rorty is interpreting and summing up the teachings of feminist writings such as Marilyn Frye,
The Politics of Reality (Trumansburg, N.Y.: Crossing Press, 1983), pp. 33 and
112, and Catharine MacKinnon, "On Exceptionality," in *Feminism Unmodified:
Discourses on Life and Law* (Cambridge, Mass.: Harvard University Press, 1987),
p. 105: "Especially when you are part of a subordinated group, your own definition of your injuries is powerfully shaped by your assessment of whether you
could get anyone do anything about it, including anything official." Rorty proceeds to comment, reformulating the insights of both Frye and MacKinnon:
"Only where there is a socially accepted remedy can there have been a real
(rather than crazily imagined) injury" ("Feminism and Pragmatism," p. 251).

55. *Shoah*, p. 12.

56. Ibid., p. 68.

57. Arendt does not see the trial as a revolution. She does not underscore or
does not fully recognize the revolutionary dimension of the trial. I argue nonetheless that it is, among other factors, her newborn interest in revolutions—the
subject of the book on which she is already working and that will become precisely the successor to the Eichmann book—that inadvertently, intuitively, draws
her to the trial in Jerusalem.

58. From a different vantage point, compare Mark Osiel's analysis of the limits of traditional criminal law in its response to administrative massacre. "Alongside such Promethean aspirations," Osiel remarks, "the traditional purposes of
criminal law—deterrence and retribution of culpable wrongdoing—are likely to
seem quite pedestrian . . . As an aim for criminal law, the cultivation of collective
memory resembles deterrence in that it is directed toward the future, where enhanced solidarity is sought. But like retribution, it looks to the past, to provide
the narrative content of what is to be shared in memory." (Mark Osiel, "Ever
Again: Legal Remembrance of Administrative Massacre," *University of Pennsylvania Law Review* 144 [1995]: 463, 474.)

My own argument concerns not simply the purposes of criminal law in their
excess of traditional conceptions, but what I have called the conceptual revolution in the very status of the victims operated by and through the Eichmann
trial. *My claim is that the posture of the Eichmann trial with respect to victims is
unique*—and different from the legally familiar definitions of the issues for debate, currently discussed in legal scholarship through its contemporary reassess-
ment and reformulation of the role of victims in criminal trials. Within the
context of these contemporary debates, Paul Gewirtz notes how "modern law
enforcement continues to struggle to find an appropriate place for victims and
survivors in the criminal process . . . Indeed, no movement in criminal law has
been more powerful in the past twenty years than the victims' rights movement,
which has sought to enhance the place of the victim in the criminal trial process"
(Paul Gewirtz, "Victims and Voyeurs: Two Narrative Problems at the Criminal
Trial," in *Law's Stories: Narrative and Rhetoric in the Law*, ed. Peter Brooks and
Paul Gewirtz [New Haven: Yale University Press, 1996], p. 139). "In 1982
alone," writes Lynne N. Henderson, "California voters approved a 'Victims' Bill
of Rights' that made substantial changes in the California law . . . Although 'vic-

tims' rights' may be viewed as a populist movement responding to perceived injustices in the criminal process, genuine questions about victims and victimization have become increasingly co-opted by the concerns of advocates of the 'crime control' model of criminal justice" (Lynn N. Henderson, "The Wrongs of Victims' Rights," *Stanford Law Review* 37 [1985]: 937). Martha Minow "worries," thus, about "the contemporary prevalence in legal and political arenas of victim stories": "One who claims to be a victim invites, besides sympathy, two other responses: 'I didn't do it,' and 'I am a victim, too.' No wonder," Minow writes, that "some describe contemporary political debates as exhibitions of 'one-downmanship' or as the 'oppression Olympics.' Victim stories risk trivializing pain and obscuring the metric or vantage point for evaluating competing stories of pain. Victim stories often also adhere to an unspoken norm that prefers narratives of helplessness to stories of responsibility, and tales of victimization to narratives of human agency and capacity" (Martha Minow, "Stories in the Law," in *Law's Stories*, pp. 31–32).

Arendt objects, precisely, to the focus on the victims in the Eichmann trial because she too prefers existential "stories of responsibility" to "narratives of helplessness." My point is different, and can summarized as follows:

(1) In 1961 the Eichmann trial gives a central role to victims, in historical anticipation of the political emergence of the question of the victim at the forefront of criminal jurisprudential debates today.

(2) What is at issue in the Eichmann trial is not (what today's scholars focus on as) *victims' rights* but rather (what I will define as) the question of the *victims'* (legal and historical) *authority* (see "Part Five: The Web of Stories" in this chapter), insofar as this newborn authority changes not simply our *ethical* perception of the victim but also our *cognitive* perception of history.

(3) The debates on victims' rights perceive the victims as individuals; the Eichmann trial creates a collective, a community of victims.

(4) Ordinarily (in current legal discourse and analysis) *the victim is perceived in opposition to the state,* or as victimized mainly by the state. (Although there are moments in which the state divides against itself to correct its own abuses, as in the case of the American civil rights laws enforced by the federal government against the resistance of individual states.) The Eichmann trial is a unique moment and a unique case in which *the state defends the victims, who were made victims by another state.* The trial performs a unique exchange between victims and state, in that, *through the trial, victims and state mutually transform each other's political identity.* The state that represents the victims plans the trial, and the victims' stories add up to a saga and create the case of the state that, in its turn, creates a transformation (here analyzed as a conceptual revolution) in the victims.

(5) My approach in this respect is therefore different both from that of Arendt and from that of her opponents: it is distinct from the accepted interpretations of the role of the victims in the Eichmann trial. In my view, the victims/witnesses are not simply expressing their suffering: they are *reclaiming legal subjecthood* and autobiographical personhood. They *change within the trial* from being merely victims to something else. *They are carrying out a prosecution* (a "J'accuse" articulated through a legal process). Through this recovery of speech

and this recovery of history, they reinvent an innovative logos that is *no longer simply victims' logos* but constitutes a new kind of legal language. In the act of claiming their humanity, their history, their story, and their voice before the law and before the world, they are actively (and sovereignly) reborn from a kind of social death into a new life.

(6) Arendt sees and takes great pains to point out the danger inherent in the fact that the state creates a monumental history: for her, the combination of monumental history with the self-authorization of the state spells fascism. My argument, however, is that, although the Eichmann trial was monumental history created by the state for political purposes that were particularist and Zionist-nationalistic, the consequences of the trial were momentous, in that the trial has in fact created (or enacted) a *universalization of the victim*. Thus, the trial as event exceeded and surpassed the intentions of its planners.

Legal scholars continue to debate the proper role for victims in criminal prosecutions. For a contemporary victim-oriented vision of criminal justice, see George P. Fletcher, *With Justice for Some: Victims' Rights in Criminal Trials* (Reading, Mass.: Addison-Wesley, 1995). Fletcher argues that "[t]he minimal task of the criminal trial . . . is to stand by victims, to restore their dignity, to find a way for them to think of themselves, once again, as men and women equal to all others" (ibid., p. 6). For a critique of Fletcher's approach, see Robert P. Mosteller, Book Review, "Popular Justice," *Harvard Law Review* 109 (1995): 487. For an overview of the law surrounding victims, see Douglas E. Beloof, *Victims in Criminal Procedure* (Durham: Carolina Academic Press, 1999).

For discussions of the modern victims' rights movement in criminal law, see, among others: Minow, "Surviving Victim Talk"; Donald Hall, "Victims' Voices in Criminal Courts: The Need for Restraint," *American Criminal Law Review* 28 (1991): 937; Robert Elias, *The Politics of Victimization: Victims, Victimology and Human Rights* (New York: Oxford University Press, 1990); Leroy Lamborn, "Victim Participation in the Criminal Justice Process: The Proposal for a Constitutional Amendment," *Wayne Law Review* 34 (1987): 125; Lynne Henderson, "The Wrongs of Victims' Rights," *Stanford Law Review* 37 (1985): 937; Andrew Karmen, *Crime Victims: An Introduction to Victimology* (Monterey, Calif.: Brooks/Cole Publishing, 1984); Josephine Glitter, "Expanding the Role of the Victim in a Criminal Action: An Overview of Issues and Problems," *Pepp. Law Review* 11 (1984): 117; Abraham Goldstein, "Defending the Role of the Victim in Criminal Prosecutions," *Mississippi Law Review* 52 (1982): 515; President's Task Force on Victims of Crime, *Final Report* (Washington, D.C.: U.S. Government Printing Office, 1982); U.S. Department of Justice, *Four Years Later: A Report of the President's Task Force on Victims of Crime* (Washington, D.C.: U.S. Government Printing Office, 1986).

On different kinds of political victims and on victimhood more generally, see above, references in notes 48, 53, 54.

On victim impact statements, see, among others: Susan Bandes, "Empathy, Narrative, and Victim Impact Statements," *University of Chicago Law Review* 63 (1996): 361; Carole A. Mansur, "*Payne v. Tennessee:* The Effect of Victim Harm at Capital Sentencing Trials and the Resurgence of Victim Impact Statements,"

New England Law Review 27 (1993); Angela P. Harris, "The Jurisprudence of Victimhood," 1991 *Sup. Ct. Review,* 77; Vivia Berger, "Payne and Suffering: A Personal Reflection and a Victim-Centered Critique," *Florida State Law Review* 20 (1992): 22; Victor Vytal, "*Payne v. Tennessee:* The Use of Victim Impact Evidence at Capital Sentencing Trials," *Thurgood Marshall Law Review* 19 (1994); Dina Hellerstein, "The Victim Impact Statement: Reform or Reprisal?" *American Criminal Law Review* 27 (1989): 371.

For a summary of the issues of identity and representation, and for an analysis of the question, "Who can speak for whom?" see Martha Minow, "Not Only for Myself: Identity, Politics and Law," *Oregon Law Review* 75 (1996): 647.

59. See, for instance, Segev, *The Seventh Million.*

60. Rorty, "Feminism and Pragmatism," p. 233.

61. "It came as a discovery to many that we were actually a nation of survivors," prosecutor Hausner noted in his memoirs of the trial: "The editor of a leading newspaper told me, after listening to the shattering evidence of a woman witness in court: 'For years I have been living next to this woman, without so much as an inkling of who she was.' It now transpired that almost everyone in Israel had such a neighbor." (Hausner, *Justice in Jerusalem,* p. 453.)

62. Semantic authority is, among others things, what endows a story with transmissibility and unforgettability. "Not only a man's knowledge," writes Walter Benjamin, "but above all his real life . . . first assume transmissible form at the moment of his death. Just as a sequence of images is set in motion inside a man as his life comes to en end—unfolding the views of himself under which he has encountered himself without being aware of it—suddenly in his expressions and looks the unforgettable emerges and imparts to everything that concerned him that authority which even the poorest wretch in dying possesses for the living around him. This authority is at the very source of the story.

"Death is the sanction of everything that the storyteller has to tell. He has borrowed his authority from death" (Benjamin, "St.," 94).

On "the mystical foundation of authority" in law and jurisprudence, see Jacques Derrida, "Force of Law," in *Deconstruction and the Possibility of Justice, Cardozo Law Review* 11 (1990): 919.

On Arendt's views of the theorist as storyteller, see Melvyn A. Hill, "The Fictions of Mankind and the Stories of Man," in *Hannah Arendt: The Recovery of the Public World;* David Luban, "Explaining Dark Times: Hannah Arendt's Theory of Theory," in *Hannah Arendt: Critical Essays,* pp. 79–110; and Benhabib, *The Reluctant Modernism of Hannah Arendt,* pp. 91–95.

63. Walter Benjamin, "On Some Motifs in Baudelaire," *Ill.,* p. 159.

64. Benjamin, "St.," 102.

65. Ibid., p. 98.

66. Cover, "The Folktales of Justice: Tales of Jurisdiction," in *Narrative, Violence, and the Law,* p. 176.

67. Cover, "Nomos and Narrative," in *Narrative, Violence, and the Law,* pp. 95–96.

68. Compare Lawrence Douglas, "The Memory of Judgment," *History and Memory* 7 (1996): 100, at 114, 120, underscoring "the failure of the Nurem-

berg trial [to] adequately address the Nazi genocide" of the Jews, and observing that the Nuremberg tribunal adopted an "approach that placed the Holocaust on the margins of the legally relevant."

69. *Report to the President by Mr. Justice Jackson, Oct. 7, 1946,* in U.S. Department of State, Report of Robert H. Jackson, U.S. Representative to the International Conference on Military Trials, p. 437; quoted by Robert Cover in *Narrative, Violence, and the Law,* p. 196 (emphasis mine).

70. Arendt regrets "the extreme reluctance of all concerned to break fresh ground and act without precedents" (*EiJ,* 262), and charges: "The court . . . never rose to the challenge of the unprecedented, not even in regard to the unprecedented nature of the origins of the Israel state . . . Instead, it buried the proceedings under a flood of precedents" (263). "I think it is safe to predict," Arendt concludes, "that this last of the Successor trials will no more, and perhaps even less, than its predecessors, serve as a valid precedent for future trials of such crimes. This might be of little import in view of the fact that its main purpose—to prosecute and to defend, to judge and to punish Adolf Eichmann—was achieved, if it were not for the rather uncomfortable but hardly deniable possibility that similar crimes might be committed in the future . . . If genocide is an actual possibility of the future, then no people on earth—least of all, of course, the Jewish people, in Israel or elsewhere—can feel reasonably sure of its continued existence without the help and the protection of international law. Success or failure in dealing with the hitherto unprecedented can lie only in the extent to which this dealing may serve as a valid precedent on the road to international penal law" (*EiJ,* 272–273).

71. "Thus," Cover insists, "the claim to a law is a claim as well to an understanding of a literature and a tradition." "The Folktales of Justice," p. 177.

72. Compare Jacques Derrida's analysis of the principle of "man's sacrality" (as understood by Walter Benjamin) in Derrida, "Force of Law," pp. 920, 1028–1029 (emphasis added): "'Thou shall not kill' remains an absolute imperative . . . which forbids all murder, *sacralizes life* . . . Benjamin . . . stands up against the sacralization of life *for itself,* natural life . . . *What makes for the worth of man* [*what makes for "man's sacrality"*] . . . *is that he contains the potential, the possibility of justice,* the yet-to-come of justice, the yet-to-come of being just, of his having-to-be just. *What is sacred in his life is not his life but the justice of his life."*

On the foundational value of the Eichmann trial's inadvertent testimonial constitution of a "sacred narrative," compare Mark Osiel's analysis of the way in which legal proceedings constitute foundational narrative events: "All societies have founding myths, explaining where we come from, defining what we stand for. These are often commemorated in the form of 'monumental didactics,' public recounting of the founders' heroic deeds as a national epic. Some societies also have myths of refounding, marking a period of decisive break with their own pasts, celebrating the courage and imagination of those who effected this rupture. Myths of founding and refounding often center on legal proceedings or the drafting of legal documents: the Magna Carta (for Britain), the trial and execution of King Louis XVI (for France), and the Declaration of Independence and the Constitutional Convention (for the United States) . . . Such legally induced transformations of collective identity are not confined to the distant past . . . These events are both 'real' and 'staged,' to the point of problematizing the distinction between true and false representations of reality. In these ways, law-related activities can and do contribute to the kind of social solidarity that is enhanced by shared historical memory" ("Ever Again: Legal Remembrance of Administrative Massacre," pp. 463, 464–466).

However, as Osiel points out, "sometimes the memory of a major legal event will initially unify the nation that experienced it, but later be interpreted so differently by contending factions that its memory becomes divisive" (ibid., p. 476). Thus, the act of founding can become "the focal point for later disputes about its meaning and bearing . . . on contemporary disputes." This has been the case of the foundational legal event of the Eichmann trial. The canonical meaning of the victims' solidarity amounting to (what can be called) the trial's "sacred narrative" later gave rise to decanonizing and desacralizing critiques of the political, commercial, and manipulative uses and abuses made of the memory of the Holocaust and of the trial. Arendt's was in fact the first *decanonizing and desacralizing reading* of the "sacred narrative" offered by the trial. For other desacralizing political critiques of the fantasies, distortions, and political abuses born of, or sanctioned by, the Eichmann trial, see Lahav, "The Eichmann Trial, the Jewish Question, and the American-Jewish Intelligentsia," pp. 555, 574–575; Segev, *The Seventh Million;* Idith Zertal, "From the People's Hall to the Wailing Wall: A Study in Memory, Fear and War," *Representations* 69 (2000): 39–59.

73. Paul Celan, "Conversation in the Mountain," in *Last Poems* (San Francisco: North Point Press, 1986), pp. 207–212.

4. A Ghost in the House of Justice

1. Friedrich Nietzsche, *The Use and Abuse of History for Life,* trans. Adrian Collins, introduction by Julius Kraft (New York: Liberal Arts Press, 1949, 1957), pp. 12–17. See Chapter 3, section II, subsection entitled "History for Life."

2. Robert Jackson, "Introduction," in Whitney Harris, *Tyranny on Trial: The Evidence at Nuremberg* (New York: Barnes and Noble, 1954, 1995), pp. xxxv–xxxvi.

3. "Novelist Rebecca West, covering the first 'historic' Nuremberg trial for the *New Yorker,* found it insufferably tedious," writes Mark Osiel (Rebecca West, "Extraordinary Exile," *New Yorker,* Sept. 7, 1946, pp. 34, 34). "This reaction was not uncommon. As one reporter notes (Alex Ross, "Watching for a Judgment of Real Evil," *New York Times,* Nov. 12, 1995, section 2, p. 37): 'It was the largest crime in history and it promised the greatest courtroom spectacle. [But] . . . What ensued was an excruciatingly long and complex trial that failed to mesmerize a distracted world. Its mass of evidence created boredom, mixed occasionally with an abject horror before which ordinary justice seemed helpless.'" Quoted in Mark Osiel, *Mass Atrocity, Collective Memory and the Law* (New Brunswick, N.J.: Transaction Publishers, 2000), p. 91.

4. Gideon Hausner, *Justice in Jerusalem* (New York: Harper and Row, 1968; orig. pub. 1966), pp. 291–292.

5. In a short text called "The Witness," Jorge Luis Borges writes:

Deeds which populate the dimensions of space and which reach their end when someone dies may cause us wonderment, but one thing, or an infinite number of things, dies in every final agony, unless there is a universal memory . . . What will die with me when I die, what pathetic and fragile form will the world lose? (Jorge Luis Borges, *Labyrinths: Selected Stories and Other Writings* [New York: New Directions, 1962], p. 243)

It is because humans, unlike documents, do not endure that the Eichmann trial calls upon each witness to narrate the singular story that will die when he or she dies. Transience is inscribed within this legal process as the witness's death is, from the start, implicitly inscribed within each testimony.

While documents—unlike the living witnesses—exclude death as a possibility inherent in the evidence, and while the Nuremberg trials claim authority precisely in the act of sheltering the courtroom from the death it talks about, in the Eichmann trial, on the contrary (to use Walter Benjamin's expression), "Death is the sanction of everything the storyteller has to tell. He has borrowed his authority from death" (Benjamin, "St.," 94).

6. Attested to by the chief prosecutor's widow in *The Trial of Adolf Eichmann*, a PBS documentary Home Video (B3470), a coproduction of ABC News Productions and Great Projects Film Company, 1997.

7. The Eichmann trial was the first trial televised in its entirety. The complete trial footage is kept in the archives of the State of Israel.

8. "Our memory," writes Paul Valéry, "repeats to us the discourse that we have not understood. Repetition is responding to incomprehension. It signifies to us that the act of language has not been accomplished." Paul Valéry, "Commentaires de *Charmes*," in Valéry, *Oeuvres* (Paris: Gallimard, Bibliothèque de la Pléiade, 1957), vol. 1, p. 1510; my translation.

9. The writer published the English translation of his works under the pseudonym Ka-Tzetnik 135633. An alternative orthography of the author's name, the one used in the trial's English transcripts and in Arendt's *Eichmann in Jerusalem*, is K-Zetnik (since the name is modeled on the German letters KZ, pronounced Ka-tzet, from *Konzentrationslager*, "concentration camp"). This latter orthography is the one I will use.

10. See Criminal Case 40/61 (Jerusalem), *Attorney General v. Eichmann* (1961). English translation of the trial transcripts in *The Trial of Adolf Eichmann: Record of Proceedings in the District Court of Jerusalem*, vol. 3, Session 68 (June 7, 1961), Jerusalem 1963, p. 1237. I use here the modified English version quoted by Hannah Arendt in *Eichmann in Jerusalem* (*EiJ*, 224).

11. K-Zetnik, *Tzofan: Edma* (Tel Aviv: Hakibbutz Hameuchad Publishing House, 1987), p. 32; in English, Ka-Tzetnik 135633, *Shivitti: A Vision*, trans. Eliyah Nike De-Nur and Lisa Hermann (San Francisco: Harper and Row, 1989), p. 16. I will hereafter refer to this text by the abbreviation *Shivitti*. The letter H (Hebrew) will designate the original Hebrew edition; the letter E (English) will

refer to this American edition. The abbreviation tm (translation modified) will mark my occasional modifications of the English translation according to the Hebrew original.

12. The narrative that follows is a literal transcription of the trial footage (session of K-Zetnik's testimony), as seen in the PBS documentary *The Trial of Adolf Eichmann*. See also Criminal Case 40/61 (Jerusalem), *Attorney General v. Eichmann* (1961), in *The Trial of Adolf Eichmann: Record of Proceedings in the District Court of Jerusalem*, vol. 3, Session 68 (June 7, 1961), Jerusalem 1963, p. 1237. Hereinafter abbreviated *Proceedings*.

13. Yehiel Dinoor was forty-five years old at the time of the trial. He passed away in his house in Tel Aviv in July 2000 at the age of eighty-four. Born in Poland as Yehiel Feiner (Segev, *The Seventh Million*, 4), he had changed his legal name to the Hebrew name Dinoor, meaning "a residue from the fire." The name Dinoor is spelled alternatively as Dinur (in the trial's English transcripts, see *Proceedings*, vol. 3, p. 1237), as De-nur (in *Shivitti* and, consequently, in Segev), and as Dinoor (in Arendt, *Eichmann in Jerusalem*). I am following Arendt's orthography because it best corresponds to the Hebrew pronunciation of the name.

14. "All Israel held its breath," Tom Segev will remember thirty years later. "It was the most dramatic moment of the trial, one of the most dramatic moments in the country's history" (Segev, 4).

15. Haim Gouri, *Facing the Glass Cage: The Jerusalem Trial* (Tel Aviv: Hakibbutz Hameuchad Publishing House, 1962), p. 124; my translation from the Hebrew.

16. Nietzsche, *The Use and Abuse of History for Life*, pp. 12-17. On the difference between the monumental and the critical versions of the Eichmann trial, see Chapter 3, section II, subsection "History for Life."

17. Compare Karl Jaspers, *The Question of German Guilt*, trans. E. B. Ashton (New York: Fordham University Press, 2001; orig. pub. 1947).

18. Hannah Arendt, letter to Karl Jaspers of August 18, 1946 (letter 43), in Arendt and Jaspers, *Correspondence: 1926-1969 (AJ Corr.)*, p. 54; emphasis mine. In cited passages the emphasis is mine unless otherwise indicated.

19. Letter 46 (October 19, 1946), *AJ Corr.*, 62.

20. Letter 50 (December 17, 1946), ibid., p. 68.

21. Letter 173 (December 16, 1960), ibid., p. 413.

22. Letter 274 (December 23, 1960), ibid., p. 417.

23. Arendt refers to the common sense of the situation. But, as Robert Ferguson notes, "common sense, as anthropologists have begun to show, is basically *a culturally constructed use of experience to claim self evidence;* it is neither more nor less than 'an authoritative story' made out of the familiar." Robert Ferguson, "Untold Stories in the Law," in *Law's Stories: Narrative and Rhetoric in the Law*, ed. Peter Brooks and Paul Gewirtz (New Haven: Yale University Press, 1996), p. 87, referring to Clifford Geertz, "Commonsense as a Cultural System," in Geertz, *Local Knowledge: Further Essays in Interpretive Anthropology* (New York: Basic Books, 1983), pp. 73-93.

24. In the PBS and ABC News documentary *The Trial of Adolph Eichmann*,

Hausner's wife corroborates this fact, explaining why her husband chose to call K-Zetnik despite the reluctance of the writer.

25. I analyze this *missed encounter* and this *professional misunderstanding* for different purposes than simply to contrast (as does, for instance, Mark Osiel) *disciplinary differences.* "It is this confessedly subjective experience—irrelevant to criminal law," writes Osiel, "that oral historians have only recently sought to explore. In this respect, scholars have perceived the need to overcome what they perceive as a 'legal' concern with the factual accuracy of personal testimony in order to apprehend its historical significance. That is, these scholars try to grasp the meaning of the period's most traumatic events through the continuing memory of those who lived through its trauma. One such scholar writes:

"'Testimonies are often labelled as 'subjective' or 'biased' in the legal proceedings concerning war crimes. The lawyers of war criminals have asked the most impertinent questions of people trying to find words for a shattered memory that did not fit into any language . . . They demand precise statements of facts . . . A lawyer's case is after all merely another kind of story . . .

". . . It is not the task of oral historians to give the kind of evidence required in a court of law . . . [Some historians attempt to uncover] the ways in which suffering is remembered and influences all other memory . . . One is dealing with an effort to create a new kind of history that cannot be used as legal evidence since it explicitly records subjective experience." (Selma Leydersdorff, "A Shattered Silence: The Life Stories of Survivors of the Jewish Proletariat at Amsterdam," in *Memory and Totalitarianism,* ed. Luisa Passerini [New York: Oxford University Press, 1992], pp. 145, 147–148. Quoted and surveyed in Mark Osiel, *Mass Atrocity, Collective Memory and the Law* [New Brunswick, N.J.: Transaction Publishers, 2000], pp. 103–104.)

My own interest is not in contrasting the historical recording of trauma with that of the law, but in exploring and in analyzing, on the contrary, ways in which collective trauma is apprehended (and misapprehended) by the law, and ways in which the very *limits of the law* in its encounter (or its *missed encounter*) with the phenomenon of trauma *reveal* precisely cultural aspects of its traumatic meaning.

26. *Shivitti,* H 50, E 32, tm.

27. For an elaborate analysis of my own "jurisprudential trauma theory," see Chapter 2, in particular sections I, IV, V. For the philosophical and psychoanalytic insights of trauma theory in general, see, in particular, *Trauma: Explorations in Memory,* ed. Cathy Caruth (Baltimore: Johns Hopkins University Press, 1995); and Cathy Caruth, *Unclaimed Experience: Trauma, Narrative and History* (Baltimore: Johns Hopkins University Press, 1996).

28. On the phenomenon of intrusive memory and of traumatic repetition prevalent in the aftermath of trauma, see, for instance, Bessel A. van der Kolk and Onno van der Hart, "The Intrusive Past: The Flexibility of Memory and the Engraving of Trauma," in *TEM,* ed. Caruth, 158–182.

29. This terrified collapse is at the same time an improbable act of resistance, a gesture of defiance of the court and of its ruling.

30. *Shivitti,* H 24, E 9, tm. I will use this literary, autobiographical narrative, written subsequently by K-Zetnik to describe his psychiatric therapy for his re-

current Auschwitz nightmares, to retrospectively illuminate the drama of the courtroom scene.

31. Ibid., H 107, E 95.

32. Ibid., H 57, E 40, tm. Compare: "But I have no choice. I am unable to answer questions. In general I cannot sustain interrogation. This is a trauma whose origin is in the torture cellar of the Gestapo in Katowice." *Shivitti*, H 37, E 20, tm.

33. *Shivitti*, H 8–9, E x–xi.

34. Ibid., H 32, E 16, tm.

35. Ibid., H 33, E x–xi, tm.

36. Ibid., H 34, E 18, tm.

37. *Proceedings*, vol. 1, Session 6 (April 17, 1961), Jerusalem 1962, p. 62. Quoted in Hausner, *Justice in Jerusalem*, pp. 323–324; Arendt, *EiJ*, p. 260.

38. Under this name with which he signs his literary work and which materializes his oath to the dead, Dinoor continues not just to remember those who left him, but also, as a writer, to give literary voice to their last look and to their final silence.

39. "It now appeared," writes Arendt, "that the era of the Hitler regime, with its gigantic, unprecedented crimes, *constituted an 'unmastered past'* not only for the German people or the Jews all over the world, but for the rest of the world, which had not forgotten this great catastrophe in the heart of Europe either, and had also been unable to come to terms with it. Moreover—and this was perhaps less expected—general moral questions, with all their intricacies and modern complexities, which I would never have suspected would haunt men's minds today and weigh heavily on their hearts, stood suddenly in the foreground of public concern" (*EiJ*, p. 283, emphasis mine).

40. On the relation between trials and historical and cultural abysses, see Chapter 2, section V.

41. This abyss, this epistemological rupture, is what the Eichmann trial and its monumental history (at once the prosecution's case and the text of the judgment) precisely fails to perceive, in Arendt's eyes. "I have insisted," Arendt writes, "on . . . how little Israel, and the Jewish people in general, was prepared to recognize, in the crimes that Eichmann was accused of, an unprecedented crime . . . In the eyes of the Jews, thinking exclusively in terms of their own history, the catastrophe that had befallen them under Hitler, in which a third of the people perished, appeared not as the most recent of crimes, the unprecedented crime of genocide, but on the contrary, as the oldest crime they knew and remembered. This misunderstanding . . . is actually at the root of all the failures and the shortcomings of the Jerusalem trial. *None of the participants ever arrived at a clear understanding of the actual horror of Auschwitz, which is of a different nature from all the atrocities of the past* . . . Politically and legally, . . . these were 'crimes' different not only in degree of seriousness but in essence" (*EiJ*, 267; emphasis added).

Compare Arendt's insistence in her 1946 letter to Jaspers on the abyss that, henceforth inhabiting both guilt and innocence, explodes the tool of law in bursting open all legal frameworks: "The Nazi crimes, it seems to me, *explode the limits of the law* . . . this guilt, in contrast to all criminal guilt, oversteps and *shatters any and all legal systems*. That is the reason why the Nazis in Nuremberg are so smug . . . And just as inhuman as their guilt is the innocence of the victims. . . *This is the abyss that opened up* before us as early as 1933 . . . and into which we have finally stumbled. I don't know how we will ever get out of it" (letter 43 [August 18, 1946], *AJ Corr.*, 54; italics mine).

42. Hannah Arendt, "'What Remains? The Language Remains': A Conversation with Günter Gaus," in Hannah Arendt, *Essays in Understanding, 1930–1954*, ed. Jerome Kohn (New York: Harcourt Brace, 1994), pp. 13–14.

43. Ibid., p. 14.

44. Susan Sontag, "Reflections on *The Deputy*," in *The Storm over* The Deputy, ed. Eric Bentley (New York: Grove Press, 1964), p. 118. This comment was, of course, an utterly astonishing remark whose value lay in the surprise that it reserved, in its unsettling power with respect to any simple-minded or reductive legalistic understanding of the trial.

Provocatively, Sontag argued that there was a dimension in the trial that was excessive to its legal definition. She called this dimension "art," because she felt the trial left an impact on the audience that was, in its strength and depth, comparable to the expressive power of a work of art. The trial moved her and existentially and philosophically engaged her. Sontag insisted, therefore, that the trial had a *literary meaning* in addition to its *legal meaning*, and that this extralegal meaning was somehow utterly important for a full grasp of what was at stake in this event of law. The value of Sontag's interpretation lies, in my eyes, not in its axiomatic categorization of the trial as a work of art (a categorization I cannot accept), but in the power of this unexpected categorization to destabilize the category of the legal and to open it for further thought and for a larger cultural interrogation.

45. Ibid., pp. 118–119. Art, says Sontag, no longer stands in opposition to reality: while twentieth-century reality becomes more and more hallucinated, more and more divorced from what we used to call reality, art moves closer to reality than it ever was before, and mixes in with its jurisprudential gestures. Art no longer is a statement: it is an intervention in a conflict, an action, a commitment, an engagement. It is *politicized* and *de-aestheticized*. A "work of art" no longer is aesthetics, it is politics.

46. Compare Robert Cover, "Violence and the Word," in *Narrative, Violence, and the Law: The Essays of Robert Cover*, ed. Martha Minow, Michael Ryan, and Austin Sarat (Ann Arbor: University of Michigan Press, 1995), pp. 203–238.

47. *Shoah* borrows some of its main witnesses from the Eichmann trial. The most striking example is that of Simon Srebnik, whose extraordinary testimony was first heard during the proceedings of the Eichmann trial. See *Proceedings*, vol. 3, Session 66, pp. 1197–1201, and *Shoah*'s extraordinarily moving opening scene, in *Shoah: The Complete Text of the Film by Claude Lanzmann* (New York: Pantheon Books, 1985).

48. Like the Eichmann trial, Lanzmann's film puts in evidence before the audience a fact-finding process whose goal is—like that of the legal process—to

elicit truth and to prohibit its evasion. Lanzmann borrows his procedures—his techniques of cross-examination and of detailed, concrete interrogation—from the legal model of a trial. Like the Eichmann trial, *Shoah* hears testimonies in a multiplicity of languages and uses an interpreter to simultaneously translate them into the language of its legal process. And like the Eichmann trial, the film wishes not only to *prove* but to *transmit*. "My problem," Lanzmann says, "was to transmit. To do that one cannot allow oneself to be overwhelmed with emotion. You must remain detached . . . I tried rather to reach people through their intelligence." (Claude Lanzmann, interview in *L'Express*, quoted in Shoshana Felman and Dori Laub, *Testimony: Crises of Witnessing in History, Psychoanalysis and Literature* [New York: Routledge, 1992], p. 239.) For a more elaborate study of the film *Shoah*, see Felman, "The Return of the Voice," in Felman and Laub, *Testimony*, pp. 204–283.

49. Arendt, "Truth and Politics," in *Between Past and Future* (New York: Penguin, 1993; orig. pub. 1961), p. 261.

50. Claude Lanzmann, interview with Deborah Jerome ("Resurrecting Horror: The Man behind *Shoah*"), *The Record*, October 25, 1985.

51. Claude Lanzmann, "From the Holocaust to 'Holocaust,'" *Dissent* (Spring 1981): 194, my emphasis; French original in *Les Temps modernes* 395 (June 1979), reprinted in *Au Sujet de* Shoah: *Le film de Claude Lanzmann*, ed. Michel Deguy (Paris: Belin, 1990), pp. 306–316.

52. On the historicizing role of the judges and more generally on the relation between law and history, compare the remarkable analysis of Michal Shaked, "History in Court and the Court in History: The Opinions in the Kastner Trial and the Narratives of Memory," *Alpayim* 20 (2000): 36–80 (Tel Aviv: Am Oved), in Hebrew.

53. *Shivitti*, H 49, E 31–32.

54. Compare Arendt, *EiJ*, 231: "During the few minutes it took Kovner to tell of the help that had come from a German sergeant, a hush settled over the courtroom; it was as though the crowd had spontaneously decided to observe the usual two minutes of silence in honor of the man named Anton Schmidt."

There were moments in which even the prosecutors were overcome by silence and, for a minute, could not go on. On these inadvertent moments of silence, compare the retrospective testimony of Justice Gabriel Bach, at the time assistant prosecutor in the Eichmann trial, in the documentary film *The Trial of Adolf Eichmann*, and Hausner, *Justice in Jerusalem*, pp. 324–325: "The story of the extermination in Poland followed, and the wholesale killings by the *Einsatzgruppen* . . . There, I knew, words could not describe the mass shooting of close to a million and four hundred thousand people before open pits. I cut short the address and read, instead, a lullaby composed at the time in the Wilno ghetto . . . When I finished reading there was silence for a moment. I simply could not go on. Fortunately it was almost 6 P.M., about time for the adjournment of the session. The presiding judge must have realized my predicament; he asked whether this was a convenient place to stop. I nodded thankfully."

55. Gouri, *Facing the Glass Cage*, p. 244; my translation from the Hebrew.

56. "Reading of the Judgment of the District Court," *Proceedings*, vol. 5, Session 121 (December 15, 1961), Jerusalem 1994, p. 2218.

57. "Hence," Arendt concludes, "to the question most commonly asked about the Eichmann trial: What good does it do?, there is but one possible answer: It will do justice" (*EiJ*, 254).

58. "Reading of the Judgment of the District Court," *Proceedings*, vol. 5, Jerusalem 1994, p. 2146; emphasis mine.

59. In her own turn, Arendt narrates not only the totality of facts, but also what is different from, and more than, that totality. Arendt's encounter with the Eichmann trial in turn partakes not only of law's story but also (mutely, indirectly) of art's story, or, more precisely, of the way in which law's story in the trial is transpierced, pervaded by the writer's testimony.

60. "Perhaps it is symbolic," said the judges, "that even the author who himself went through the hell named Auschwitz, could not stand the ordeal in the witness box and collapsed."

61. "The telling of factual truth comprehends much more than the daily information supplied by journalists . . . Reality is different from, and more than, the totality of facts and events which, anyhow, is unascertainable. Who says what is . . . always tells a story, and in this story the particular facts lose their contingency and acquire some humanly comprehensible meaning." Hannah Arendt, "Truth and Politics," in *Between Past and Future* (New York: Penguin, 1993; orig. pub. 1961), p. 261.

62. Walter Benjamin was a friend of Arendt's during their exile years in Paris. She admired his works and wanted to help him emigrate to the United States, but she learnt soon after her own arrival in America that he had committed suicide during his illegal and aborted escape from France (see Chapter 1). In 1942, when Arendt first learnt about the existence of the Nazi death camps, she wrote "a poem for her dead friend, a farewell and a greeting," entitled simply "W.B.": "Distant voices, sadnesses nearby / Those are the voices and these the dead / whom we have sent as messengers ahead, to lead us into slumber." (Quoted in Elisabeth Young-Bruehl, *Hannah Arendt: For Love of the World* [New Haven: Yale University Press, 1982], pp. 162–163.)

The last time Walter Benjamin saw Hannah Arendt, in Marseilles, he entrusted to her care a collection of manuscripts he hoped she could deliver to the United States. After his death, Arendt traveled to the cemetery of Port Bou on the Franco-Spanish border only to discover that her dead friend, who was buried there, does not even have an individual, *named* grave. In a letter to Scholem written on October 21, 1940 (less than a month after Benjamin's death), Arendt describes the shock of her realization that in this cemetery, "the most fantastic . . . and beautiful spot" she has ever "seen in [her] life," there is nothing left to bear witness to Benjamin's life and death: "[His grave] was not to be found, his name was not written anywhere." (Quoted in Gershom Scholem, *Walter Benjamin: The Story of a Friendship*, trans. Harry Zohn [Philadelphia: Jewish Publication Society of America, 1981], p. 226.)

In 1968, Arendt redeems Benjamin from namelessness by publishing his manuscripts in the United States. In her introduction to Benjamin's *Illumina-*

tions, Arendt narrates (and mourns) her friend's absurd, untimely, and tragically ironic (needless) suicide (*Ill.*, 5–18). She recapitulates this narrative and briefly mentions her own mourning in her letter of May 30, 1946, to Gertrude Jaspers, the Jewish wife of the German philosopher (the letter is discussing another dead mutual acquaintance and the two correspondents' common personal relation to the Jewish problem): "Or perhaps he was just tired and didn't want to move on again, didn't want to face a totally alien world, a totally alien language, and the inevitable poverty, which so often, particularly at first, comes close to total destitution. *This exhaustion,* which often went along with *the reluctance to make a big fuss, to summon so much concentration for the sake of this little bit of life,* that was surely *the biggest danger we all faced.* And it was *the death of our best friend in Paris, Walter Benjamin,* who committed suicide in October 1940 on the Spanish border with an American visa in his pocket. This atmosphere of sauve qui peut at the time was dreadful, and suicide was the only noble gesture, if you even cared enough to want to perish nobly . . . What you wrote about *'our' problem* moved me very much . . . and today that means *our dead"* (letter 36, *AJ Corr.,* 40–41; emphasis mine).

63. There is another witness who, in contrast to K-Zetnik, did prove the ability to tell a story. His name is Zyndel Grynszpan, and the story he narrates is that of his forced deportation, at the beginning of the war, from Germany to Poland. He is, in Arendt's eyes, the ideal storyteller—the ideal witness—although no other witness in the trial can live up to his example. His plainly factual and chronologically coherent narrative stands in contrast to the disjointed account of K-Zetnik. *"Now he had come to tell his story,"* Arendt writes, "carefully answering questions put to him by the prosecutor; *he spoke clearly and firmly, without embroidery, using a minimum of words"* (*EiJ,* 228; italics mine). Compare Benjamin's similar stylistic preference in "The Storyteller": "There is nothing [writes Benjamin] that commends a story to memory more effectively than the *chaste compactness* that precludes psychological analysis. And the more natural the process by which the storyteller forgoes psychological shading, the greater becomes the story's claim to a place in the memory of the listener, the more completely is it integrated into his own experience, the greater will be his inclination to repeat it to someone else" ("St.," 91). Arendt indeed repeats verbatim Grynszpan's testimony and does not paraphrase or summarize it, as she does with K-Zetnik's discourse. Arendt is so remarkably and deeply moved by Grynszpan's testimony that she steps out of her boundaries and (for a moment) pleads against her own legal objection to the victim's story and against her own puristic, legalistic emphasis on strict legal relevance: "This story took no more than perhaps ten minutes to tell, and when it was over—the senseless, needless destruction of twenty-seven years in less than twenty-four hours—one thought foolishly: *Everyone, everyone should have his day in court.* Only to find out, in the endless sessions that followed, *how difficult it was to tell the story,* that—at least outside the transforming realm of poetry—it needed a purity of soul, an unmirrored, unreflected innocence of heart and mind that *only the righteous* possess. No one either before or after was to equal the shining honesty of Zindel Grynszpan" (*EiJ,* 229–230; emphasis mine).

The reason Arendt is so overwhelmed with emotion, I would suggest, is that her own traumatic story of *the loss of Germany* is unwittingly, unconsciously reflected back to her from Grynszpan's modest story. This narrative of a forceful removal across national borders is also Benjamin's story (and the cause of his death).

What is significant for my point here, however, is that Arendt describes Grynszpan *in Benjamin's literal words*. The apotheosis of Arendt's uncharacteristic pathos in this passage is a literal stylistic echo, a literal rhetorical and verbal reminiscence of Benjamin's concluding sentence in "The Storyteller." Benjamin writes, in his signature phrase: "The storyteller is the figure in which *the righteous man* encounters himself" ("St.," 109). Similarly, resonantly, Grynszpan is described by Arendt as having "a purity of soul" that *"only the righteous possess"* (*EiJ*, 229).

Another reference to "The Storyteller" makes itself evident at the beginning of the book. In the first chapter, in one of her rare moments of self-inclusion, Arendt situates herself as part of the audience of the trial whose task it is *"to face the storyteller."* "[The audience] was filled with *'survivors,'* with middle-aged and elderly people, immigrants from Europe, like myself, *who knew by heart all there was to know,* and who were in no mood to learn any lessons . . . As witness followed witness and horror was piled on horror, *they sat there and listened in public to stories* they would hardly have been able to endure in private, when they would have had *to face the storyteller*" (*EiJ*, 8; my emphasis). Arendt here places herself significantly among the *survivors,* those who inadvertently *share with those who took the stand the knowledge* of how difficult it is to tell the story of survival (to testify at once to life and to the death—the dying—the survival has entailed). The expression "to face the storyteller" (in which Arendt as a listener and as a survivor also faces herself) is reminiscent again of Benjamin's "Storyteller," in which *the listener becomes a storyteller* in her turn. "For storytelling is always the art of repeating stories," writes Benjamin: "The more self-forgetful a listener is, the more deeply is what he listens to impressed upon his memory . . . [The listener] listens to the tales in such a way that the gift of retelling them comes to him all by itself" ("St.," 91). It is as though Arendt, facing Eichmann in Jerusalem and judging the trial at the level of her statement, were also at the same time, at the level of her utterance, listening to the whisper of Benjamin's voice reciting, as it were, "The Storyteller" from his deathbed (like the original narrator in his essay): "It is . . . characteristic that *not only a man's knowledge or wisdom,* but *above all his real life*—and this is the stuff that stories are made of—*first assumes transmissible form at the moment of his death.* Just as a sequence of images is set in motion inside a man as his life comes to an end, unfolding the views of himself under which he has encountered himself without being aware of it—suddenly in his expressions and looks the unforgettable emerges and imparts to everything that concerned him that authority which even the poorest wretch in dying possesses for the living around him. This authority is at the very source of the story" ("St.," 94).

64. Compare Arendt, *EiJ*, 6: "Justice . . . demands seclusion, it permits sorrow rather than anger."

65. Arendt borrows this sentence from Isak Dinesen, "who not only was one of the great storytellers of all times but also—and she was almost unique in this respect—knew what she was doing." Arendt, "Truth and Politics," p. 262.

66. Compare the prosecutor's opening statement (see above and note 37).

67. I am arguing that Benjamin and Heidegger are the two *absent addressees* of *Eichmann in Jerusalem* (symbolically, the German-Jewish casualty and the compromised German philosopher: a lost friendship and a lost love).

68. "Even where there is only a rustling of plants," Benjamin writes lyrically, "there is always a lament. Because she is mute, nature mourns . . . [and] the sadness of nature makes her mute." Walter Benjamin, "On Language as Such and on the Language of Man," *SWI*, 73.

69. Ibid.

70. This speechless story is a story of mourning and of the inability to mourn: the story of a trauma and of the trauma's silencing and willful disavowal.

In the middle of the writing of *Eichmann in Jerusalem*, Arendt also was in a violent car accident in which she almost died: another brutal inner rupture, another intimate relation to death that similarly, equally, was silenced and has left no visible mark on the tight argument of the book. Arendt tells Jaspers about this nearly fatal accident: "It seemed to me that for a moment I had my life in my hands. I was quite calm: death seemed to me natural, in no way a tragedy or, somehow, out of the order of things. But, at the same time, I said to myself: if it is possible to do so *decently*, I would really like, still, to stay in this world." (Quoted in Young-Bruehl, *Hannah Arendt: For Love of the World*, p. 335; emphasis mine.)

71. "It is only for convenience that we speak of . . . 'traumatic memory,'" writes the psychiatrist Pierre Janet. "*The subject is often incapable of making the necessary narrative which we call memory regarding the event;* and yet he remains confronted by a difficult situation in which he has not been able to play a satisfactory part." Quoted in van der Kolk and van der Hart, "The Intrusive Past," in *TEM*, ed. Caruth, p. 160; emphasis mine.

72. On Benjamin's relation to the First World War and on the role of silence and of trauma in his work, compare Chapter 1, Part Two, "Benjamin's Silence."

73. *Shivitti*, H 34, E 18, tm.

74. The importance of the story element in trials is by now a commonplace in legal scholarship. What is less well known is that, to the extent that trauma is what cannot be narrated (Benjamin, Janet), it also incorporates the paradoxical story of an inherent resistance to storytelling. Every trauma thus includes not only a traumatic story but a *negative story element*, an *anti-story*. I argue that the Eichmann trial is an unprecedented legal event that articulates at once a monumental *legal story* and a collective, monumental *anti-story*, the unanticipated story of the impossibility of telling.

On trauma theory as incapacity for narration, see, among others, van der Kolk and van der Hart, "The Intrusive Past," pp. 158–182, and Caruth, *Unclaimed Experience*.

For general discussions of the relation between law and narrative, see, among others: James R. Elkins, "On the Emergence of Narrative Jurisprudence: The Humanistic Perspective Finds a New Path," *Legal Studies Forum* 9 (1985): 123–156; Derrick Bell, *And We Are Not Saved: The Elusive Quest for Racial Justice* (New York: Basic Books, 1987); Mari Matsuda, "Looking to the Bottom: Critical Legal Studies and Reparations," *Harvard Civil Rights–Civil Liberties Law Review* 22 (1987): 323–399; James R. Elkins, "The Quest for Meaning: Narrative Accounts of Legal Education," *Journal of Legal Education* 38 (1988): 577–598; Richard Delgado, "Storytelling for Oppositionists and Others: A Plea for Narrative," *Michigan Law Review* 87 (1989): 2411–2441; Kathryn Abrams, "Hearing the Call of Stories," *California Law Review* 79 (1991): 971–1052; *Narrative and the Legal Discourse: A Reader in Storytelling and the Law*, ed. David Ray Papke (Liverpool: Deborah Charles, 1991); Patricia Williams, *The Alchemy of Race and Rights: Diary of a Law Professor* (Cambridge, Mass.: Harvard University Press, 1991); Robin West, *Narrative, Authority, and Law* (Ann Arbor: University of Michigan Press, 1993); Daniel A. Farber and Suzanna Sherry, "Telling Stories Out of School: An Essay on Legal Narratives," *Stanford Law Review* 45 (1993): 807–855; Richard Sherwin, "Law Frames: Historical Truth and Narrative Necessity in a Criminal Case," *Stanford Law Review* 47 (1994): 39–83; *Narrative, Violence, and the Law: The Essays of Robert Cover*, ed. Martha Minow, Michael Ryan, and Austin Sarat (Ann Arbor: University of Michigan Press, 1995); *Critical Race Theory: The Cutting Edge*, ed. Richard Delgado (Philadelphia: Temple University Press, 1995); *Critical Race Theory: The Key Writings That Formed the Movement*, ed. Kimberlé Crenshaw et al. (New York: New Press, 1995); Austin Sarat, "Narrative Strategy and Death Penalty Advocacy," *Harvard Civil Rights–Civil Liberties Law Review* 31 (1996): 353–381; *Law's Stories: Narrative and Rhetoric in the Law*, ed. Peter Brooks and Paul Gewirtz (New Haven: Yale University Press, 1996); *History, Memory and the Law*, ed. Austin Sarat and Thomas Kearns (Ann Arbor: University of Michigan Press, 1999).

75. Because the unanticipated force of the event of the impossibility of telling caught everyone off guard and must have been surprising even to the trial's architects and to its legal actors, Arendt treats it as a symptom of their oversight and of their failure. I see it as a proof of the success of their conception beyond their grasp.

In the same way that K-Zetnik's fainting could not be foreseen and was not planned, the legal narrative of the impossibility of telling could not be planned. It had to happen. It was the human and the legal meaning of what happened. *But no one could articulate this meaning at the time.* It was the unanticipated essence of the event, not part of the trial's stated ideology. It is only now in retrospect that this significance comes into view and can be recognized and formulated.

76. Segev, 4, my emphasis.

77. I now return from the "subtext" of *Eichmann in Jerusalem* to Arendt's conscious and explicit *text*: her conscious critical report as a legal historian of the trial.

78. Oliver Wendell Holmes, "The Path of the Law," *Harvard Law Review* 110, no. 2 (1997): 991, 991.

79. Ibid., p. 1006. "When we study law," Holmes asserts, "we are not studying a mystery" (ibid., p. 991). Eichmann's banality, Arendt insists, and the banality of Nazism as a whole, is not a mystery. Its essence is its shallowness, its hollow lack of depth. And this, says Arendt, is why "it is in the nature of this case that we have no tools to hand except legal ones, with which we have to pass sentence on something that cannot even be adequately represented either in legal terms or in political terms" (Arendt to Jaspers, letter 274 (December 23, 1960), *AJ Corr.*, 417). The tool is purposely, revealingly reductive: "When we study law, we are not studying a mystery."

80. Sontag, "Reflections on *The Deputy*," pp. 118–119; emphasis mine.

81. In this sense, the Eichmann trial did fulfill its function, even in Arendt's critical eyes. "Those who are convinced that justice, and nothing else, is the end of law will be inclined to condone the kidnapping act, though not because of precedents . . . This last of the Successor trials will no more, and perhaps even less than its predecessors, serve as a valid precedent for future trials of such crimes. This might be of little import in view of the fact that its main purpose—to prosecute and to defend, to judge and to punish Adolf Eichmann—was achieved" (*EiJ*, 264–265, 272–273).

82. Benjamin, "GEA," *SWI*, 355; emphasis mine.

83. Compare Pierre Nora, "Between Memory and History: *Les Lieux de mémoire*," trans. Mark Roudebush, *Representations* 26 (Spring 1989): 7–25.

84. Benjamin, "GEA," 340.

85. Benjamin (using Hölderlin's terms) speaks of "the caesura of the work" (ibid., pp. 354 and 340–341).

86. "Thereby, in the rhythmic sequence of the representations . . . there becomes necessary what in poetic meter is called the caesura . . . the counter-rhythmic rupture . . . that caesura in which, along with harmony, every expression simultaneously comes to a standstill, in order to give free reign to an expressionless power" (ibid., pp. 340, 341).

87. It is as though, summoned to court, history acquired power of speech in amplifying and in making audible K-Zetnik's own repeated yet repeatedly mute cry: "That mute cry" [K-Zetnik writes] "was again trying to break loose, as it had every time death confronted me at Auschwitz; and, as always when I looked death in the eye, so now too the mute scream got no further than my clenched teeth that closed upon it and locked it inside me. Indeed that was the essence of that cry: it was never realized, never exposed to the outside air. It remained a strangled flame inside me" (*Shivitti*, H 18, E 1–2, tm).

88. Compare the strikingly resonant statements of the French philosopher Emmanuel Levinas: "The relation to the face is all at once the relation to the absolutely weak—what is absolutely exposed, what is naked and what is deprived . . . and at the same time . . . the face is also the 'Thou shall not kill' . . . It is the fact that I cannot let the other die alone, it is as though there were [from the face] an appeal to me . . . For me, he is above all the one for which I am responsible." "*It is always from the face, from my responsibility for the other, that justice*

emerges." Emmanuel Levinas, "Philosophie, Justice, Amour," *EN,* 114–115; my translation and emphasis.

89. Walter Benjamin, *The Origin of German Tragic Drama* (1928; London: NLB, 1977), p. 166.

90. "And indeed, before we come to any conclusion about the success or *failure* of the Jerusalem court, we must stress the judges' firm belief that they had no right to become legislators, that they had to conduct their business within the limits of Israeli law, on the one hand, and of accepted legal opinion, on the other. It must be admitted furthermore that *their failures* were neither in kind nor in degree greater than the failures of the Nuremberg Trials or the Successor Trials in other European countries. On the contrary, part of *the failure of the Jerusalem court* was due to its all too eager adherence to the Nuremberg precedent" (Arendt, *EiJ,* 274; emphasis mine).

91. Asked what was his concept of the Holocaust, Lanzmann answered: "I had no concept. I had obsessions, which is different . . . The obsession of the cold . . . The obsession of the first time . . . The obsession of the last moments, the waiting, the fear. *Shoah* is a film full of fear . . . You cannot do such a film theoretically. *Every theoretical attempt was a failure, but these failures were necessary . . .* You build such a film in your head, in your heart, in your belly, in your guts, everywhere." (Interview given by Lanzmann on the occasion of his visit to Yale University, and filmed at the Fortunoff Video-Archive for Holocaust Testimonies at Yale on May 5, 1986. Tape transcription, pp. 22–23; emphasis mine.)

Index

abyss, 86–96, 122, 138, 150–151, 164, 207n56 (*see also* Simpson trial; Tolstoy)
  of trauma, 90–92, 94, 150–151, 207n56
  of sexuality, 88–89, 94
  of difference, 89, 94
  of memory, 90, 93, 96
  of repetition, 94–96
  and law, 8, 90–96, 209n60
  and literature, 92–96, 209n60
  between law and literature, 94–96
  of Auschwitz, 150–151
  truth as, 92
African Americans, 6, 12, 204n46 (*see also* black(s)/blackness; Simpson trial; King, Rodney)
Althusser, Louis, 82, 201n35
anti-Semitism, 115–117, 120–122
anti-story, 156–160, 240nn71,74 (*see also* narration; storytelling)
Arendt, Hannah, 8, 19, 21, 23, 50, 64, 106–130, 131, 137–166, 183n7, 187n32, 210n1
  Eichmann in Jerusalem, 106–130, 131, 137, 140, 156, 158, 160, 162, 182n10, 187n32, 240n70 (*see also* storytelling; narration; anti-story)
  "Truth and Politics," 157–158
  "Isak Dinesen," 106, 240n65 (*see also* storytelling)
art, 13, 54, 65, 77, 106–107, 116, 151–156, 235n44
  and the Holocaust, 106–107 (*see also* Celan; K-Zetnik; Lanzmann)
  and law, 107, 151–156, 162,

235nn44,45 (*see also* Tolstoy; Zola; K-Zetnik; Kafka)
  as witness, 152 (*see also* Tolstoy; Zola)
Attorney General v. Eichmann, 109, 210n1 (*see also* Eichmann trial)
Auschwitz, 114, 125, 135–136, 142–154, 150–151, 159–160
autobiography, 24–25, 34–39, 42, 103, 187–188n42

banality of evil , 107–112, 139, 161, 212–213nn4,5 (*see also* Arendt; Jaspers)
beating, 75, 81–85, 202–203nn36,38–40 (*see also* Simpson trial; King, Rodney; Tolstoy)
  wife-, 75, 202–203nn38–40
  of Rodney King, 81, 84–85, 202n36
  and invisibility, 81–83, 202n38
  as political act, 82
  and seeing, 85
Ben Gurion, David, 109–112, 119, 141, 215n13
Benjamin, Walter, 3, 8, 10–53, 83, 127, 131, 158, 160–166, 182n10
  suicide of, 3, 48–50, 182n10
  silence of, 18, 22–53
  body of, 49
  presence in *Eichmann in Jerusalem*, 156–160, 237n62, 238–239n63
  A Berlin Chronicle, 24, 36–39, 42–43, 46–51
  "Critique of Violence," 15–18

245

Freud, Sigmund *(continued)*
"Thoughts for the Times on War
and Death," 1
Moses and Monotheism, 62–63, 84,
174–175n3, 198n13, 204n45,
219n29 (*see also* trauma; Caruth)
Beyond the Pleasure Principle,
190n70 (*see also* trauma; repetition)

gender, 6, 12, 60–61, 64, 83, 91–95,
206–207n56
trauma of, 6, 60–61, 91, 206–
207n56 (*see also* feminism)
and the law, 91–93
genocide, 6, 12, 113, 119, 150
Germany, 19–21, 29, 35, 115, 118–
119, 150, 238–239n63, 174n3
ghost, 10, 58, 62, 131–166 (*see also*
K-Zetnik; Eichmann trial;
Simpson trial; King, Rodney;
repetition)
and justice, 10, 62, 155
Arendt's mourned and unmourned
ghosts, 58
of Rodney King, 62
Goldman, Ronald, 58, 104, 194n3
(*see also* Simpson trial)
Gouri, Haim, 137, 154

Hausner, Gideon, 110, 113, 133,
136, 142, 144, 149, 216n14 (*see
also* Eichmann trial)
Heidegger, Martin, 158, 240n67
Heinle, Fritz, 34–35, 39–43, 49, 51–
52, 190n7, 191n85 (*see also*
Benjamin; Scholem)
suicide of, 34, 41, 43, 49
Herman, Judith, 173n2, 176n3, 181–
182n3
historicism, 29–30, 188n50
history, 1, 11–53, 61–64, 84–85,
111–123, 132, 138, 174n3
and trauma, 1, 33, 62–63, 83–85,
174n3
and justice, 11–53, 54–105, 204n46
on trial, 12–13
critiques of, 13, 184n11

and silence, 14, 22, 30
philosophy of, 28–32, 34, 48, 112,
120–123
and speechlessness, 33–34
angel of, 47–48
and repetition, 61–64, 84–85
legal, 108, 112–120, 138
"monumental," 111–123, 132, 138
(*see also* Nietzsche)
"critical," 111–112, 120–123 (*see
also* Arendt; Nietzsche; Zola)
for life, 111–112 (*see also* Nietzsche)
historical dualities, 62, 84, 198n14
Hitler, Adolf, 19, 29, 47, 113, 122,
139, 188n51, 221n40,
234nn39,41
Hölderlin, Friedrich, 35–36, 39–40, 43
Holmes, Oliver Wendell, 161, 242n79
Holocaust, 4, 7, 106–130, 131, 151–
153, 156–159, 165

invisibility, 79–85
of trauma, 79–85
of domestic violence, 79–85,
202n38
of the battered face, 79
Irving v. Lipstadt, 12
Israel, state of, 106, 109, 113, 120,
122, 126, 128, 213–214n10

Jackson, Robert (Justice), 129, 132,
134–135, 145 (*see also* Nuremberg
trials)
Jameson, Fredric, 185n19
Janet, Pierre, 240nn71,74
Jaspers, Karl, 63–64, 109, 138–139
Jews/Jewish people, 4, 12, 18–19,
113–116, 119, 122, 126, 128,
138–140 (*see also* Eichmann trial;
Arendt; Scholem)
Johnson, Barbara, 192–194n1
judges, 55, 113, 131, 149, 164
Judgment Day, 14–15, 17–18 (*see also*
Benjamin)
jury/jurors, 5, 91–92
justice, 3–4, 9, 10–54, 80–82, 106–
130
theaters of, 4, 9, 80, 106–130